The Intellectual Origins of the Global Financial Crisis

GVLA.

THE INTELLECTUAL ORIGINS OF **THE GLOBAL FINANCIAL CRISIS**

Edited by Roger Berkowitz and Taun N. Toay

FORDHAM UNIVERSITY PRESS   New York 2012

Frontispiece: Gluttony, from *The Seven Deadly Sins*, engraved by Pieter van der Heyden
(c. 1530–72) 1558 (etching and engraving) (b/w photo), Bruegel, Pieter the Elder (c. 1525–69)
(after) / The Israel Museum, Jerusalem, Israel / Vera & Arturo Schwarz Collection of Dada
and Surrealist Art / The Bridgeman Art Library International

Fordham University Press has no responsibility for the persistence or accuracy of URLs for
external or third-party Internet websites referred to in this publication and does not
guarantee that any content on such websites is, or will remain, accurate or appropriate.

Fordham University Press also publishes its books in a variety of electronic formats.
Some content that appears in print may not be available in electronic books.

Library of Congress Cataloging-in-Publication Data is available from the publisher.

Printed in the United States of America

14 13 12   5 4 3 2 1

First edition

Contents

Preface

As world markets crumbled in the fall of 2008, I was teaching a seminar on Hannah Arendt's book *The Origins of Totalitarianism*. The second main section of Arendt's exploration of twentieth-century totalitarianism is called "Imperialism." In it, Arendt shows how the imperialist insistence that political power expands infinitely is one of the root causes of totalitarian governance. Arendt describes imperialism as the importing of the economic principle of unlimited growth into the realm of politics. She argues, convincingly, that while growth may be an important principle of economics, politics demands limits. A state requires borders, and a citizenry depends on a sense of themselves as sharing a common sense of right and wrong. In short, politics requires judgment and limitation, both of which are overwhelmed by the economic and imperialist imperatives for infinite expansion.

Arendt's insight into the political implications of the subordination of political to economic thinking struck me as deeply relevant to the emerging financial crisis. Although the financial crisis has many economic, political, and psychological causes, it is, in important ways that Arendt makes visible, a result of a crisis in political judgment. In our globalized world, political limits fall prey to economic rationality. Tax havens and rent seeking allow global corporations to evade national regulation; nations are set into competition for business; a growing economy becomes the foundation of national security; and the free market—the absence of government—is seen as the epitome of good governance. In the frenzy for growth and the confidence in the invisible hand, governmental institutions around the world ceded their authority to regulate, set limits, and to govern. In Arendtian terms, the financial crisis emerged from our elevation of the economic rationality of infinite growth over the necessarily limited practice of political judgment.

Arendt's book made cogent the fact that the financial crisis shared with totalitarianism a rootedness in the elevation of economic over political modes of governance. The rise of economic thinking is central to

Arendt's lifelong concern with the retreat of political judgment in our times and our willingness to be ruled by technocratic and bureaucratic rationality instead of insisting on our collective freedom. Arendt, I realized, offered a profound and underappreciated way to think the depth and danger of the current financial crisis.

It was around this time that I was working to institutionalize the Hannah Arendt Center for Politics and Humanities at Bard College. I approached Alex Bazelow, a Bard graduate and friend of both Arendt and her husband, Heinrich Bluecher. Alex generously agreed to help support a conference exploring the intellectual origins of the financial crisis. I also approached Dimitri B. Papadimitriou, president of the Levy Economics Institute at Bard and Taun Toay, of the Levy Economics Institute; I asked them to commit the Levy Institute to cosponsor a conference that took a broad and Arendtian look to the origins of the financial crisis. They generously agreed. The ensuing conference, "The Burden of Our Times: The Intellectual Origins of the Global Financial Crisis," took place in October 2009 at Bard College.

As do all Hannah Arendt Center conferences, the "Burden of Our Times" conference brought together public intellectuals, artists, journalists, businesspeople, and academics from across the disciplines to address the relevance of Arendt's thinking to a contemporary political event. The effort is to spur thinking about politics in the spirit of Hannah Arendt and to encourage people to "think what we are doing."

The conference produced a unique blending of discourses, with humanities professors speaking about derivatives and tax havens and economists and business leaders thinking through the philosophical implications of thinkers such as Arendt, Max Weber, and Michel Foucault. Richard Bernstein, writing in the *International Herald Tribune* and the *New York Times*, advised the Financial Crisis Inquiry Commission, created by Congress to investigate the causes of the recent and ongoing financial crisis, to consider the Arendtian analysis presented at the Bard conference. There was a clear sense that doors had opened that should not simply be allowed to shut.

Taun Toay and I asked the participants to expand and polish their essays for publication. At the same time, we asked that they make an effort to preserve the style and form of the original oral presentations. The essays that follow are the result. They are as a whole shorter than typical academic essays, and they have fewer footnotes and scholarly trappings.

Instead, they present efforts to think with and, at times, against Arendt in her call for thinking what we do.

—*Roger Berkowitz*

This volume is a work of twenty-six contributors and two editors and would never have been finished without the assistance of many others. From the beginning, Bard's President, Leon Botstein, encouraged and supported our efforts. Funding for the conference, which also supported publication of this book, was generous and came from Wendy and Alex Bazelow, Mischa Frusztajer, Alice and Nathan Gantcher, Richard Gilder, Amy and Jeffrey Glass, James Grosfeld, Robert and Martha Lipp, Jack Nusbaum and Nora Ann Wallace, Marshall Rose, Barbara and Jon Roth, and Will Weinstein.

In planning the original conference, we were assisted greatly by Debra Pemstein and Mary Strieder. In addition, a number of Bard students—especially Alice Baker—assisted in preparing the manuscript for publication. Finally, we are deeply indebted to Helen Tartar, Thomas C. Lay, and Eric Newman at Fordham University Press, and the copy editor, Teresa Jesionowski. Fordham Press has been a strong supporter of the Hannah Arendt Center, and their engagement and professionalism are extraordinary.

—*Roger Berkowitz and Taun N. Toay*

The Intellectual Origins of the Global Financial Crisis

The Burden of Our Times

:: ROGER BERKOWITZ

A crisis becomes a disaster only when we respond to it with preformed judgments, that is, with prejudices. —HANNAH ARENDT, *BETWEEN PAST AND FUTURE*

An accomplished businessman, one deeply involved in the housing industry, wrote me when I solicited his views on the intellectual causes of the financial crisis. The cause of the crisis is really quite simple he said: Cheap money—the combination of low interest rates, lax regulation, financial innovation, and excess leverage—led to unprecedented speculation.

From an economic point of view, the cheap money hypothesis is unassailable. But in a volume on the *intellectual* origins of the financial crisis, we need to go further. For starters, we might ask: What is cheap money?

Cheap money means money that can be borrowed at little cost. When interest rates are low, those with money have no incentive to keep it in the bank. When low interest rates are combined with lax regulations, the chances of successful investments are increased, and incentives for risky speculation are increased. In an era of cheap money, saving is discouraged, and speculation is encouraged.

If cheap money is behind the bubble, what is behind cheap money? And when did the era of cheap money begin?

Some, like Charles Morris, say it began in the aftermath of 9/11 and the bursting of the technology bubble, when the Federal Reserve reduced the federal funds rate to 1 percent and kept it there until 2004, financing the bubble in housing prices that lasted until 2007.[1]

Others, like George Soros, say that it began with the free-market fundamentalism of the 1980s. Globalization, deregulation, and financial innovation led to an unprecedented increase in leverage and speculation. Credit market debt in the United States exceeded 350 percent of GDP in

2007. Limitless and unregulated credit creation helped create a "super-bubble" in asset prices.[2]

Still others argue that the epoch of cheap money began on August 15, 1971, the day that the United States abandoned the gold standard. As a fiat currency, the dollar is not backed by hard assets, and the potential supply of dollars is limited only by the imagination and demand of the citizenry. For William Fleckenstein, the loss of the gold standard in a democratic political system that rewards politicians for their largess cannot but lead to an ever-increasing supply of dollars. "In a social democracy with a fiat currency," he writes in his motto that was long emblazoned on his website, "all roads lead to easy money."[3]

Another chorus of experts—like Hunter Lewis in his essay in this collection—argues that the rise of easy money is rooted in government policies developed in response to the Great Depression in 1929. When governments flood markets with easy money in times of economic contraction, well-meaning intervention encourages a moral hazard, incentivizing speculators to employ ever-greater amounts of leverage with the expectation that they will profit in good times and be bailed out in bad times.

Yet still others would say that the era of cheap money is much older, that it began on May 5, 1716, the day that John Law founded "Law and Company," as the national bank of France. Law's radical innovation was that paper money—as opposed to silver and gold coin—could be printed, and thus the supply of money could exceed the amount of gold and silver on which its value was based.

What this little tour of the last three hundred years tells us is that if cheap money is the economic cause of the financial crisis—and my friend is right in at least a strict economic sense that it is—it is an answer that tells us very little.

John Stuart Mill, writing amid the great financial crisis of 1826, argued that cheap money will expand irrationally in times of speculative optimism, inaugurating a vicious cycle of boom and bust. Some booms are longer. Some busts are deeper. But the boom-bust cycle of cheap money is part of the speculative nature of capitalism itself. In his essay "Paper Currency and Commercial Distress," Mill argues that the factual unavoidability of economic crises generated by speculation was an adequate defense of cheap paper money against those who would use the crisis to criticize it. For Mill, cheap money and the speculative frenzies that cause cheap money are simply unavoidable parts of a capitalist economy.[4]

Mill is certainly not the only defender of cheap money who points to the inevitability of boom-bust cycles. On the contrary, most economists see booms and busts as simply part of the capitalist system, predictable and necessary crises that cannot be avoided. Thus, Joseph Schumpeter has written that business cycles "are not like tonsils, separable things that might be treated by themselves, but are, like the beat of the heart, of the essence of the organ that displays them."[5] And Arthur F. Burns, the great student of business cycles, wrote back in 1947: "For well over a century business cycles have run an unceasing round. They have persisted through vast economic and social changes; they have withstood countless experiments in industry . . . ; they have confounded forecasters without number, belied repeated prophecies of a 'new era of prosperity' and outlived repeated forebodings of 'chronic depression.'"[6] For Burns and Schumpeter, as for Mill, cheap money and the crises it engenders are part and parcel of capitalism. We have no choice, they suggest, but to accept the inevitability of crises.

The impulse to normalize the recent financial crisis by pointing to the realist inevitability of easy money, booms, and busts, harbors a danger. By familiarizing, analogizing, and making understandable the 2008 crisis in global finance, the easy money thesis also reconciles us to the crisis. It is all too easy for us today to simply shrug and say that crises are part of capitalism. To do so, to say that the crisis was caused by cheap money, is to say that there is nothing more to say. To explain the 2008 financial crisis as an inevitable by-product of capitalism is to forestall further inquiry, to overlook personal and corporate fraud, to refuse to judge individual and collective wrongs, and to abandon ourselves not simply to the vagaries of the market, but also to the misdeeds of miscreants. Above all, such an approach risks thoughtlessness.

When this crisis hit, I happened to be teaching Hannah Arendt's *The Origins of Totalitarianism*. Two of Arendt's insights struck me as having particular relevance to our present situation. First, Arendt confronted a similar phenomenon in which the crisis of totalitarianism was being normalized. The world has long known dictators. Hitler and Stalin, so it was said, were proof positive of the continuity of human frailty. Against this view, Hannah Arendt argued that it was mistaken to understand totalitarianism as simply the latest form of tyranny. Indeed, one should not understand totalitarianism, for to understand it is to normalize it and to desensitize ourselves to the fact of its extraordinary evil.

Against the effort to understand, Arendt counsels comprehension. By comprehension, she means, "the unpremeditated, attentive facing up to, and resisting of, reality—whatever it may be."[7] The factual reality of totalitarianism, as Arendt comprehended it, was that in our world today any and every evil is possible and can even be rationally justified by otherwise well-meaning people. What is needed, she argued, was that we face up to the fact that totalitarianism, genocide, and administrative massacres were now ever-present dangers in our times. Originally titled *The Burden of Our Time*, Arendt's book *The Origins of Totalitarianism* seeks not to explain totalitarianism but to face up to its singular actuality. Arendt's passion was, as she later wrote, "to think what we are doing."[8]

Crises offer particularly good opportunities to think what we are doing. A crisis "tears away façades and obliterates prejudices" and thus allows us "to explore and inquire into whatever has been laid bare of the essence of the matter."[9] When she discusses the crisis of education, Arendt affirms that the essence of education is natality—the fact that, born into a preexisting world, human beings must be educated both to fit into and also to remake that world. What we need to ask amid our contemporary crisis is: What is the essence of economics today that the crisis lays bare?

Surprisingly, since she is rarely cited as an authority on economic affairs, Arendt offers an original and thoughtful road map to think through the financial crisis, one that begins with the insight that the essence of economics is unlimited growth. In her telling, the seeds of the financial crisis are not in economics itself, but in the importation of economics into politics, or rather the dominance of infinite growth—an economic principle—in the realm of politics, where it does not belong.

Arendt develops her thesis about the dangerous subordination of politics to economics in *The Origins of Totalitarianism*. She argues that imperialism is the most important intellectual foundation of totalitarianism. At the root of imperialism is the transfer of the economic principle of unlimited growth to politics. Imperialism has its economic roots in the "realm of business speculation"—specifically the bursting of an investment bubble in the 1870s. As national entrepreneurs sought new markets, they enlisted state support for economic expansion. "Expansion as a permanent and supreme aim of politics is the central idea of imperialism."[10] The rise of imperialism, Arendt argues, means that politics becomes subservient to economics.

Arendt fears the confusion of economics and politics and especially the elevation of economics over politics. Since politics demands the imposition of limits and "stabilizing forces that stand in the way of constant transformation and expansion," she argues that imperialist expansion brought with it a grave and destabilizing threat to the political order. When politics under the sway of economic imperatives is forced to expand on the world stage, political leaders must offer ideologies that give meaning to an ever-larger, undefined, disconnected, and homeless mass, a population that replaces a citizenry. Under the economic imperatives of growth, politics becomes world politics.

It is an open question today whether politics can return to a political activity that sets moral, ethical, and economic limits on human action. The prevalence of economic and scientific thinking—thinking that by their natures evades limits—means that politics is caught up in discourses that make the central boundary-setting idea of politics immensely difficult, if not impossible. Those who, in the name of community, defend the purity of national boundaries confront the same inexorable economic laws that defeat advocates for local ownership against chain stores as well as those who defend some notion of biological humanity in the face of a seemingly inexorable advance of human implants, genetic modification, and prosthetic medicine. The economic and scientific spirit of our age supports the implacably modern maxim that whatever can be done, should be done. Thus political judgment limiting action—economic, global, or scientific—is increasingly an anachronism.

The confusion of economic and political thinking is rampant today. I refer not only to George W. Bush's claim to be a CEO president, the increasing appeal of businessmen as politicians, and President Barack Obama's pragmatism, but to the more general confusion today between prosperity and happiness. We now believe that if we achieve a certain—apparently ever-increasing—level of material prosperity, we will be happy. The welfare state is inseparably part of democratic capitalism, and politics—to a degree unimaginable in the recent past—now defines the common good as the commonwealth. Political legitimacy, as countries like China make clear, is guaranteed more by economic security than political liberty. As Michel Foucault observed nearly fifty years ago, economic prosperity "produces legitimacy for the state that is its guarantor."[11] Economics, not politics, is increasingly the foundation of modern politics.

Not only politics but also who we are—as a matter of personal identity—is defined by economic thinking. Amid productivity gains that offer riches that were unimaginable decades ago, let alone centuries ago, we continue to labor away—and not out of need. Freed from need, and yet deprived of a publicly meaningful religious, cultural, or civil life beyond economic concerns, modern economic citizens work to consume. *Homo sapiens* is replaced by *homo oeconomicus*. As economic beings, we treat ourselves as consumers. Every consumer is an entrepreneur, the CEO of his personal corporation that invests in the right schooling, training, and universities—all of which promise a certain return on the investment. Even health care, as President Obama reminds us, is justifiable primarily as a good investment in our future productivity. The economic foundation of our present worldview is so natural that we rarely today perceive its strangeness. When we hear human rights advocates proclaim that human rights is good for business or antiwar activists discourse on the economic costs of war, we forget that other cultures in other times did not reduce ethical and martial considerations to economic calculus.

Our philo-economism also obscures the fairly obvious fact that "a man does not 'by nature' wish to earn more and more money."[12] Take that statement by Max Weber seriously, and let it sink in. Throughout history, humans have wanted to live well, but they have generally sought to avoid work whenever possible; they have wanted to be rich, but they have sought wealth to attain power or to avoid work; when they have worked, they worked from need. Those who succeeded became aristocrats and paid others to work for them, so that they could pursue the more meaningful activities of politics, leisure, and pious devotion.

How did *homo oeconomicus* overcome man's natural hedonism? How did econocentrism overcome the religious prescriptions against acquisitiveness and the love of money? How did capitalism emerge as the natural and dominant way of assessing value in the world?

The most famous answer to this question was given by Max Weber in his book *The Protestant Ethic and the Spirit of Capitalism*. Put aside Weber's controversial historical thesis about the importance of Protestantism to capitalism—a thesis that Liah Greenfeld has brilliantly adopted and adapted in her book *The Spirit of Capitalism* and in her essay in this volume. At the heart of Weber's account is his claim that the rise of an unnatural and specifically capitalist ethic—to earn more and more money combined with the a strong work ethic that limits the spontaneous enjoyment of life outside of work—is rooted in the increasing rationalization of society, culture, and humanity itself. What capitalist rationality demands is that humans act according to the reason of profit and loss.

Capitalist rationality is enormously powerful in allocating resources efficiently and increasing general prosperity. But such rationalization is also dehumanizing. For if humans must act rationally, they must abandon spontaneous feelings, passions, instincts, even commonsense moral sensations—all of which are rejected as irrational. The great paradox that Weber discovered in capitalism is that the pure rationalism of capitalist activity is irrational. And yet, the power of capitalist rationality is, it seems, irresistible.

The irresistibility of capitalism is part and parcel of the demand for certainty. Capitalism offers the certainty of a balanced ledger and the clarity of profit and loss. Capitalism thus offers objective criteria on which to rationally evaluate all decisions. In its promise of objective certainty, capitalism is a symptom of what Hannah Arendt calls the experience of homelessness. Our world, the world defined by the loss of the authority of religions and the decay of traditions, is also a world defined by the loss of a spiritual home. Capitalism—the social system that defines good and bad, winners and losers, status and power, by clear and certain criteria of salary and wealth—is one way that a homeless humanity sets itself on a certain and stable foundation, albeit one of its own making.

In a *New York Times* op-ed essay in the midst of the financial crisis, Calvin Trillin presented the thesis that the origin of the financial crisis is that smart guys began working on Wall Street. There is no doubt truth to this, and it goes hand in hand with the extraordinary rise of the entire financial and banking industries in the world. What needs to be seen, however, is that the reason smart guys have come to Wall Street is not simply because they wanted or needed that second ocean-faring yacht. Rather, it is that in an era of unbridled capitalism, self-worth and purpose are determined above all by one's standing in the game of workplace success. When all higher culture and spiritual values have been devalued, the one way that a person can secure meaning and sense to life is through the objective measurement of success that capitalism offers. In such a world, the pursuit of wealth, as Max Weber saw, is stripped of all need for spiritual justification, and emerges simply as a sport, a game in which not only the spoils but also the sense of significance and wholeness go to the winners.

Our challenge, the burden of our time, is facing up to and also resisting this reality: that our public world has no values outside of those objectively recognizable values of profit and loss. In this sense, the crisis must not merely be seen as an inevitable hiccup in the advance of capitalism.

The point in such a volume as this is not to "solve" the crisis, but to "think what we are doing." For it is in thinking what we are doing, Arendt writes, that we erect obstacles to oversimplifications, compromises, and conventions. Following Arendt, our challenge is to think what we are doing amid the crisis in the global financial system. That means facing up to the inescapable connection between crisis and capitalism without thereby reconciling oneself to the crisis. What is needed, in other words, is a facing up to the realities of easy money, financial crises, and the subordination of politics to economics without losing our ability to resist those realities.

It is to this task, to thinking through, facing up to, and resisting the foundational elements of the global financial crisis, that the essays in this volume are dedicated. Although Arendt is often thought to have ignored the concerns of economics, this is, as Tracy Strong argues, quite misleading. Arendt's defense of politics is to be understood as an engagement with what she takes to be an illegitimate elevation of economics over politics, a transformation that she explores and resists throughout her work. Even her first book, *The Origins of Totalitarianism*, shows that the predominance of economics over politics is at the very heart of the potential for totalitarian government in our age. For Strong, we must confront not simply the economic but also, more importantly, the political dangers revealed by the financial crisis. To think what we are doing today, he writes, is to rethink and reimagine citizenship and politics in an imperialist world.

The essays by Strong, Jerome Kohn, and Antonia Grunenberg in Part 1 of this volume directly engage Arendt's thinking about imperialism and economics as a prod to think through the intellectual origins of our contemporary financial crisis. For Kohn, imperialism and its explosion of all political limits names the unresolved problem of politics in an age in which politics, at least in its traditional sense, has become very nearly impossible. He turns to Arendt's own discovery of Thomas Hobbes as the philosophical origin of the modern contempt for politics; Hobbes's elevation of self-interest over the public good, Kohn argues, is the intellectual foundation for the loss of political limits on the economic pursuit of self-interest. We must, he writes, take the opportunity of the financial crisis to think politically in a way that reclaims our public world, to the extent that this is possible.

Grunenberg agrees that we as citizens must judge the political origins and lessons of the financial crisis, even though we are not experts in financial affairs. She worries that the political body seems to have been converted into an appendix of economic self-interest and that we are increasingly less able to use the political body to control overarching economic powers. This loss of political control over the economy, she argues, is at the core of our contemporary reality.

In the essays, interviews, and round-table discussions that form Part 2 of this volume, ten businesspersons from outside the academy offer their accounts, frequently inspired by Hannah Arendt, of the intellectual and cultural sources of the financial crisis. At the root of many of these contributions is the sense that our economic and political worlds have undergone a transformation of values. David Callahan finds the foundation of the crisis in the relentless, amoral logic of self-interest, profit, and the bottom line, a logic that has grown ever more dominant as it has squeezed out the fuzzier bonds of human connectivity and our integrity in dealing with other people. Callahan follows the increased incidences of cheating that pervade our culture and argues that now is the time to tell a moral story about capitalism that can restore values supportive of a more benign capitalism.

Following Callahan's call for a new moral narrative are a series of interviews with successful business leaders, which focus on the values of business in modern American capitalism. Paul Levy, managing director of JLL Partners, asks, Who are the people who made loans and sold the derivatives that led to the financial crisis? They are, he answers, generally good, law-abiding people. Like Callahan, Levy understands that reckless financial actions are often undertaken by decent people who simply get caught up in the clichés of the day and cut corners or push legal limits from a thoughtless desire to secure their position rather than from monstrosity or evil. Levy bemoans the loss of a liberal arts background, an education in the literary and historical classics that binds a society together and gives people something to live for besides simply earning more money. What is being lost, he writes, are the good lives, the happy lives, without which people live simply for gain and acquisition.

Vincent Mai, chairman of AEA Investors, seconds Levy's insistence on the apparent loss of the upright businesspersons engaged in work for intellectual satisfaction and the reputational goods that come from personal integrity rather than mere financial gain. Mai writes of the transformation of the business world in which the old rules have been turned upside down, so that a culture of making as much money as you can has replaced a culture where reputation and honor mattered equally as much if not more than the drive for large bonuses. For Mai, as for Levy, there is a strong sense that the unlimited drive for profit has replaced other ends as the driving force of the financial industry and that this shift in the values of business contributed greatly to the oversized bubbles that were the proximate cause of the financial crisis. Mai argues that the financial community must come to understand that there are things more important than its immediate self-interest.

One potential response to the crisis in values described by Callahan, Levy, and Mai is the development of corporate social responsibility. Alex Bazelow, who worked with Hannah Arendt for five years before her death, discusses the film *Twelve Hours to Midnight—How Brazil Has Responded to the Global Financial Crisis*, a film exploring the work of business leaders in Brazil who have set out to reform capitalism. Bazelow describes the corporate social responsibility movement and later the Instituto Ethos in Brazil, which have evolved into powerful instruments of social reform and now include over a thousand corporations responsible for up to 33 percent of Brazil's gross domestic product. For Bazelow, Brazil is a model for a meaningful reform of capitalism along ethical and socially responsible lines.

Bazelow then supplies the questions for an interview by human rights scholar Cláudia Perrone-Moisés with one of the leaders of Brazil's corporate social responsibility movement, Raymundo Magliano, who is also the former president of Bovespa, the Brazilian stock exchange. For Magliano, the financial crisis is a crisis of values centered on the instrumentalization of human beings. As humans have been reduced simply to means, we witness the dehumanizing side of market logic—a market logic that Arendt understood and opposed throughout her work.

Following the interviews is a round-table discussion led by Taun N. Toay and including Raymond Baker, director of the Global Financial Integrity Project; Rebecca Berlow of Sandelman Partners; Jack Blum, chairman of the Tax Justice Network (USA); Zachary Karabel, president of River Twice Research; and Tom Scanlon, attorney adviser to the U.S. Treasury Department. Discussing the free market, tax evasion, and governmental regulation, the participants in the round table provide a provocative window into their thoughts and opinions as business leaders struggling to understand the deeper intellectual grounds and consequences of the financial crisis.

Part 3 moves from the question of values to the dangers of finance capitalism. For Sanjay Reddy, the distinctive aspect of the 2008 financial crash versus other manias, crashes, and panics is that this crisis has its roots in an epistemic problem. Market prices were largely opaque, concealed by complicated technical products that exacerbated the proclivity toward bubbles that is inherent in capitalism. More specifically, the rise of what Reddy and others in this section call finance capitalism, has created a financial industry that is so enormous and influential that it escapes political and ethical oversight. The challenge, Reddy writes—invoking an Arendtian voice—is to somehow allow a new form of public sovereignty emerge—a new way of energizing public politics to assert control over and limits upon the financial world.

Hunter Lewis, cofounder of Cambridge Associates, offers a controversial and impassioned rejection of Keynesian economics, which he associates with the rise of finance capitalism. The essence of Keynsianism, Lewis writes, is the fundamental belief in the benefits of debt and low—or even nonexistent—interest rates. Because Keynes supports a debt-driven economy, Lewis associates Keynes with the very system of finance capitalism that Reddy, Papadimitriou, Matias, and Burress argue is behind the crash. The bottom line, Lewis argues, is that Keynes's ideas may be helping the financial elite get richer, since they are first in line to borrow the cheap money. At the same time, Keynes's counsel to lower interest rates punishes the masses who save money, including the people clinging to life on a dollar a day. The Crash of 2008, Lewis writes, was caused by too much debt leading to a finance-induced housing bubble. Invoking common sense against Keynsian economics, he insists that we will not solve the crisis by adding more debt.

Against Lewis, Dimitri Papadimitriou enlists the economist Hyman Minsky, famous for arguing that finance was the cause of instability in a capitalist system, to defend Keynsian stimulus programs. Beyond his policy recommendations for more stimulus, Papadimitriou argues that Minsky has shown that economic stability is impossible, even with intelligent regulation and policy, because rational behavior leads to speculative booms. This means that we have undergone a shift, first from "commercial capitalism" to "industrial capitalism," and now from "paternalistic, managerial and welfare state capitalism" to "money-manager capitalism." It is money-manager capitalism that requires a supply of credit ever more elastic and the corollary hypercomplex financial innovations that justify that credit.

Along similar lines, David Matias and Sophia Burress also attribute the financial crisis to the emergence of a new idea of financial capitalism. For Matias and Burress, the growth of the financial industry is only one side of the story. Alongside the meteoric rise of the finance industry in the United States, they trace the rise of a consumer society. It is the combination of a consumer mentality that demands unlimited consumption with a financial industry that promises unlimited access to debt that makes possible the magnitude of bubbles that characterized the financial crisis. The focus on consumption at the expense of the public good means that the economic calculation of private interest has supplanted all attempts to imagine a common public good outside of economic growth. With no higher values to constrain economic expansion, we come to be ever more at the mercy of the unstable boom and bust cycle of capitalist cycles.

The essays in Part 4 turn to the tradition of political thinking from Max Weber to Karl Marx and from Michel Foucault to Rosa Luxemburg in order to seek to understand the intellectual origins of the financial crisis. Liah Greenfeld offers a provocative argument that the origins of capitalism as well as its present crisis are found in nationalism. Building on and departing from Max Weber's thesis that capitalism emerged from Calvinist Protestantism, Greenfeld argues that the emergence of a distinctly capitalist value system is tied to the modern rise of the nation-state. Specifically, the competitive national exertion unleashed by nationalism is what explains the willingness of capitalists to sacrifice and save in order to grow both their personal and national fortunes.

Robyn Marasco, Miguel de Beistegui, and Olivia Custer offer essays that in different ways trace the foundations of modern capitalism to neoliberalism. Neoliberalism, Marasco explains, is the steady reorganization of everyday life according to the logic of competitive market behavior. If Arendt worried that economic thinking was diminishing the realm of political judgment, neoliberalism celebrates the privatization of public services and the subordination of politics to economic principles of efficiency. As government of a vast and complex social economy comes to be understood as an attempt to manage and maximize economic resources, neoliberal government trades in calculable risks, and mobilizes powers and technologies of risk management through its dispersal across populations. Marasco sees this attempt to manage risk to be the underlying feature of modern capitalist society, one that had a central albeit unacknowledged role in spawning the bubble and the crash of the financial crisis.

Miguel de Beistegui agrees that the intellectual foundations of modern capitalism are found in the neoliberal elevation of market metrics over political judgment; what he disputes, however, is that the near collapse of the financial system in 2008 constitutes a crisis. A crisis involves a questioning and confronting of the existing system. Although the crisis should have been an opportunity to raise the question of the relation between economics and politics today, and especially between the market and the state, he worries that the submission of the state to the market is taken for granted and its rethinking is off limits. Beistegui argues that the state itself has progressively fallen under the scrutiny and undisputed authority of the market, so much so that the state is increasingly powerless and unnecessary.

One hallmark of neoliberalism is the value it places on "short-term thinking" and, in particular, the elevation of efficiency and success as measures of worth. Although it is common for politicians and commentators to rail against such short-term thinking, Olivia Custer argues that we need, at least in some scenarios, to accept the victory of neoliberalism and embrace its short-term thinking. Any political response to the dominance of economic logic may have to take on the "short-termism" of neoliberal logic neither as a regrettable myopia nor as a sign of insensitivity to moral values higher than mere economic ones but as the perspective that shapes our reality. For Custer, this does not mean that we meekly submit to the economic victory over politics, but that resistance is only possible with modern weapons.

Finally, Drucilla Cornell turns to Rosa Luxemburg, whom Arendt also credits with understanding the deep connection between capitalism and imperialism, as well as with the overwhelming of politics by economics. For Cornell, Luxemburg articulates the deep need for constant accumulation and thus constant violence that is ineradicably part of capitalism. Turning to South Africa and the profound effects of finance capitalism, imperialism, and the triumph of economics over politics, Cornell points to that country as offering an ethical and political response to the economic drivers of our world crisis.

The volume ends with Taun Toay's economic epilogue that furthers the spirit of interdisciplinary provocations found in this volume. If economics, politics, and the humanities too often reside in different worlds, the effort here is to begin the necessary efforts to bring humanist concerns to economics as well as to insist that humanists take seriously the logic and power of the economy in our time. Without such a dialogue, the continuing victory of economics over politics will not merely continue; it will increasingly overwhelm all residual political and ethical resistance, abandoning us to a world of infinite growth and unknowable shallowness.

PART I

Hannah Arendt and the Burden of Our Times

Can Arendt's Discussion of Imperialism Help Us Understand the Current Financial Crisis?

:: T R A C Y   B .   S T R O N G

In 1898, William Jennings Bryan had been protesting the imperialism of the U.S. annexation of the Philippines. Theodore Roosevelt responded in this manner: "If you were not opposed to the taking of California, you cannot be opposed to the taking of the Philippines." This is imperialism based not so much on the acquisition of resources—though those may come too—but on the desire for universal expansion. In this the United States was already not like earlier imperialisms—it was the expansion of an idea, an expansion of a way of life, an expansion that knew no natural limits. We have seen some of this in the last decade in the Middle East, but also before.

Hannah Arendt's discussion of what she calls "imperialism"—the second major section of her book *The Origins of Totalitarianism*—contains the following points.

1. The modern age is the age of *world* politics.

2. The modern age has seen a shift from localized and limited goals of national interest to the limitless pursuit of power after power with no certain nationally and territorially prescribed purpose and hence with no predictable direction. (*Origins of Totalitarianism*, 160–61).[1] This is what she calls modern imperialism. She quotes the great English imperialist in

Africa, Cecil Rhodes, who gave voice to the expansionary essence of imperialism: "I would annex the planets if I could."

3. Part of this shift to limitless power entails the growth of the invisible government over against the visible government (that is, the government that is not in the sight of the citizenry).

4. This rise in invisible governance in turn leads to an erosion, perhaps even a disintegration, of the nation-state, that is, of the space in which human beings belong and live as citizens. The erosion of the nation-state, she argues, is *consequent* to imperialism, a movement that "proved to contain nearly all the elements necessary for the subsequent rise of totalitarian movements. . . . Before the imperialist era, there was no such thing as world politics, and without it, . . . the claim to global rule would not have made sense" (164).

Arendt's worry is that the present age might turn out to be analogous to the period immediately prior to World War I, when a small incident triggered an unprecedented disaster. Statelessness is the danger, a danger that, it is worth noting, Nietzsche had already identified in 1871.

In *Origins of Totalitarianism*, Arendt seems not directly concerned with the economic realm: The Great Depression of 1929 and following does not even make the index to her book. This is misleading. She was nowhere near as hostile to the affairs of the *oikos* as many have made her out to be, but it is important to her to maintain a clear distinction between that which is political and that which is economic. Like Carl Schmitt (whom she had read extensively), she drew a sharp line between politics and economics. Thus the argument of the book on totalitarianism is that the infinite political expansionism of imperialism is a transposition to the political realm of the economic tendencies of capitalism, and this in turn is an essential component of totalitarianism.

So the first question we must ask is how the kind of imperialism that she describes—this new modern imperialism—might be related to the political in the modern world. She distinguishes modern imperialism from the acquisition-of-territory imperialism—on the model of Rome or China. What has happened in modern imperialism is that a principle characteristic of capitalist economic behavior has become the driving engine of what passes today for politics. Consider the basic form of capitalist commodity exchange: I have two bushels of wheat that I sell to you for twelve pairs of shoes that I sell to someone else for three front doors that I sell to you again for five pit bulls . . . and so on. The fundamental insight that Marx had into capitalism is that production was for the purpose of *exchange* (thus hopefully of making money) and only secondarily for the purpose of *use*. (I should note that Marx did not think this incompatible with an expanding economy—but that is a longer story.) The point here is that it is the nature of economic production under modern conditions not primarily to be for a goal, but to be constantly oriented toward the future, *a future that has no natural ending point, no goal*. This has increasingly become the dominant form of economic behavior and is characteristic of the behavior Arendt calls imperialist.

Although I do not need to go into detail about them, the elements of this transformation to an unlimited and goal-less economy are as follows:

1. There has been an enormous increase in capital transfers around the entire world. By 1997, on a typical day world capital markets would move $1.3 trillion at a time when the total yearly value of world exports was $3 trillion. In 2007 daily capital market transfers were $3.2 trillion which is equivalent to $2.2 billion *a minute*. Yearly total world exports are now up to $17.09 trillion.

2. Political aims are by definition specific and limited; economic aims have no closed end.

3. There has been a rise of regional and international policy-pursuing bodies. Worldwide there are at least 49,411 registered NGOs with the WANGO (World Association of Non-Governmental Organizations), of which, tellingly, the fewest proportionally and almost absolutely are in China.

4. Global corporations and financiers have made great efforts to divorce themselves from state regulations and tax regimes. With a few exceptions, it no longer makes sense to think in terms of national financial markets: They are increasingly being integrated into a single global one, as cross-border holdings of financial assets and cross-border flows of capital grow. Today, for example, foreigners hold 12 percent of U.S. equities, 25 percent of U.S. corporate bonds, and 44 percent of Treasury securities, up from 4, 1, and 20 percent, respectively, in 1975. Cross-border capital flows create stronger links among national markets and clearly

show that despite the past decade's financial crises and the backlash against globalization, the world capital market continues to integrate and evolve.

5. The governing of nations is increasingly based on principles of economic growth.

6. The rise of businesspersons where there once were politicians. As Peter Mandelson, the EU trade commissioner, said recently, "It's most likely that businessmen and entrepreneurs, rather than diplomats, ministers and special commissioners, will provide for economic and political rapprochement between Russia and the EU."[2]

Against this we see the particular genius that Arendt saw in the nation-state. The nation-state is about a nation—that is, a group of people who understand themselves as sharing a common historical identity. Should a *nation-state* engage in conquest as in the early pursuit of colonies, it will, she argues, necessarily eventually arouse national feelings in that which it conquers, which will in turn lead the conquered land to rebel in a national consciousness (171–73). Hence the French conquest of Algeria eventually produces the National Liberation Front (FLN) and an independent Algeria, despite France's having declared Algeria a department of France. Colonialism is thus distinct from what Arendt sees as contemporary imperialism. As she remarks, "What the imperialists actually wanted was expansion of political power without the foundation of a body politic" (181). She continues:

> For the first time, investment of power did not pave the way for investment of money, but export of power followed meekly in the train of exported money, since uncontrollable investments in distant countries threatened to transform large strata of society into gamblers, to change the whole capitalist economy from a system of production into a system of financial speculation, and to replace the profits of production with profits in commission. (181)

Echoing a passage in Nietzsche, Arendt laments the consequences of developments that gave rise to "the existence of people [who] live outside the common world, [who are] human beings in general—without citizenship, . . . representing nothing but [their] own absolutely unique individuality" (383). Like Weber and Schmitt, she is worried here about the demise of the political and thus of citizenship, both consequent in our times to the loss of saliency of the territorial nation that is its contemporary cradle. The seemingly uplifting Baha'i proclamation that "the Earth is but one country, and mankind its citizens" is dangerously misleading to her, a false rationalization of precisely the imperialism she deplores.

Ironically, the same terms can be applied to international finance actors, who, however, do not lament the nonrelevance of their citizenship (or often citizenships), but on the contrary revel in it. It is also clear that in this globalized world the traditional domestic instruments of politics in the economic realm—taxation and regulation—have lost much of their effectiveness. Such policies now require the coordination of several states, a coordination that is always extremely hard to accomplish. From Arendt's point of view, this is the worst of two worlds: The erosion of the nation-state gives rise to imperialism; the residue of the nation-state structure now impedes the solution to the problems of what she calls imperialism (remembering her understanding of its nature). Thus the globalization of economic actors, of media, and of financial transactions escapes to a great degree the control of nation-states. In relation to these developments, most governments—in particular that of the United States—flail or bewail their powerlessness. It is possible that in Europe we are beginning to see developments that go beyond this—Nietzsche predicted that "Europe wants to become one." We shall see.

And here there is a paradox. The French distinguish between *globalization* and *mondialisation*. The former designates the extension of economic rationality to all human activities—it is the basis of Arendt's notion of imperialism. It is the march toward an integrated global market. This is McDonald's in Tiananmen Square. *Mondialisation*—from the French *monde*, the world—refers to the extension to the planet of all forms of exchange, be they cultural, political, social, philosophical, or other.

However, these two realities interact. To take just one aspect: The consequences for the physical environment—loss of biodiversity, deforestation, pollution, and global warming are consequences that take place on a planetary level and are clearly the interaction of cultural, social, and political factors with economic factors—those of Arendt's imperialism. *The fiscal crisis has the same origins as the environmental one.*

Now these considerations seem at some point remote from what are generally taken to be Arendt's concerns. Indeed, she has often been criticized for amateurish dabbling in social science. I do not wish to enter into that debate here. It is, however, the case that Arendt thinks that developments such as those described above have profound and deleterious effects on humans in the world. Consider this passage:

> From a philosophical viewpoint, the danger inherent in the new reality of mankind [the realization or idea of the "unity of mankind"] seems to be that this unity, based on the technical means of communication and violence, destroys all national traditions and buries the authentic origins of all human existence. This destructive process can even be considered a necessary prerequisite for ultimate understanding between men of all cultures, civilizations, races and nations. Its result would be a shallowness that would transform man, as we have known him in five thousand years of recorded history, beyond recognition. It would be more than mere superficiality; it would be as though the whole dimension of depth, without which human thought, even on the mere level of technical invention, could not exist, would simply disappear. . . . It would ultimately arrive at a denominator of which we have hardly any notion today.[3]

Note a few points that might be made more salient. The destruction of "national traditions" buries the "authentic origins" of all human beings. This tells us that the *polis*—as the space in which humans encounter each other in speech and in which the political is present for political beings (*Dasein*, to fall back into Heideggerese)—requires that there be *different* communities of humans, each with its own qualities. Should this disappear, all that is of depth to human beings—the very possibility of thinking itself—would disappear. This is what Benjamin Barber has taught us to call McWorld.[4] Before one gives up on the nation-state—and its sins are many—one should think of what one would thereby be giving up.

Thus we have problems that are predicted by Arendt but for which the solution may not be clear in Arendtian terms. I have recently returned from two weeks in China where I was impressed by the concerted effort to deal with carbon emissions (a necessary effort—you will know why if you have tried to breathe the air in Beijing. Industrializing in thirty years focuses the mind marvelously). Compared to the United States, however, the coherence of their policies is striking. One can only ask if the present American nation-state is simply unable to deal with these problems.

Congress was unable to have a coherent policy by the Copenhagen Summit in December 2010.

Arendt spoke of the importance of inclusion *and* exclusion for a viable conception of citizenship. As Jean-Luc Nancy, in an essay called "La Comparution/Compearance," concludes in an explicitly Arendtian vein:

> Community . . . always excludes and on principle. . . . At the bottom, that which the community wants to exclude is that which does not let itself be identified in it. We call it the "other." . . . But to exclude, exclusion must designate: it names, identifies, gives form. "The other" is for us a figure imposed on the unpresentable (*infigurable*).[5]

Can we still do this? Can we still have political community? It seems doubtful. Modern developments, the ones Arendt described as imperialism, have undermined the foundation of the political, a foundation that must rest on exclusion and those who are not included. Everything seems double-edged—that which puts me in face-to-face contact by computer teletalk with a friend in Beijing also allows the transfer of $2.2 billion a minute.

I see a number of problems that are hard to deal with in terms of our "traditional" notions of citizenship. First, I think, is the fact that in modern times it has become increasingly difficult, in principle, to exclude anyone from claiming membership in a particular polity. This means, however, that all are members or can claim to be. One thinks here of the struggles in America over those coming across the border for work, or those in Europe who seek asylum in Germany, or Denmark, or the Netherlands. There is presently a large group of *sans papiers*—we call them "undocumented"—in France claiming the right of residence and membership. On what grounds do we exclude them? Most arguments are economic or atavistically nativist, and not political in Arendt's sense.

Second, in our modern age decisions arise on a whole range of issues that concern simply what Giorgio Agamben calls *"zoe"*—bare life. These include genetic modification of crops, medical technologies, surrogate mothering, cloning, and so forth. Biological life itself is presently becoming subject to changes that escape any conceivable sovereignty. The domain of potentially political concerns is thus dramatically extended by technology. But often these are thought in economic terms. There are already widely substantiated rumors of international traffic in human organs. It will prove feasible in the not too distant future to clone organs as replacement parts. Think of the market that will open up!

Third, as noted briefly above, the modern world has produced a whole new kind of people: These may come from what we call "failed states," or they may be asylum seekers from culturally oppressive regimes; they may be "illegal aliens" in search of employment that cannot be found "at home"; they may be prisoners at Guantánamo. Arendt notes that we now call them "displaced persons," not even, as we used to call them, "stateless persons." Approximately 3 percent of the world's population (200 million people) live outside the country of their birth, and for the greatest part, not by their own desire.

What to do about imperialism?

I suspect that while we will in the end recover from the present fiscal crisis (though, as Keynes remarked, "in the end we are all dead"), the deep structures and transformations that have given rise to it will not go away and will return in one form or another. Perhaps we need an equally deep transformation. It will involve a certain amount of reeducation. Although I understand the enthusiasm with which the Chinese have embraced the automobile, it has been unfortunate. Maurice Strong (the moving force behind the 1972 Stockholm Earth summit, the 1992 Rio Earth Summit, and the 2009 Copenhagen one, and today a major player in China's policies toward the environment) once said: "It is clear that current lifestyles and consumption patterns of the affluent middle-class . . . involving high meat intake, consumption of large amounts of frozen and convenience foods, ownership of motor vehicles, small electric appliances, home and work place air-conditioning, and suburban housing are not sustainable. . . . A shift is necessary toward lifestyles less geared to environmental damaging consumption patterns." On this issue at least, we must realize that we are part of nature, and that nature is not something out there for us to take from, a "standing reserve" as the philosopher Martin Heidegger called it, simply ready to be turned into energy. If the nature of what Arendt calls imperialism is to acquire without limit, humans will have to set limits, or nature will impose them and not kindly. If we do, however, then perhaps what Arendt called "love of the world" will be the basis for a new form of politics.

TWO

"No Revolution Required"

:: JEROME KOHN

for Alexander Bazelow

In the moment between sleep and waking one sometimes sees, not unconsciously as in a dream but prior to the actual consciousness of thinking, images of intense clarity. After Roger Berkowitz invited me to say a few words about the relevance of Hannah Arendt's analysis of late nineteenth-century imperialism to an economic event in the twenty-first century—which struck me as both intriguing and slightly daunting, since Arendt was wary of looking at the present through the prism of the past—I saw such an image. In it Arendt and Karl Marx were together in heaven, and she., gazing down on our current financial crisis, tugged him by the sleeve: "Look here, Marx," she said, "they did it all by themselves: *no revolution required.*" Though not a product of thinking, thinking about that image led me in the direction of thinking about the "they" who "did it all by themselves."

Let me say, first, that although Arendt agrees with Marx that socialism is the logical outcome of capitalism, she fundamentally differs from him in her understanding of imperialism as "the first stage in political rule of the bourgeoisie" rather than, as he understood it, "the last stage of capitalism." That difference is of considerable importance to us, since Arendt writes of imperialism in *The Origins of Totalitarianism*, the elusive masterwork whose overall intention is to demonstrate, through the examples of Nazi Germany and Stalinist Russia, that totalitarianism is *Entpolitisierung*—the abandonment of politics—wherever it appears. She treats imperialism not as a cause but as an "origin" or "element" of totalitarianism, which as such, and unlike a cause, does not disappear with the disappearance of totalitarian regimes. Thus to discern imperialism in the twenty-first century is to recognize neither the resurgence of totalitarianism nor the end of capitalism and the beginning of socialism, but something entirely different: the unresolved problem, in a later stage of bourgeois rule, of maintaining political order in a world whose political borders are increasingly transgressed by, among other technological innovations, electronic transfers of vast sums of money.

Second, what Arendt means by imperialism is neither colonialism, national aggrandizement, nor empire building in the old Roman sense. She defines imperialism as "expansion for expansion's sake," a concept that entered politics via a new *mentalité*, a new vision of Europe's position in the world, a new *Weltanschauung*, if you will. To her, imperialism, as distinct from the age-old practice of conquest, gives an entirely new meaning to politics, and the ironic reason is that its principle of ever-increasing expansion has its source in the *necessity* of economic activity, which since antiquity had been thought of as a subsidiary condition of the *freedom* that can be realized only in political activity. Expansionism was born in the late nineteenth century from the export of capital from Europe to the noncapitalist world, an economic necessity dictated by the accumulation of surplus, or, as Arendt prefers to call it, "superfluous" money at home—superfluous because its lopsided distribution radically diminished the capacity of domestic markets to make it productive. After the disastrous financial swindles of the 1870s and '80s, which were on a scale Bernard Madoff might admire, the need to protect their far-flung capital investments, and the huge profits derived from interest on them—not only from unscrupulous swindlers but also, and more importantly, from straightforward inter-European competition for the same markets—provoked capitalists, for the first time, to ensure their enterprises by backing them up with the power of the state. It was then that Europe's principal nation-states, Britain foremost among them, also for the first time took or mistook the economic principle of "expansion for expansion's sake" as their own aim and goal. Arendt finds the well-known saying that "the British Empire was acquired in a fit of absent-mindedness" unfortunately true, the result not of deliberate political policy, but, on the contrary, of self-propelling economic processes. Much more might be said about the revaluation of politics that followed its absorption of economic practices, and the gradual overcoming of the resistance of traditional statesmen to that absorption, not least in Britain itself. This is how Arendt sums it up:

The significant fact about this . . . revaluation, which began at the end of the [nineteenth] century and is still in effect, is that it began with the application of bourgeois convictions to foreign affairs and only slowly was extended to domestic politics. Therefore, the nations concerned were hardly aware that the recklessness that had prevailed in private life, and against which the public body always had to defend itself and its individual citizens, was about to be elevated to the one publicly honored political principle.[1]

That said, let me jump ahead to the preface Arendt wrote for a new edition of the "Imperialism" part of *Origins* in 1967, a year when tens of thousands of American soldiers were embroiled in combat on the other side of the earth. In seeing an essentially nonpolitical use of military might exemplified in a war fought in Vietnam, a small faraway nation that presented no threat to America—a war that, had we not been defeated in it, would have precluded the self-determination of the Vietnamese people— Arendt brings her work on imperialism up to date. She admits no analogy between Lyndon Johnson's 1965 decision to escalate the war in Southeast Asia in the name of the cold war's "domino theory" and Neville Chamberlain's 1938 decision to appease Hitler by ceding him Czechoslovakia's Sudetenland for the sake of "peace in our time"—which, when Hitler attacked Britain a couple years later, appeared as futile as it was ill-fated. That analogy was often invoked in defense of our action in Vietnam, as if we had gone there to avert further communist aggression, as it more recently has been invoked in defense of our action in Iraq, as if we went there to avert further acts of terrorism after 9/11. In both cases the analogy was far-fetched, and in retrospect appears absurd: Would Ho Chi Minh's unification of the Vietnamese people have prompted him to attack the United States? And what did the invasion of Iraq accomplish, other than wreaking havoc on the land and lives of the people of Iraq (who, by the way, constituted a far more literate society than our own), and what did it prove, other than that Iraq had no weapons of mass destruction and had nothing to do with the events of 9/11, in which not a single Iraqi participated?

I think the likelihood that those distant wars were not propelled by principles consonant with the common interest of American citizens legitimizes revisiting what Arendt has to say about the short-lived first stage of European imperialism, short-lived because it began in 1884 and ended only thirty years later, in 1914, with the outbreak of World War I. The fact that the worldwide dispersal of European nation-states' military power to protect their economic expansion boomeranged in the first total war in Western history was suggestive, I think, vis-à-vis the as yet unknown political fallout of the worldwide economic collapse of 2008.

To no small extent that collapse was caused by extraordinary recklessness in the marketing of debt derivatives, which were packaged and profligately sold by Wall Street, repackaged and resold to whoever would buy them, until their exchange value evaporated into thin air. The resulting situation is not comparable to the overproduction of a commodity, say coffee beans, that can at least be dumped in the sea with no one, and certainly not national treasuries, left holding the bag. Washington's legislators, bolstered by economic experts, plan to recover from the current crisis by stimulating the economy with infusions of public money, and to forestall its repetition by regulating and (one hopes) limiting the activities of the largest banks and financial institutions. But calculating economic risk is one thing, and thinking politically about the power potential in the constraints of law, which might have prevented the crisis in the first place, is another. I had thought that lawmakers on their own might have been alert to this other thing.

Moreover, the coincidence of the political application of the economic principle of "expansion for expansion's sake" and the waging of war is all too apparent, and not only in hindsight. In the ongoing war in Afghanistan a number of Washington's military experts take it as virtually self-evident that our power, which they conceive as force, must increase even to maintain our presence there, that is, to avoid the debacle of another Vietnam. Does the nature of the war in Afghanistan alter the fact that escalation was the strategy America adopted in Vietnam? The alternative, as they see it, is to endure the humiliation (of capitulating to the Taliban) and hazard the danger of a resurgent al Qaeda by pulling up stakes and exiting. Thus an opaque curtain seems to separate the economic calculation of "progress," that is, the cost-benefit analysis of losses suffered against harms inflicted, from the political thought that the division of power between federal, state, and city governments, and the branches of those governments, might generate sufficient public power—the opposite of force—to ward off remote offensive wars that willy-nilly bear the earmark of imperialism.[2]

To increase public power by dividing it is central to the Constitution of the United States, the founding document of a polity whose self-understanding was to "establish Justice, insure domestic Tranquility, provide for the common defense, promote the general Welfare, and secure the Blessings of Liberty for ourselves and our Posterity." A voluntary union of independent states for the sake of its political potential to realize the Founders' intentions is by definition adverse to every manifestation of imperialism within it. Nonetheless, no amount of reflection on the Constitution can assure the preservation of its principles, just as no amount of expertise can foresee the consequence of either horn of the dilemma facing us in Afghanistan. Both of these distinct cautions are implicit in the last sentence of Arendt's preface: "No matter how much we may be capable of learning from the past, it will not enable us to know the future."

Power is among the oldest political concepts, indeed a "conceptual pillar" of all forms of government since Plato first defined them. But the question here concerns the "power-thirsty" individuals who desire the power of the state for their private benefit, those individuals, that is, who are unwilling to acknowledge the public benefit of political power— namely, the freedom of the polity from which power accrues. In one of her most dramatic rereadings of political thinkers, Arendt finds both the source and the consequence of the incursion of bourgeois economic values into the public realm, and thus also of nineteenth-century imperialism, in the seventeenth-century philosopher Thomas Hobbes, "the only great thinker," in her words, "who ever attempted to derive public good from private interest." Claiming, or at least pretending to claim, that when properly understood private interest *is* public good, Hobbes sets forth in *Leviathan* a commonwealth that has no basis in "divine law, the law of nature, or the law of social contract;" that is, the commonwealth is not based on one or the other or some combination of those realms on which traditional pre- and post-Hobbesian definitions of commonwealths have always been anchored. To put it differently, Hobbes foresees a form of government rooted in and growing from the *acquisition* of power, of "power after power."

It may be helpful to recall that *Leviathan* was written in a time of instability in Britain, the result of the civil wars fought over the distribution of power between Crown and Parliament, of the regicide that removed the Crown from that equation, and of the dictatorship that replaced it. Hobbes designs Leviathan—whose familiar image, a huge body composed of the bodies of more or less identical men, literally incorporating its members—for the sake of stability, and from a perspective that would take three hundred years to become fully valid.[3] The bourgeoisie was only emerging in the seventeenth century as that class of society for which power is "the accumulated control that permits the individual to fix prices and regulate supply and demand in such a way that they contribute to his own advantage." But the individual, being a minority of one, is aware that his private advantage depends on the power of a majority, the power *accumulated* from a majority of individuals, one after the other. It follows from what Arendt calls "the unequaled magnificence of Hobbes's logic" that when—which was by no means the case in his time—each man is driven by nothing but his own interest, then the thirst for power will be "the fundamental passion" of all men, and that therefore the philosopher's answer to the question about "power-thirsty" individuals lies in the nature of man, that in which every human being shares equally.[4]

The equality of men, to Hobbes, is manifest in their ability to kill one another, whether by strength, duplicity, or conspiracy. Their consequent fear of dying violently is the *raison d'être* of Leviathan, a "mortal god," in Hobbes's words, whose power "over-awes" its members, thus holding out to them the possibility of a life that is not "solitary, poor, nasty, brutish, and short." Those famous words are usually read, as Hobbes clearly wants them to be read, as describing life in the prepolitical or postpolitical or in any case apolitical state of nature, but not by Arendt.

On the contrary, Arendt sees in them a wholly different intention on Hobbes's part, namely, to describe the lives of those who, in ruthless competition with each other, so crave the protection of an irresistible power that they willingly sacrifice their political rights, whether as subjects of a monarchy or citizens of a republic, to create Leviathan. The obverse of Hobbesian man's fear is his *self*-interest, which disables him from founding a polity wherein his own interest would weigh as much but no more than any other man's.

What Hobbes envisions is not a polity, a political association that balances diverse interests, but a monolithic power that crushes them. Leviathan's members are mutually equal in their capacity to overcome and surpass one another, either by force or what Hobbes calls "wit," but their forfeiture of political equality before the law of justice deprives them of the traditional source of public power, namely, the ability to weave bonds of fellowship, responsibility, and solidarity between them. Hobbes derives law not from a universal or generally agreed-upon standard of justice, as philosophers since Plato have done or tried to do, but from a different sort of standard altogether, namely, *success*. It follows that law is whatever Leviathan decrees it to be for the sole purpose of liberating the pursuit of its members' self-interest from "external impediments," a purpose that can be imagined as the lack of constraint in a freely flowing river. Whereas the "artificial chains" of civil law check man's brutality and ruthlessness, within that image an *indeterminate* human freedom is never anything but an illusion.[5]

On the one hand, Hobbes's commonwealth is a national security state carried to the *n*th degree, a state that logically is owed no loyalty by its members should it be defeated in war. On the other, and Hobbes knows this better than anyone, Leviathan is a tyranny, the classical perversion of polities, but a tyranny whose own interest—and this is entirely new in the history of political thought—is nothing but the collective self-interest of its members. Thus, and again logically, its members retain the right embedded in their fear of violent death, their "natural" or pre-Leviathan right to defend themselves by any means if under any circumstances, including the commission of capital crimes, the absolute power of Leviathan, to which they submit only in exchange for their security, threatens them. In other words, at one and the same time Leviathan casts out from its protective shield any of its members whose self-interest is thwarted by other members' selfsame interests *and* sanctions behavior from the unsuccessful or unlucky that would be judged criminal, if not treasonous, in a polity. With acerbity Arendt remarks, "Hobbes foresees and justifies the social outcasts' organization into a gang of murderers as a logical outcome of the bourgeoisie's moral philosophy."[6]

So it turns out that the stability of Leviathan is provisional, to say the least, and this is where Arendt's rereading of Hobbes becomes really interesting. Three preliminary considerations, however, should be mentioned. First, when power is looked upon as the means by which man's self-interest is secured, it must constantly grow. Even "to guarantee the status quo," power conceived in the means-ends category, rather than as a polity's telos, will atrophy if it has no obstacle to overcome and, in Arendt's words, "collapse . . . into the . . . chaos of the private interests from which it sprang." Therefore, Hobbes restores "the condition of perpetual war," the *bellum omnium contra omnes*, not to individual men but to individual states or, which in *Leviathan* comes to the same thing, individual corporate bodies. Arendt notes, not without irony, that the "ever-present possibility of war" lends Leviathan a "prospect of permanence," that is, a prospect of continuously increasing its power "at the expense of other states."

Second, Arendt sees confusion in the meaning of liberalism and conservatism when a free market economy, which theoretically rejects state intervention, requires (as it does today) precisely that intervention. In the nineteenth century it was the bourgeois *liberal* class that sought the power of the state, not to intrude on, but to safeguard the profitability of its investments, and the first advocates of imperialism as a political policy were liberals, not conservatives. Those who now see an opportunity for limitless expansion in a global economy, and in theory are opposed to any regulatory measures imposed on it, are called *conservative*. Yet they are the true heirs of those nineteenth-century liberals; they are our bourgeoisie, our imperialists, and more Hobbesian than they may care to admit in assuming that the riches flowing from a worldwide economy are and ought to be *pro bono publico*, in fact the overriding public good.[7]

Third, and this is Arendt's principal point, Leviathan is the artificial entity Hobbes constructs to fit men who are essentially the *same*, that is, identical in their self-interest, into a society. To be a member of bourgeois society is ipso facto to be ignorant of the common interests that arise not in the midst of socialized self-interests, but on the contrary, between men who are alike only in their *distinctness* from each other. The interests that distinct human beings discover they share in common link them in political friendship (Aristotle's *philia politikē*) and are a condition sine qua non of political life (Aristotle's *bios politikos*). The very possibility of a public political life lies in its separation from private interests, and also from the management of those interests, which Aristotle calls *oikonomia* and we call economics. *Oikonomia* is therefore not of interest in traditional political life, not *inter esse*, not *between* men who lead that life. To ancient Romans, the most political of people, *non inter homines esse* (not to be among [distinct] men) meant to be dead. Of course, Hobbes scorns all such distinctions because his extraordinary imagination foresees a time when economic life will supplant political life and economic societies replace polities.

Now comes the part that is of interest to us. If the power of Leviathan transcends traditional legal, moral, and political limits, it is no less true that the individual, in Hobbes's words, "cannot assure the . . . means to live well, which he hath at present, without the acquisition of more." Thus the acquisitiveness of self-interest is "objective" and need not be associated with human greed. If all greedy men are self-interested, the converse, all self-interested men are greedy, does not follow. One might rather say that greed is an economic *vice* that transforms magnanimity into avarice much as envy transforms courage into necklessness. Satisfaction with property already possessed, originally a conservative disposition, contravenes the tried and true economic principle of "expansion for expansion's sake." But, and here's the rub, property is not unlimited; not only is it finite in terms of the earth's resources, but it is also constantly diminished by the consumption of those resources. For that reason capitalism transmutes property into wealth, and wealth is the *beginning* rather than the *result* of acquisition.

In a chilling metaphor Arendt likens imperialists' "lifeblood" to "gold," for as life begets life, so money begets money, and wealth, as King Midas discovered when the fruit he reached for turned into gold, is in itself not consumable. Thus there are two dynamic processes going on simultaneously, a seemingly infinite increase of private wealth and a seemingly infinite increase of state or corporate power, but both are delusions, for mortality concludes the one and self-destruction the other. It is not that the life span of an individual limits the growth of his wealth, but that to exceed "all personal needs" wealth "borrows" from the public realm the indefinite "length of time . . . needed for continuous accumulation" and thereby ceases to be a private interest, except sometimes in name, as in the Carnegie Endowment and Ford Foundation, for example, or the Frick Collection and Morgan Library, and so on. The infinite progress, however, of even the most enlightened self-interest is also a delusion, nothing but a "temporary compromise," as Arendt puts it, between "political action" and "faith" in wealth as a "self-moving principle."[8]

If Hobbes sees that an endless acquisition of wealth corresponds to an endless acquisition of power, to Arendt the upshot of that correspondence is "the blind conformism of bourgeois society," which deprives men of their ability to act into the future. If men are free to act into it, the future cannot be told in advance, but Hobbes, because Leviathan (like all tyrannies) removes the ground of action from beneath its members' feet, foretells a future in which perpetual warfare—or constant competition— culminates in a final contest that "provideth for every man, by Victory or Death." But if an imperial state or corporate body were victorious and its expansion consummated in an ultimate conflict, then it could not persist, much less flourish, without "more material to devour." Thus Cecil Rhodes despaired that he could not "annex the planets."

If, however, there is nothing left for it to digest from which more wealth can be excreted, then it enters on what Arendt calls the "Road to

Suicide," for only from its ruins can imperialism's animating principle of *acquiring* wealth be regenerated. This is one reason Arendt agrees with Marx (though hardly with his dialectical reasoning) that the logical end of capitalism is socialism, a *single* enterprise, or, as she might put it, expropriation perfected. The imperialist cycle of the expansion of private wealth and state or corporate power leading to self-destruction would then begin anew. That may follow from the magnificence of Hobbes's logic, but will it necessarily come to pass in the world in which we live?

Has America already become an imperial state, as Gary Wills supposes in a recent admonitory article entitled "Entangled Giant" in the *New York Review of Books*,[9] or are we—you and I—citizens of a republic with enough freedom left between us to interrupt automatic economic processes and the pseudopolitical processes that reflect them? To put it another way, if we were to generate sufficient power to interrupt those processes and to dismantle the mechanistic system in which they function, would we not appear as actors who, acting together, discovered a public space in our midst?

Having begun these remarks by noting that our current economic collapse required no Marxian revolution, permit me to state the corollary: Reforms aimed at curbing the self-interest that moves the bourgeois economy, which had a definite beginning in time, cannot sustain it indefinitely. Though there are not important differences in Marx's and Arendt's perceptions of the rise and rule of the bourgeoisie, the difference in their perceptions of its decline is crucial. Did Marx want to see the whole capitalist economic apparatus brought to its knees and demolished? Is that what the proletarian revolution would accomplish, or would it more likely maintain the apparatus and change its management and ownership? Marx, who was far from unappreciative of the material accomplishments of capitalism,[10] might well consider that change as setting the economy right side up for the welfare and relief of the exploited working and laboring classes of his day.

But what might he have made of the October Revolution, which, as Arendt says, issued not in "an earthly paradise" but its very opposite, the "hell on earth" of total domination for everyone who came under its sway, not excluding the alienated workers and oppressed masses for the sake of whose "emancipation" it was supposedly undertaken? Of course it does not stop there. The ownership of the economic system can change again, of which there has been ample evidence in the political events of the past twenty years, in Poland's Solidarity movement, in Czechoslovakia's Velvet Revolution, in the multicolored revolutions in eastern Europe and elsewhere, in the amalgamation of East and West Germany, and within Russia itself. By and large this change has not dispelled but only redirected the people's disillusion with the previous change, sometimes to the point of nostalgia for the status quo ante. It is the system itself, or rather the more general question of the economic production of power, which is of *political* interest.

Another way to perceive the decline of bourgeois economic rule is through the public light that illuminates its own depletion in Arendt's analysis of imperialism. That may sound paradoxical but is only seemingly so, for even in periods when political action—action accompanied by speech—is enveloped in obscurity, the light that emits the power of the public realm need not be snuffed out in the human spirit.[11] On the contrary, that light inspirits the most profound political thinkers, from Plato, Aristotle, and Augustine, among the earlier, to Dante, Machiavelli, and (somewhat perversely) Hobbes, to Montesquieu, Kant, Hegel, and (also perversely) Marx, to Oakeshott and Arendt, among the later. Though less apparently so in Aristotle, Montesquieu, Hegel, and Oakeshott, that light always reveals the specific darkness of the world into which it shines, or as Hobbes puts it, "grief for the present calamities of my country." Public light surrounds Arendt's analysis of imperialism and renders imperialist phenomena transparent.

Today, for example, that light irradiates in the recesses of the human psyche the fear of dying violently, and with that fear Hobbes's insight that the weak are equal to the strong in inflicting death has once again become relevant in our nominal "war against terror." We approve that war out of fear of the violent loss of our social predilection for living companionable, abundant, decent, refined, and ever-longer lives, and yet the entire sphere of social life, even at its most accommodating, when seen in the light of the public realm appears deprived of freedom.

To *see* that deprivation may encourage us to judge ourselves, not as liberals or conservatives located somewhere on the exhausted political spectrum sagging from left to right, but as *persons* who were not born simply to reap the harvests of our work before we die, but, as Augustine says, to be *beginnings*, to be initiators of something new that can save the world, at least for the time being, from what the remarkable American philosopher and logician, Charles Sanders Peirce, calls the "indubitable result of the theory of probabilities."

All human affairs rest upon probabilities. . . . If man were immortal he could be perfectly certain of seeing the day when everything in which he had trusted should betray his trust, and, in short, of coming eventually to hopeless misery. He would break down, at last, as every great fortune, as every dynasty, as every civilization does. In place of this we have death. . . . He who would not sacrifice his own soul to save the whole world, is, as it seems to me, illogical in all his inferences, collectively.[12]

That suits Arendt well, except for the word "death." For her it is not death but *birth*, "in which the faculty of action is ontologically rooted," that can keep us from being, as Peirce says, "illogical," that is, from failing to accede to the will's ceaseless struggle against necessity in all its forms, including that of economics. Arendt goes further when she distinguishes the interminable oscillations of the will from a freedom that refutes the *rule* of necessity, for in taking action humans not only deny but also nullify and transcend the world as it *must* be. In times such as ours, when the light of the public is obscured not only by the accretion but also by the well-intentioned disbursement of socialized private wealth, the difficulty of humans joining together, acting in concert, and begetting the political power to divert the world,[13] along with its institutions, from their otherwise inevitable default, is considerable. To enter on political action has always required courage, because of the sheer inertial mass of what it sets out to displace, and even more so because of the contingencies that keep action's outcome from being known before its unrest subsides and a recharged world resettles. It is those contingencies that literally keep acting persons from knowing what they are doing, what they are bringing forth into the world, for that *cannot* be known until their deeds have become facts, that is, until what they are doing is done (*fieri—factum est*). If they knew prior to that, their action would not be free but rather the unfolding of a plan, which, as Arendt insists, *pace* Marx, is never the actual experience of humans engaged in action. To "stand guard" over facts, as she sees it, is the work of historians, whose backward glance brings the past into the present, and with it a depth to human affairs that otherwise they would lack. By respecting those facts and plumbing that depth, Hegel, the preeminent philosopher of History, discerns the emergence of an overall plan or pattern of human actions in which the *Idea* of freedom has been weaving in the human mind *and* the human world from time immemorial. In the reality of that *Idea* the appearance of contingency in action is revealed as all along having been necessary, behind the backs of actors, so to speak. If Hegel lays to rest the age-old philosophic problem of *reconciling* freedom with necessity, Arendt's conception of freedom as indeterminacy, that is, as the *opposite* of necessity, a freedom whose *conditio per quam* is the contingency or sheer accidentality that always appears when persons take action, is without precedent in the history of political thought, no less so than Hobbes's tyrannical commonwealth, in revulsion to which it is partly developed.[14]

It is true that action always aims at a particular goal, but to Arendt its political and human significance lies less in achieving that goal[15] than in clearing a public space in whose light persons in their plurality,[16] that is, persons not related by kinship but through friendship in their distinctness from one another, can appear and be recognized as the nonidentical but identifiable *who* each of them is. That alone is their political identity, the condition of the possibility of their political equality, power, and, in the memories of those who come after them, their "earthly immortality." From the beginning of the modern age, and especially since what Arendt calls "the rise of the social," the originally Christian withdrawal from political life has issued in a general indifference to the appearance and mutual recognition of the uniqueness of persons in public. But today, in our perplexities over what can be done and which choices should be made, regarding not only bailouts and bonuses but also joblessness, abject poverty, and homelessness—in short, worldlessness—and in the felt need that our own voices be heard and our own opinions heeded, we might stop to think that our right to be free *from* politics comes at the price of our right to be free *for* politics.

As political beings, we have the right to exercise our ability to speak and act in public, to face up to and, as best we can, guide the fluctuations and capriciousness of human affairs, and, not least, to fend off the dissolution of the world by welcoming newcomers into it; for the odds are favorable that in becoming and being recognized as *who's*, that is, in achieving their individual political identities, these new persons will *spontaneously* initiate new speech and new action to supersede what we who welcome them have said and done before them. The miracle of natality—of preventing the world, generation after generation, from betraying the trust vested in it by plural men—is, in Hannah Arendt's view, the birthright of every human being and the dignity inherent in every human life.

THREE

Judging the Financial Crisis

:: ANTONIA GRUNENBERG

When Hannah Arendt published her book on totalitarianism in England, she gave it the title *The Burden of Our Time*. More than fifty years later, this title sounds like a metaphor for the current world crisis. A fundamental fragility of the financial system seems to be the "burden of our time." Behind that surface, the interrelations between economy and politics as well as between politics and financial interest are at stake. Ever and ever again questions come up: How much power and control do governments have? How much influence can they exert on processes that run beyond the boundaries of nation-states? It is a challenge to analyze these phenomena and to judge the consequences and the contingencies that accompany them. As a political theorist, I am not a specialist in financial affairs. But still, I have to judge. As citizen of whichever country, I want to understand what happens and what consequences the financial crisis may have for the political future of democracy.

Asked to reflect on the question, "Can Arendt's discussion of imperialism help us understand the current financial crisis?" I will first summarize Arendt's historic-analytical understanding of imperialism and totalitarianism. Then, I will discuss the striking parallels between her analysis and the reality of today. Finally, I turn to the validity of her thesis today.

I.

It is well known that Hannah Arendt has written often on the issue whether analogies can help us understand historic events. She cautions that trying to understand the events of any time means first to look at the singularity of the event and its specific historical appearance before comparing it to any other events. Arendt questioned the effort to understand the events of today with the conceptual instruments of the past. She insisted that a close look at the very core of present events would be necessary in order to gain new categories. One basic analytical conclusion *The Origins of Totalitarianism* was that totalitarianism is a structurally new form of domination that did not have any precedents. Or to put it in the famous words of René Char, which were quoted by Arendt on several occasions: "Our heritage is not preceded by any testament."[1] We alone are asked to understand the event history confronts us with.

At the time when Arendt started reflecting about the phenomenon of totalitarianism, many of Arendt's colleagues did the same. Mainly European scholars—Franz Neumann, Ernst Fraenkel, Sigismund Neumann, Carl J. Friedrich, and Eric Voegelin—analyzed the economic and political aspects of totalitarianism. Arendt criticized their basic assumption that totalitarianism was a specific form of dictatorship. She was opposing the argument that one should qualify totalitarianism as a form of bad rule. However, she concluded: One has first to study what is unprecedented in totalitarianism, then uncover the appropriate analytical instruments that underlie it, and only then can one understand it. And that she did, revealing that at the origins of this new form of domination there was a foregoing inner erosion of democratic nation-states and their political bodies. Nation-states, she argued, fell apart under the pressure of the imperialist expansion of capitalism. Corruption poisoned democratic institutions; financial scandals ruined the middle class. Governments were not able to correct these failures. As a consequence, the trust of the people in institutions faded. Part of that process was the rise of mass movements and organizations with "leaders" at their front who promised to solve the crisis and to punish the "culprits." Out of it came a new, modern type of Jew-hatred, which aimed at the annihilation of the Jews. From Arendt's perspective, the erosion of nation-states as well as the breakdown of the parliamentary system and the reemergence of anti-Semitism, provoked traditional European elites to ally with the mob toward the end of destroying democratic political structures. For her, totalitarianism was not just a change in type of government, but the emergence of a new form of total domination. Regarding the unprecedented nature of totalitarianism, Arendt argued that the new leaders established a regime that was based on a combination of ideology and terror that had never existed before. Its goal and its practice were the annihilation of humanity within societies. Her book laid out the specificity of the multilayered origins of totalitarianism and also characterized the unprecedented form of totalitarian rule itself. What she offered was—as I have just sketched out—an argument about the interrelation between totalitarianism and imperialism.

In the following I focus on Arendt's analysis of imperialism as being at the origin of the breakdown of democracies. Thereafter I will list several points that Arendt highlights as important to the very essence of imperialism—linking them to questions that we are confronted today.

II.

Notwithstanding Arendt's sharp criticism of false analogies, it is tempting to read her study of imperialism as a commentary on the current crisis, that is, to analogize her criticism of imperialism with our perception of globalization and liberal financial capitalism. Let me explain what in the current situation attracts my attention.

First, let me take Arendt's thesis that the imperialist bourgeoisie "succeeded in destroying the nation-state."[2] She means that economic expansion and political conquest in the imperialist era were undermining and corrupting democratic institutions in the home countries. There are lots of examples in French and British history that support her thesis that the political body was corrupted by the promise of imperialist profit. If we transfer this insight from the world of yesterday into the reality of today, could we not say that global financial networks destroy national political bodies? It is tempting to say so, but if we take a closer look, we can see a big difference. Global actors need a stable political system in order to be backed by laws when they act. They need to act in a regulated and protected way, which means they need to act within international legal procedures. They seem to have no interest in destroying the nation-state as long as the state works in their interests.

Second, like V. I. Lenin and Rosa Luxemburg, Arendt understands that "expansion as a permanent and supreme aim of politics is the central political idea of imperialism" (125). Isn't it true that globalization and the freely floating streams of real and symbolic capital are supposed to be aims in themselves? Yes, and yet, we can see also that there is no expanding imperialism any more. Instead of imperialist empires, we have the World Bank, the World Trade Organization, and the International Monetary Fund, all of which regulate the economies of the world on an unimaginably wide scale. And then there are the oil companies and the military industry. One need not be a Marxist to conclude that multinational corporations and international organizations have supplanted the state in the modern world. Since the one who regulates the market controls the political body, states and nations are not the primary drivers of global expansion. The only interest national politicians seem to have is to satisfy people in providing jobs by getting the market going. So here the difference lies in the fact that financial capitalism moves beyond imperialist expansion based within nation-states.

Third, in an almost sarcastic style Arendt comments: "The only grandeur of imperialism lies in the nation's losing battle against it" (132). If we transfer this insight into the reality of today we would say that the grandeur of financial capitalism lies in the dependence of national institutions (including the legislative powers) on the health of the market. It seems as if nation-states have never been able to recover from their defeat that left them dependent on interest groups.

Fourth, responding to the question of how to counteract this tendency, Arendt judges the historic opposition to the state that exists within European nation-states: "The tragedy of this half-hearted opposition was not that many national representatives could be bought by the new imperialist businessmen; worse than corruption was the fact that the incorruptible were convinced that imperialism was the only way to conduct world politics" (132). Are not Western politicians preaching that there is no alternative to liberal market capitalism? This rationale comes to us in an ideological form. It is said that beyond liberal capitalism there is supposed to be only terrorism and poverty. This maxim seems to be at the core of the issue: After the end of socialism, capitalism is said to be self-evident. There are supposed to be no alternatives. The only way to change seems to lie within the system, not beyond it. The answer the political system provides is to ameliorate the legal system in order to repair damages already done and to prevent further damages. This reformist rationale has now been practiced for about three decades, without preventing any financial catastrophes.

Fifth, regarding politics in times of imperialism, Arendt reflects on the circumstance that politics has been replaced by the exertion of pure power. She points at the "aimless accumulation of power" (137). She defines "power as the essence of political action" (138), power being "the only content of politics" (138). However, Arendt has a very distinct concept of political power. It is therefore important to add that with her criticism she aims at the mere accumulation of means in the hands of groups or individual persons. Power within this context has lost its bond with the people. Looking at history, Arendt identified the inner bond between "the people" and power as one of the basic maxims of the American founding fathers. Throughout the history of liberalism, power was claimed to belong to the people. A government should not "own" power, but power should be lent to it. This is formulated in the documents of the American revolution, beginning with the Declaration of Independence in 1776. The consequence of this understanding of power was: If power is cut off from the people and the people do not claim it, then there is, Arendt adds, a "lack of interest in public affairs" (138). With that she focuses on the retreat of the people into their private lives. Exactly that was what the founding fathers foresaw as the nightmare of democracy: antipolitical apathy. They kept warning that if interest groups and factions were to take over society, people would be cut off from power, and power would spiral out of control. It seems as if the warning of the founding fathers has become true. Aren't the power groups of today even imitating the founding fathers in saying, "We hold these truths to be self-evident"?

What I am trying to say in this analysis is that while it is very tempting to follow Hannah Arendt in analogizing her analysis of imperialism to the reality of postmodern financial capitalism, we must be wary of doing so. Today is not yesterday.

III.

Those who want to understand the financial crisis can find a lot of enriching ideas in Arendt's thinking. But they are nevertheless confronted with the question: What is unprecedented in the present stream of events? What is new compared to the economic-financial and political situation of the time period of classical imperialism (1888–1914)? What does not fit into that image Arendt presents about the political impact of the imperialist era? And how does that affect our political structures?

Arendt's starting point was that in the time of imperialism the European bourgeoisie did not take a stand against economic interest groups (123). Today we can say: Financial groups, industrial groups, political pressure groups are intermingled in such a way that they are transformed into new power groups: the oil group—the bank group—the military group—not to forget the big rating agencies and their CEOs who are deciding the future of states. But we have to appreciate that this is a new type of economic-politics in which the basic question in the history of political ideas—*cui bono*? Who benefits? Is it in the common interest?—plays a different role than before; now, as never before, the so-called common interest is supposed to be identical with economic growth. So the situation of today seems to be structurally different from that of yesterday because economic and financial processes run along their own dynamics. They do not have to defeat democracy because they have functionalized it. They are legitimated by laws that protect them. They force the political body to follow them into that process. There will be no opposition to economic and financial processes as long as those processes are seen to be without any alternative. The loss of the ability of the political body to correct the course of economic-finance deeply affects our political system and our way of thinking.

There is no class struggle anymore because there are no more classes who can clearly be identified as such; all social layers and groups seem to be intertwined economically and financially. Whenever a bank crashes, a worker can tell himself that within five or three or seven months I am going to lose my job. Whenever a corporation such as Lehman Brothers fails, a teacher at an American college may know that his school is going to be in trouble because there will be fewer donations to the college. However, in a European capital the Catholic cathedral will not get a new roof because the financial administration of the Vatican has speculated on the world market. Or, to take a more serious example, the social welfare fund undergoes huge losses because its CEOs have been speculating without taking responsibility. Everybody is dependent in a different way: the state, politics, the legal system, the financial groups, social groups, churches, families, individuals. There is no separation between the public and the private or between the political and the economic spheres. There is only the overarching maelstrom of economic and financial profits, seemingly without any alternative. Even the critics believe that there is no alternative to this system.

It is not just the nation-state that loses the battle against monetary powers. What Arendt saw is that the political body also was losing its capability to judge what benefits the community and how to control counteracting interest groups. What is new, therefore, is that democracies have provoked a kind of financial capitalism without reflecting on the consequences. They wanted to get rid of the "social costs." What they have got instead is a total economization of the political discourse, as well as of the concepts of thinking. And the result is a loss of social care.

At the same time we do have the basic instruments that constitute the political body (division of powers, a legal system, a constitutional court, regular processes of decision making, a political class). But the political body seems to be converted into an appendix of the economic and financial processes whose representatives are members of that body or act as lobby groups in order to follow their interest in the various sections of the political body. We are less able to use the various parts of the political body to control overarching powers. The legal system may work as if the world of business were under control, but it itself is undergoing a structural change. Compared with Arendt's view of an independent legal system that can control and limit political and economic forces, the modern legal system has been of uprooted. It is forced to follow the ups and downs of global financial streams instead of guiding and controlling them. This is something new in our reality: We still have all the forms and instruments of control, but they may work against the purpose they were set up for.

Paradoxically enough, the financial groups do need the political body for their business. They rely on the protecting forces of the state against all the threatening forces: Al Qaeda in the Middle East or pirates off the coast of Somalia, terrorists in India or populist movements in South America or in Europe. Power groups of today want to be protected by nation-states and by an international legal system that allows them to act in their interest, which is said to be in the common interest at the same time.

In Arendt's analysis, the great dangers that came from the downfall of the European nation-states were that any form of political organization melted away and that anonymous masses were crying for new leaders. In our times there are neither masses organized around political interests and demands nor are there masses crying for a new leader; if any do, they are just a small minority. There is not the radical rejection of the parliamentary system as in the period between World Wars I and II. Everybody thinks today that either political institutions are without any real power, or they are corrupt. At the same time, many are convinced that the political body cannot regain power because it is exposed to anonymous global forces. The "little man" always suspected the political class of being corrupt, but that criticism is much older than imperialism. The new phenomenon is that people take no interest in politics because they know beforehand that they cannot gain any influence in it. It is true that the so-called middle class fears being ruined by financial capitalism and is looking for culprits—whether it finds those culprits in the president of the United States or the CEOs in the global financial networks. But there are no charismatic leaders promising real alternatives. Western democracies seem to be condemned to follow the new power groups into all the visible and yet unavoidable traps that the dynamics of the world financial system offers in the future. There simply seems to be no interest in and no pride in the political bodies that were created hundreds of years ago by citizens out of their free will. In such a situation, no institution and no leader can take responsibility for the catastrophes of tomorrow. If anonymous groups are supposed to have taken over rule on a global scale, then no one has to take responsibility.

Taking seriously our predicament pushes us to look at the other side of our political passivity. For a couple of years now, groups of mainly younger people have been questioning the supposed self-evidence of economic growth and financial profit. This process has partly reached the institutional level. Laws have been advanced to protect nature, animal rights, water supplies, and so on. Improvements have been made concerning the survival of the human species and the preservation of natural resources. But the will to change has not yet brought to the level of a public discourse serious discussion about how to reinstitute political power by the people over our economic processes. We witness a beginning. But it is still not clear if people do want to understand themselves as part of a political power as opposed to just being parts of an economic machine. Maybe the era of politics has gone forever, and the documents of the founding fathers are only a relic of ancient times. The words are still there, but their meaning has been fundamentally changed.

IV.

My concluding remarks ask: What can be done by political scientists and political theorists? It seems as if political theory has not caught up with the need for critical reflection. It is not enough for political theorists to adapt old concepts to new constellations. It is not enough to talk about "good governance" if governments are reduced to being agencies of economic growth and financial profit.

Among many others there are four avenues that are worthy of research:

1. Analysis of the power structure: Who are the power groups? Where does their power come from, and why can it not be controlled? What are

the conditions for the fact that the people in the West do not reclaim political power as people do in other regions of the world?

2. Reflecting the gap between the institutional existence of the political body and its powerlessness: What are the structural changes the political body is undergoing as a consequence of liberal laissez-faire financial politics?

3. Considering the space between the principles of the polity and the practice of daily politics: What kind of political and social processes are going on within this space?

4. Reflecting on the paradoxical role of the state, weakened by globalized economic and financial processes, functionalized by the need of legal services by global players, and needed by the poor, which the state wants to get rid of.

In the end there is no general answer to these questions. The need for more critical analysis aiming at the singularity of the events of our time is still there. Before changing the world, one has to understand it. That is what lies at the bottom of Arendt's analysis.

PART II

Business Values and the Financial Crisis

FOUR

Capitalism, Ethics, and the Financial Crash

:: DAVID CALLAHAN

In the wake of financial crashes, most postmortems tend to focus on poorly designed economic or regulatory systems. Explanations of the great crash of 2008 have been no exception, and we are all now familiar with such causes of the meltdown as cheap money, lax government watchdogs, and shady financial engineering. Inevitably, as well, there is a fair bit of moralizing that follows periods of greed and speculation, and this time around has been no different. Wall Street figures such as Richard Fuld have been demonized, and the investment bank Goldman Sachs has been cast as something of an evil empire. Also demonized have been over-leveraged Americans who bought homes that they can't afford and the front-line mortgage brokers who signed people up for mortgage time bombs.

What has been missing, though, is a more serious probe into how the ethical climate emerged that fostered and legitimized all the bad behavior that led to the crash. This is no small gap in our understanding. If it is true that the crash can be traced as much to a decline in ethics as to any other cause, then it suggests that even the most ambitious regulatory reforms will not prevent future crises. Instead, we'll have to deal more fundamentally with those factors that are responsible for a deterioration in ethics.

This is not as hard it sounds. Because, as it happens, any probe into what's wrong with America's ethics leads inevitably back to familiar terrain related to the overreach of markets and the failures of regulation. Recent scandals illuminate a growing conflict between *market* values and *human* values. Indeed, the great moral struggle today is not between traditionalism and modernism, or between faith and secularism—the long-standing battle lines of the culture war. Rather, it is between, on the one hand, the relentless, amoral logic of self-interest, profit, and the bottom line, a logic that has grown ever more dominant in this age of turbo-charged global capitalism, and, on the other hand, the fuzzier bonds of human connectivity—our integrity in dealing with other people, our empathy for others, and our obligations to others. Fundamentally, we must understand the financial crisis as yet more evidence that human values have been losing and place all efforts at reform in that larger context.

The link between capitalism and moral turpitude is by no means a new idea. Since the days of Adam Smith, social critics have remarked on how the pursuit of profit, efficiency, and creature comforts can change people's values for the worse. More than thirty years ago, the sociologist Daniel Bell famously argued in *The Cultural Contradictions of Capitalism* that modern capitalism elevated the pursuit of short-term gain and pleasure over the more traditional values of self-restraint and obligation toward others. Bell was writing at a time when rising individualism and materialism, propelled by postwar affluence, seemed to be turning America into a more hedonistic and narcissistic society.

The picture turned much darker starting in the 1980s, as American capitalism went into overdrive and laissez-faire ideas came to dominate policymaking. In particular, ethical problems exploded as three features of contemporary U.S. capitalism took hold: high levels of inequality, widespread financial insecurity, and lax rules governing economic life. All these features would reach an apex in President George W. Bush's second term, in the years leading up to the financial scandal.

Bigger Carrots for Winners

Start with inequality. It makes sense that granting ever-larger rewards to economic winners might lead to bad behavior. Such fat carrots, which are endemic to what the economist Robert Frank has called a "winner-take-all society," create obvious incentives to behave dishonestly or take excessive risks with other peoples' money. George Washington once said, "Few men have virtue enough to withstand the highest bidder." Very true it would seem, especially on Wall Street. Although the issue of executive pay has received much attention lately, there is a clear if less discussed link between the recurrent wrongdoing of U.S. business elites and the outrageous amounts of money these people are paid.

Let's be clear: The criminality and extreme risk-taking by key actors in the mortgage meltdown were motivated by financial incentives of a magnitude that didn't exist a few decades ago, before inequality soared and norms changed around executive compensation. For instance, one of the central figures in the disaster—Angelo R. Mozilo, the founder and chief executive of Countrywide Financial Corp.—earned up to $470 million between 2001 and 2007, making him among the highest paid CEOs in America. One reason Countrywide was so successful, according to lawsuits filed by several state attorneys general, was that it engaged in widespread deceptive lending practices.

The incentives on Wall Street for unethical or risky practices were nearly as great. Richard Fuld made $354 million as CEO of Lehman Brothers between 2002 and 2007, a period when the company earned vast profits from mortgage-backed securities. Joseph Cassano, who presided over AIG's credit-default swap operation, made $315 million during his time at the company. Stanley O'Neal made nearly $90 million in compensation during the boom years as he aggressively led Merrill Lynch into the profitable but highly risky mortgage-backed securities business.

Populist critics tend to demonize the executives and bankers who orchestrated the financial crisis. But on closer scrutiny, many of the key figures in the crisis don't seem especially malevolent, or all that different than anyone else. For the most part, they are ordinary business leaders who were exposed to extraordinary temptation. And this is a key point: When people do bad things to make huge sums of money, the problem is usually not the moral failings of specific individuals as much as the distortions of an economy that offers outsized rewards to winners. As Alan Greenspan commented in 2002, about the dot-com era: "It is not that humans have become any more greedy than in generations past. It is that the avenues to express greed had grown so enormously."

This point was appreciated, briefly, when Greenspan made his comment, in the wake of the scandals that destroyed Enron, Worldcom, and other companies. Back then, there was much talk of how overly lavish stock options created huge incentives for CEOs to pump up, or prop up, stock values by reporting false earnings. The result was the 2002 Sarbanes-Oxley Act, which imposed stiffer penalties for earnings fraud and sought to ensure that the auditors of company books weren't compromised. But that reform did nothing to reduce the vast incentives to cut corners that existed in other parts of the economy, such as the mortgage business.

Thus, just a few years after the biggest corporate frauds in U.S. history, the business world has found itself roiled by a crisis of even larger proportions.

To be sure, some inequality is necessary to make capitalism function. People who work harder or have better ideas deserve bigger rewards, and in this way, inequality can help nurture positive behavior. But when the gaps get too big and the winners get paid too much, bad things happen. And this is a point that bears repeating by anyone who seeks to make a deeper, more resonant case against laissez-faire ideas.

A Harsher Bottom Line

Something similar is happening regarding the corrosive effects of growing bottom-line pressure and financial insecurity. It is not just that the carrots have been getting bigger for winners lately; it also that the sticks of economic life have been hitting harder for everyone, another trend that brings out the worst in people.

Even before the economy plunged into recession, the middle class—and even the upper middle class—was feeling squeezed by the high costs of housing, health care, child care, and college tuition. Meanwhile, corporations—their employers—are ever more focused on profit maximization as large investors look for growth in earnings every single quarter. Thanks to globalization and new technologies, competition is growing fiercely in many industries. The heat is on in the executive suite, and that heat is passed down through the entire corporation. Employees have come under greater pressures to perform than in the past and even more so now amid the widespread layoffs of recent months.

People have incentives to behave badly when they're pinched financially or when they perceive that their job—or their future—is at risk. You can see this motive at work in any number of areas where ethical misconduct is common. Take cheating by students, which has gone up since the early 1990s, with two-thirds to three-quarters of high school and college students admitting to some recent cheating. Students are cheating more even as young people are less likely to drink and drive, use illicit drugs, engage in binge drinking, smoke cigarettes, get pregnant, or commit violent crimes. Why the dichotomy? One reason, cited by cheaters themselves, is the rising economic stakes of education. Getting into college is more competitive than ever, and the costs of college are higher than ever. Maintaining a high GPA while at college is increasingly essential, as more students depend on scholarships, which are conditional on academic performance, to defray soaring tuition. And as the BA has become less valuable, good college transcripts matter more for getting into professional school, which is also more competitive than ever. In justifying her cheating, one student told a researcher: *"Good grades* can *make the difference between going to medical school* and *being a janitor."*

Many professionals are similarly tempted to trade personal integrity for financial security. A poll by Harris Interactive of 1,200 Americans workers in February 2009 found that 28 percent of respondents said they would act immorally—including lying or backstabbing—to keep their jobs. That was certainly clear amid the widespread dishonesty around property appraisals. At the height of the real estate boom, surveys found that over half of all appraisers had felt pressure, typically from mortgage brokers, to overstate home values. While the appraisal process is meant to be a key safeguard in the lending process, ensuring that borrowers and lenders alike are making sound judgments, it became commonplace for appraisers to take their marching orders from brokers and "hit the number" needed to close loans. This fraud made it easier for people to overborrow against their homes, mainly through refinancing, and helps explain why so many homeowners now owe more than their homes are worth.

Appraisers were typically not the villains in this story. Rather, as I pointed out in a 2005 study for Demos, appraisers felt they had no choice but to succumb to pressure from brokers and banks if they wanted to keep getting business or even get paid for work already done—and this was well before the crash. In turn, former mortgage brokers at large firms like Countrywide or ReMax have talked about the tremendous pressures they were under to close large numbers of loans—even if that meant cutting corners. Worse still, subprime lenders often tied compensation, in the form of "yield spread premiums," to a broker's success in steering borrowers to higher interest loans.

Similar pressures to act unethically have become common in many parts of the economy—from discount retail stores to white shoe law firms—amid a rising obsession with the bottom line. The rampant "wage theft" exposed in recent years at chains such as Wal-Mart, Family Dollar, and Target offer another vivid illustration of the corrupting nature of such pressures. In *Wage Theft in America*, Kim Bobo estimates that workers lose billions of dollars every year because of illegal employer practices, like denying overtime. Many of the revelations of wage theft at large chains reflect a common pattern: Managers at local stores were instructed to keep down payroll costs, with implicit or explicit threats to their compensation or job security if they failed to achieve this goal. But because they had limited flexibility to reduce store hours or staffing, the managers turned to a variety of illegal tactics, like forcing employees to work off the clock, denying overtime, or manipulating computerized time sheets so that workers were paid for fewer hours.

Rampant overbilling by lawyers shows a similar dynamic at work, albeit in more upscale environs. Over the past few decades, as corporate law firms have come to operate much more like businesses with a greater focus on profits, there has been an upsurge of accusations of overbilling by such firms. In early 2009, three tech companies sued Foley & Lardner, one of the largest corporate law firms in America, alleging overbilling. In 2002, a group of associates at Clifford Chance, then the largest law firm in the world, wrote an extraordinary memo that condemned the firm's requirement that every associate bill 2,420 hours a year. The memo stated, "the requirement is profoundly unrealistic, particularly in slow areas of the firm. Moreover, associates found the stress on billable hours dehumanizing and verging on an abdication of our professional responsibilities insofar as the requirement ignores pro bono work and encourages 'padding' of hours, inefficient work, repetition of tasks, and other problems."

Weak Regulation and Sleeping Watchdogs

Finally, weak government and lax oversight have served to exacerbate the moral problems of extreme capitalism. Sleeping watchdogs create obvious temptations to lie and cheat for financial gain, and the need to wake up these watchdogs extends far beyond Wall Street and corporate America.

Americans cite honesty as a top values concern in part because they confront its absence daily. Auto repair shops overbill consumers by billions of dollars annually while the tab from unethical contractors may be much higher. Insurance companies routinely refuse to pay out deserved claims, while the health-care sector is notorious for padding the bills of patients or performing unnecessary work. And, of course, the vast scope of predatory lending is by now well known—as it was long before the crash. Across the country, government agencies and better business bureaus deal with an unending flood of complaints from consumers who have been ripped off in ways large and small.

Conservatives have a ready explanation for all this bad behavior, which is that permissive liberalism and "moral relativism" have clouded the difference between right and wrong. Yet Americans are behaving better on many fronts, and there is no evidence of a broad-based decline of morality in recent years. Rather, behavior has worsened almost exclusively in areas where there are financial gains to be had, and rampant dishonesty has been spurred on by weak watchdogs and lax rules.

The prosecution of consumer abuses and low-level frauds is a case in point. In many states and localities, law enforcement agencies do not investigate frauds where losses are under a certain amount, such as $100,000, for lack of resources. Indeed, law enforcement agencies at all levels have generally given low priority to consumer fraud and white-collar crime, a reflection of both an underinvestment in government and the tendency of stratified societies to focus its punitive powers on its poorest members.

Things are made worse by the abysmal state of professional ethics and the failure of key institutions to police themselves. For instance, enforcement of the American Bar Association's code of ethics is left to state bar associations, which are notoriously ineffective. A 2006 survey by the American Bar Association found that out of 123,927 complaints about lawyers, only 3.5 percent led to formal discipline and less than 1 percent resulted in disbarment. The American Medical Association has been sluggish in barring gifts to doctors from drug companies, and, anyway, the AMA's ethics code is enforced by state medical societies that—like their legal counterparts—are not known for their vigilance. Meanwhile, the epidemic of steroid use in major league baseball occurred because for many years MLB had no serious drug-testing policy, and players faced no negative consequences for juicing up.

One particularly insidious effect of weak watchdogs is the pressure that otherwise honest people can feel to behave unethically. If your competitors are cutting corners, and getting away with it, it puts you at a disadvantage. Come back to the example of wage theft. In 2007 the U.S. Labor Department's Wage and Hour Division oversaw 130 million workers with only 750 investigators, less than half the number it had 60 years earlier to police a vastly smaller labor force. What this hollowed-out regulatory structure has meant, Kim Bobo writes, is that "ethical employers are placed at a competitive disadvantage by employers who steal wages from workers." In this sense, the problem with lax oversight is not just that it makes Americans vulnerable to predation or undermines fair play; it is also that even the best among us can be drawn into immoral and illegal behavior. Our economic system, it turns out, routinely helps turn ordinary people into criminals.

A side effect of all this is pervasive cynicism: When society's rules are routinely flouted or enforced selectively on those with little power, people lose faith in equal justice and feel license to make up their own rules. Add widespread feelings that the social contract is broken, and that hard work no longer assures economic security, and the result is a moral free-for-all.

A New Moral Conversation about Capitalism

So what is to be done about all this? Well, the good news is that we have a president who would seem to have the intelligence and insight to understand how economic and regulatory systems can drive a breakdown in ethics. The bad news is that Obama, along with other Democrats, has resisted opening up a full-fledged *moral* attack on the economic and regulatory policies of the past thirty years. In a February 2009 speech on the mortgage crisis, for instance, the president never mentioned how predatory practices and milder forms of deception by subprime lenders helped create the current crisis. More often, he has deployed familiar Democratic language about salvaging the American Dream and ensuring middle-class security. That helps in a recession, but it will provide little guidance once the economy picks up.

A tough moral critique of unchecked markets, however, will find a receptive audience among Americans, who often already understand the ethical risks that arise in such a system. Many people intuitively know that bigger temptations can lead more people to lie and cheat in a society where the winners live like kings. They know that financial anxiety can tempt even those with integrity to cut corners. And they know that more bad things happen when nobody is watching. The basic dynamic here is not very complicated, and with the right push from up high, this story can become central to the national conversation about why and how to temper capitalism.

The Obama administration is already advocating many of the needed policy changes. Its tax plan, along with its economic and education policies, aim to reduce inequality, while its health-care reform and other social protections will help alleviate insecurity. The administration has also promoted greater regulation along a wide front, not just in the financial sphere.

But the administration still needs to think bigger. What is needed is a targeted, high-profile presidential initiative that can serve as a focal point for a new and distinctively progressive push to strengthen America's values. Why not create a White House Office of Ethics, Integrity, and Character that would work with federal agencies, state and local governments, and nonprofit organizations to address serious ethical problems in different sectors of American society?

The "to do" list of a new White House ethics office would be quite long. For instance, it might mount a sweeping effort to reduce the rampant fraud and conflicts of interest found in the health-care sector and medical profession. In recent years, the Justice Department has gone after many large pharmaceutical companies for corrupting doctors, promoting the "off label" use of drugs, and overbilling government programs such as Medicare. These efforts should be ongoing, but also be linked to a softer campaign to raise the ethical standards among doctors and health-care administrators, encouraging better self-policing by these professionals. A similar campaign could target the decrepit state of ethics among lawyers and look at how the federal government could either push the legal profession to better police itself or take on some of these oversight functions directly. The government could also play a constructive role in pushing for strong codes of ethics in industries where nearly no such infrastructure now exists, such as in the construction industry.

Or, to take another example, the White House might work with the Internal Revenue Service to change American attitudes about tax avoidance. Despite a strong majority of Americans who say tax evasion is wrong, the IRS has estimated that $350 billion is lost annually to tax avoidance. One common excuse of tax cheats is that the rich don't pay their fair share of taxes, thanks to various loopholes, and so it's okay for the little guy to level the playing field. As the Obama administration moves to change the tax code, including closing the loophole on "carried interest" that allows hedge-fund managers to pay lower taxes than their secretaries, there should be an opening to encourage better tax compliance among Americans. Such a soft campaign to instill ethical citizenship would go hand in hand with long-overdue efforts to bolster IRS resources, especially so that it can go after wealthy tax cheats.

A White House push on ethics should also focus on character building among young people. Recent decades have seen any number of efforts to change the behavior of young people when it comes to drugs, smoking, alcohol, and sexuality. These campaigns reflect America's narrow values conversation since the 1970s, which has been dominated by social conservatives and a cramped definition of personal responsibility. What young people haven't much heard is another set of messages about how to be a good person in a culture and economic climate that is so much about self-interest. Young people need to hear why it's important to help others, how to resist getting caught up in materialistic pressures, what to do when the heat is on to cut corners, and why it's important to value integrity over financial gains.

There is already a growing universe of service programs that help young people look beyond their own self-interest and feel a sense of obligation to others. That universe is about to get much larger thanks to a new law that triples the size of AmeriCorps. As well, there are national initiatives to teach character, such as Character Counts, that could be revamped and greatly expanded. A White House office could work to fit these efforts into a broader national strategy to raise America's ethics.

But the window of opportunity won't stay open forever; recent polls already show a glimmer of returning economic optimism among Americans. Now is the time to tell a moral story about capitalism that has the chance to imprint on the public mind and still have resonance when the malls are packed once more. Now is the time for progressives to try to move beyond their reflexive bread-and-butter frame and their relentless focus on the material dimensions of American life. Even in hard times, people hunger for leadership at the moral and spiritual level. If Obama and the Democrats can get ahead of the curve, reinventing how America talks about both values and the economy, there is a good chance that this nation's values will never be the same.

An Interview with Paul Levy

:: R O G E R   B E R K O W I T Z

ROGER BERKOWITZ: Tell us a bit about yourself and your background in business.

PAUL LEVY: I'm Paul Levy. I run a firm in New York City that is in the leveraged buyout business, something that has been much in the press recently—it's also called private equity. I've been in the business now since 1983, and I had the exciting experience of working at Drexel-Burnham from 1983 to '88. Drexel is a much-maligned, or was a much-maligned, institution when it was alive. I think my experience there has really informed a lot of what I've done since then, so again if that's a good basis for questions, I'd be happy to handle some.

RB: As a businessman with wide-ranging interests, how do you understand the intellectual origins and moral impact of the financial crisis?

PL: In trying to figure out what's gone on in this crisis, I've come at it from two directions: One is to try to construct some sort of sense of a moral framework in which this thing played out.

This is not the last bubble. It may be the last bubble *I* live though. There are students here who will probably be living through another one, and it brings to mind an article that was in the *Wall Street Journal* this past week about the Nobel Prize. Somebody was lamenting the fact that the Nobel Peace Prize has become a prize that is given to people who really haven't done much for peace. They talked about the prize that was given to Frank Kellogg, who was the American secretary of state in 1928 when the Kellogg-Briand Treaty was entered into. That was the treaty, as you may know, which outlawed war as an instrument of national policy, quote unquote. The first three signers were Italy, Japan, and Germany, and by 1931 Japan had invaded Manchuria; in 1935 Italy had invaded

Abyssinia, which is Ethiopia; and by 1939, of course, we know that Germany had invaded Poland to start World War II. The Nobel Prize was *not* given to Winston Churchill, who rallied the West from an abject state of depression and near-defeat, was *not* given to FDR for what he did in America in fighting the depression, or in rallying, again, America to help save Europe, nor was it given to Charles de Gaulle who held out to the very end and asserted the great liberty and power of the French spirit; so you have got to wonder who the prize goes to. My point is that memories are short; it is hard to predict the future; and we forget history at our peril: First and foremost, bubbles repeat themselves.

So, what I've been thinking about is "How do bubbles happen?" and the only thing I can think about—putting aside some of the arcane analyses of regulation and bank theory and things of that nature—is that you really have to look at this on an atomistic basis. Every day banks don't get out of bed and go to work at a bank; *people* get out of bed and go to a bank. People get out of bed, and they go to work at an investment bank. They work at a buyout shop like mine, and they do this all across America, in many different ways. That's what people *do*—they do something. So the question is, Who are the people that go and do this? And what is their training? And why are they doing the things they're doing?

Fortunately, we live in a society where people generally do roughly good things: People are law-abiding, for the most part; people care about their communities; people are good to their families; and they do a lot of wonderful things. It so happens, though, that we have this recurring problem in the financial area. You don't read about terrible corruption cases, or bubbles, in big, good law firms or universities, you name it—it seems to keep happening in the financial arena.

One of the things I keep coming back to is that the people that go into business aren't particularly well trained. They are increasingly good at arcane elements of finance but not particularly well trained in the humanities, and this is a subject that I'm close to. I was not an MBA; I was a JD. I wound up going into business. I have one brief story that I remember vividly, from around 1985: I had a French-born neighbor who was a very successful person, who died in 1985, and he had a terrific collection of French literature, and I used to go over there once in a while and talk to him (I speak French; I lived a year in France), and I would read his books and just take them off the shelf and look at them. He was always encouraging me. So he passed away, and his wife called me and said, "Would you like to buy his collection?" and I said, "Sure, I'd love to buy his collection." And so, I bought his collection, and I got an original edition of Proust, *In Search of Time Past*. I went to work the next day, and I said to one of my office colleagues—he said, "How was your weekend?"—and I said, "Oh my God, it was great! I actually bought an original edition of Proust." He of course went to Harvard Business School and some other fancy place, and he said, "Who's Proust?" I said, "You gotta be kidding me!" So I figured I was onto something. I walked down the hall. I walked into some other guy's office. His name was Doug. I said, "Doug! How are you? How was your weekend?" seeing if I could get him to ask about mine, and he told me, and he said, "How was yours?" and I said, "It was great!" I told him the same story. He graduated from Harvard Business School—he didn't know who Proust was! And it's a small example, but that's over twenty years ago and that sort of thing has been happening all the time.

I interact with the biggest and the best investment banks and the biggest and the best private equity firms, and the people are generally very nice, very affable, very, very intelligent, very energetic, but there is always something lacking. I mean, we've hired any number of young analysts from the best schools, I won't mention one in particular, but they go to business school; they get training; and they come out; and they're incredibly bright; they come straight from college; and some of them are bright enough to realize that they've missed everything that binds our society together. They haven't done much history; they were smart in high school; they exempted out of college history. They exempted out of literature in college. They exempt out of everything, so they wind up having a full four-year career that consisted of accounting, corporate finance, things of that nature, and they just sort of lack the kind of fiber that I think keeps society together and fully integrated.

RB: Many attribute the Great Recession to an overabundance of greed in our society or the erosion of values within capitalism. To what extent was the last crisis a product of losing our moral compass?

PL: That's the kind of thing that bothers me a lot, and I've been playing for years with a kind of mental thought experiment. You've all heard of Warren Buffet. There are stories all the time about people who are Buffet-millionaires, people who knew Warren when he was just a kid back in Omaha, and you get a little schoolteacher who put ten thousand dollars with Warren, and you get a professor of physics who's at some university somewhere, and *he* put ten thousand dollars with Warren. The years go by quickly, and all of a sudden Warren's doing incredibly well, and the ten thousand dollars turns out to be two hundred thousand dollars. Twenty times their money. But they hold on. And then the two hundred thousand dollars in no time becomes a million dollars. But they hold on. And then the million becomes fifty. Fifty million! From ten thousand! And they hold on. And then it goes to a *hundred* million dollars. And they hold on until ultimately willing it to a charity.

Think about what was going on in the mentality of the person who never sold. I think about that all the time because, you start to say, "Why didn't they sell?" because the ten thousand dollars probably represented significant money to them when they gave it to Warren, and therefore the million, the ten million, the fifty million, the hundred million, also represented significant money, but they didn't sell. The only thing I can think of, not knowing these people, is that these were people who had good lives anyway—that their lives weren't built around money. It may be the manifestation of the expression that "the rich person is the one who's happy with what he has." These people were profoundly rich on both levels, both the philosophical level and the fact that it was in the bank, but they didn't need it.

These stories make you think about what kind of value structures are brought to work every day when people get out of bed and go to work at these fancy institutions on Wall Street. I am no saint, but I can tell you that when I started my working career as a corporate lawyer I wanted to be financially successful, although I did not have a firm view on how to get there. What I focused on, and I wish the young people today would do this, was just developing my skills, meeting people, and making myself a better asset. The long-term goal was in place and the desire intense, but in the short term I didn't think about money that much. I wanted to be creative, take risks, and make something out of nothing. I simply assumed that by painting an attractive, balanced, broad picture of myself on the canvas of my life, that the picture that would emerge, if you pardon the metaphor, would be a winning one. The money would follow everything that had come before. Now, however, everyone wants to collapse their career into a short period, as though they knew they would die young, or at least that their intensity would wane in short order. I don't understand the impatience. Getting money has become the goal, instead of building the person.

And it seems that no amount of compensation is enough. College graduates routinely make $150,000 per annum. A few years later, and I mean a few, they are making $300–400,000 a year. Then it quickly gets really bad because five years out they expect to make $1 million a year, and they let you know it. They know what their buddies make, and they all view themselves as exceptional, so the high amount they know to have been earned by someone else is the amount to which they are entitled. It's not only tedious, it's sick. And these are the people who, over time, and much less than you'd think, are the ones running the mortgage programs, the CDO [collateral debt obligation] and CLO [collateral loan obligation] pyramiding schemes and financings, and the more they do, the better they are paid and the sooner their goal—their one and only goal of having money—is obtained. We have a big challenge. And we have to realize how early it starts. These kids are bright. They do well in high school; they take AP classes; they exempt out of college-level courses; they graduate early so they can get into the working world and start making money as soon as possible. We have an entire system that feeds this impatience for wealth creation.

Changes that allowed for this culture did not happen all at once, and they are not solved all at once. It takes tiny steps and one of the biggest small steps we can take is to focus on the humanities and liberal arts more. A good economist or accountant is not necessarily a good citizen, and the best in the field are often trained in other professions. Education, though, is the key. We might have better bankers if they spent less time with technical analysis and more with Proust and other greats not well known on the Street.

RB: Hindsight is twenty-twenty, but what lessons can we learn from the crisis that can carry forward? Or was there a specific event that committed us to the path of crisis?

PL: I think you have to look at the bipartisan obsession with increasing and promoting home ownership. I'm not a big defender of all of the subprime activity, and you have to realize that some of the newspaper accounts of what happened are actually accurate. Much of this began with the Community Reinvestment Act of 1977 (CRA)—an act that was originally passed by Congress and signed by Jimmy Carter that was amended and strengthened by every administration, Republican *and* Democratic, since then. There was not much resistance to the idea of subprime loans to increase home ownership. Here and there, a few questions were asked, but all told, everybody was in favor of increasing home ownership in America.

The home-ownership rates had been for years somewhere in the 60 percent range, and the goal was to get it higher, higher, higher. For those of us who are around my age, there was a religious tenet: You want to buy a house, you put up 20 percent. There was no discussion; that's what you had to save. But under the CRA, you had significant purchases of homes without a sensible down payment—without any down payment. Nobody had a stake in the outcome. No one had a stake in maintaining the home. And people walked when they could no longer afford even the most minimal of interest.

So, whom do you blame? Do you blame the consumer for doing that? Do you blame the government for pushing home ownership? Or do you blame the banking industry that pushed and later packaged the loans into a cascading pyramid of problems? I am not opposed to sensible regulation, but permitting the government to advance social value judgments by distorting markets and incentives will fail more often than not. Just look at where the Dodd-Frank legislation is heading: Banks are again too large, and risk is more concentrated than ever. Goldman Sachs rides high, undaunted, and the Federal Reserve is fueling inflation.

RB: Alan Greenspan and others have said that everyone missed the crisis. Many executives who lost their companies billions of dollars walked away with tens and hundreds of millions of dollars. Should we be blaming specific individuals for what they did?

PL: There really hasn't been a prosecution, at least none that I can think of so far, in this whole debacle. There's nothing. Nobody of importance, at an important institution, has been prosecuted for anything. I don't think necessarily that that's a result of prosecutorial lassitude, or oversight. I think there might not have been a lot of crimes committed. Maybe there were, and we haven't seen them, but it is also likely that the crimes just aren't there. I'm sure there were prosecutors out there working diligently to make their mark, but so far we really haven't found a smoking gun.

What does that mean? It means that people sort of deviate from the line a little bit at a time, and I don't think they bring particularly criminal intent to any of their activities, but if you don't have good values— permit the little pun here—you're not going to be good at figuring out value. Because if you'll do anything for money, if you have no values, you're going to lose track of what things are really worth.

Which leads me to another, more concrete comment: What happened in the buyout industry? You know I have some interest in that area. Here you basically had these very good firms that were growing by leaps and bounds. The top leveraged buyout firms in America had two or three hundred billion dollars under management—an enormous amount of money concentrated in a few hands. And I don't think that is necessarily bad, but what happened is that the fee structures were such that people were making more money just from the fees than they would make from managing the money, from investing the money, than what most of us would consider to be a fortune to be earned in a lifetime. They were making more money from just having control of the assets so that they didn't have to worry about making a profit from the assets when they were invested. So, the incentives got really, really skewed. The liquidity in the banking system—you can blame Alan Greenspan; you can blame Ben Bernanke; you can blame whomever you want—there was just enormous liquidity, and that fueled it.

When the buyout industry started it was a "cottage" industry of sorts. Teams were small; expenses were modest; and everyone was anxious to prove their worth through the profits they made. The fee structures in the industry, which haven't changed much over the years, were usually a 2 percent management fee paid on committed capital and a 20 percent profit participation in profits when and only if obtained. Take this example: A 2 percent fee on a $500 million fund is $10 million per annum. That amount comfortably paid for a team of five or ten professionals, office rent, costs of pursuing deals, and the like, but without undue money left over for "bonuses"; there weren't supposed to be bonuses from excess management fees. The bonuses were supposed to come from profits earned. Five hundred million dollars of successful investments might produce $1.5 billion in proceeds; a profit of $1 billion, on which the fund partners shared 20 percent of the profits, or $200 million. That's a handsome payday, but, high as it is, it's only from profits. Well, when the buyout funds grew to $20 billion, and the management fees were 1.5 percent of that amount, or around $300 million PER ANNUM—while the teams had grown, and costs had grown—the amount left for the firm leaders was staggering even before ANY profits had been made. And, as often happens, firm leaders became more focused on raising more and more money to generate ever-higher fees. Thus, with excessive liquidity, these firms rushed to invest their funds; funds competed with one another over scarce high-quality corporate assets; and prices inevitably rose to unrealistic and unwise levels. Not to be daunted, higher and higher prices were paid; funds were put to use more rapidly; and new funds were then raised, generating even more management fees. And the ball went round and round, and the excesses grew and grew. Profits be damned; the fees were good enough!

RB: Hyman Minsky, among others, saw relaxed regulation as intrinsic to the business cycle; namely, that during prolonged upturns political pressure relaxes regulation in the name of profit. This, in turn, encourages excessive risk and borrowing, which ushers in a crash. Out of the rubble emerges regulation that is intended to address the crisis that just occurred. Do you agree that regulation is destined to relax during good times?

PL: I do not know what to do about regulation. I'm not particularly tuned in to all of the intricacies of regulation, but I would suggest that those who advocate for and write regulations keep two thoughts in mind. Thought number one is that if I buy a stock, if I decide to take a risk, a financial risk—and we want people to do that in America since it is absolutely, I think, overall, in our collective interest—if I take a risk, and I make a mistake, I, and I alone, should suffer for that risk. Or at the very least, the circle of pain should be extremely narrow. If I borrow money, maybe my banker loses the money, but he should have to have sufficient reserves to deal with that. What we can't have is a situation where people take outlandish risks, seeking outlandish gains, and all of us pay for that. I think that we all would agree that it's okay if you want to take a shot, take it. If you lose the money, go home—as Rudyard Kipling would've said:

> If you can make one heap of all your winnings
> And risk it on one turn of pitch-and-toss,
> And lose, and start again at your beginnings
> And never breathe a word about your loss; . . .
> Yours is the Earth and everything that's in it,
> And—which is more—you'll be a Man, my son!
> So, you take your shot—but we can't have cascading risk.

And the other thing I would say is that there are transactions that each of us enters into on a regular basis where we expect to take zero risk. You put your money in the bank, you shouldn't lose it. You put your money on a prepaid credit card, you shouldn't lose it. You put your money in a mutual fund, which says that it's guaranteed by the government, you shouldn't lose it. So there you aren't taking risk; you shouldn't have risk; and you shouldn't have to incur risk. Where you are taking risk, you should have the consequences of that risk, but it shouldn't be borne by society at large. And that's where I think the regulation should go.

A third area that I think merits regulation is consumer protection. We hear stories of someone who starts off paying 5 percent on credit card debt and then it is raised to 18 percent interest. The banks shouldn't be able to change it midstream. I hope the government passes legislation to stop that. Or if you pay your credit card a day late, you pay the same full-month fees as if you had paid it thirty days late. That's ridiculous. There are times when the government is there to help, and I think these are perfect examples. So there [are] plenty of good opportunities—plenty of reasons for regulation; I'm not opposed to that at all.

Finally, the would-be philosopher in me is comfortable with the point that the investor who is taking a risk profits or suffers from his risk, but the professor of business administration in me is aware of the tremendous power of marketing, especially as our economy gets more complicated and seems to advance higher than the level of education of the people who take risks. We have to control marketing in the same way that we've learned to control the labels of pharmaceutical products, and we insist that the labels keep up as the pharmaceutical products get more complicated—we don't seem to do this in the financial sector, and I'm disturbed, for example, by the growth of the financial service sector as the manufacturing sector decreases. So these are factors that lead me to say that the investor who takes a risk must be protected as well. This already is the case: The financial sector is required to put labels on their products that say, for example, that the investor should not consider that because the history of the payoff has been good, that this is guaranteed for future investments. But that labeling has become inadequate, and for that reason the regulation of the financial sector must be accelerated.

RB: We hear the claim that "Wall Street doesn't get it." Fifty years ago, the average CEO made 24 times the average salary of the average person working at his or her firm. Today the average CEO makes 274 times the salary of their average employee. That means that the average CEO is somehow expected to be 11 times more valuable than his or her predecessors in the middle of the twentieth century. Is this cultural divide between Wall Street and Main Street part of what underlies the financial crisis?

PL: I struggle with this question all the time. My dad was a patrolman in the Holland Tunnel in the 1930s, then in the fire department for fourteen years from the end of the 1930s until 1950. Believe me, I get it. These disparities are gut-wrenching, but correcting them is not easy—certainly not without unduly intruding the government into business affairs. We have to realize, and I for one don't think this is a particularly debatable point, that our elected officials and regulators have—to generalize—very, very little experience working in businesses. President Obama, for example, whatever you think of his administration, has no personal experience in any normal workaday activity, unless you call weekly lectures on constitutional law, serving in the Illinois State Senate, briefly as a U.S. Senator, or working as a community organizer normal work. God bless him, he's done well, but it's not clear what if any experiential wisdom he brings to the subject of business regulation.

I find the progression of executive pay somewhat fascinating. When the buyout boom began in the early 1980s, one of the oft-repeated mantras was that American business was fat, dumb, and happy; we dominated the world coming out of the upheaval of World War II (we did, in fact!), but we had failed to keep pace with modern techniques, and in particular the Japanese were going to "eat our lunch." (Parenthetically, while we have made great strides—not without their own problems—they have foundered terribly.) The buyout titans were going to slim down business, reduce waste, create value for long-suffering shareholders (the 1970s were an awful period in the markets), and profit handsomely themselves. On balance, and despite the usual excesses and mistakes, American business did slim down and shape up; profit margins did expand, and, along with the Reagan tax cuts of 1982 and other factors, stock prices boomed; interest rates fell; shareholders did better; and, to your question, so did the managers of corporate America. On some level, their improved compensation was well earned. They did lead the charge, and they did, for the top few, tackle the problems holding back companies. There was no way the workers could benefit to the extent managements did.

It's a bit like the problem with taxes today: Confiscating all the wealth of the hated "millionaires" won't solve our fiscal problems; there just aren't enough of them. Government expenses and entitlement benefits will have to fall or taxes for everyone will have to rise, and that means for the middle class as well—which certainly has had a rough go of it. In rewarding leaders for the creation of billions of dollars of value at a given corporation, it really doesn't take too much to handsomely reward a few people at the top. When the denominator is thousands of workers divided into savings obtained or value created, the amount per worker is just not that impressive.

The other part of the problem relates to risk and entrepreneurship. The myth of Horatio Alger is not a bad one in a capitalist society: Be good; work hard; take risk; and you'll get ahead; you may even get wealthy. What's so bad about that? The American companies of the 1960s and 1970s that came under siege by the LBO guys, however, were not led by entrepreneurs or risk takers. To be a bit snide, they were run by the country club set, and nobody really "shook up" the troops to compel productive change. When the LBO guys started offering performance-related compensation packages to industrial managers, who previously were paid in some sensible ratio to the so-called worker bees, and those packages paid off grandly, the outside compensation consulting firms started going after the best managers to lure them into buyout activity with its pay-for-performance pay packages. Many of them, before leaving, went back to their companies to let them match the packages; many left. Boards had to react in order to retain their stars. Salaries grew but not wildly so; what grew unreasonably were annual grants of stock options. It used to be that a senior executive received a one-time package that lasted for years, and a winning company made the executive rich but not outlandishly so. All of a sudden, to thwart the brain drain to the buyout industry, option grants became huge and were repeated annually.

That's a long way of answering your question, or at least how we got here. Today, the headlines on compensation are awful. The boards have no backbone; the outside advisers (compensation experts and executive recruiters) are paid more if pay packages are higher; and shareholders are generally disenfranchised. In fact, shareholders are indifferent or even pleased as punch to pay grandly when companies succeed, and their ability to change compensation in the face of failure is limited. In the end, I do not think the government should be involved in this issue, however unfortunate the disparities may be. But going back to my opening remarks: When our boards are staffed with individuals who live by compensation charts rather than values, who are afraid of bucking the trend or not "going along with the guys," who lack the ability to discern right from wrong, who do not bring to their service a broader sense of community and discipline, then we wind up where we are. It's unfortunate in the extreme.

SIX

An Interview with Vincent Mai

:: ROGER BERKOWITZ

ROGER BERKOWITZ: When you heard from a friend that the Arendt Center was organizing this conference, you made it known you had strong opinions about the intellectual origins of the financial crisis. I appreciate your making time for this discussion. First, I'd like to start just by having you tell me a little bit about your background in business and how that affects your perspective on the financial crisis that we've just been going through.

VINCENT MAI: I grew up in South Africa on a farm in the Eastern Cape, a far cry from the financial community in New York. I had the very good fortune when I left South Africa, which I did in the sixties, to go to London, and started my career working for an extraordinary man, a great man, Sir Siegmund Warburg, the founder of S. G. Warburg & Co. There happens to be a biography just on the newsstands right now of Sir Siegmund by Niall Ferguson, *High Financier: The Lives and Time of Siegmund Warburg*.

Now, the essence of this man—and it's all relevant to what defined my approach—was just a *passionate* view that your reputation was everything and that your reputation was governed by the quality of the advice you gave to people, and the correctness of your advice. He saw himself as the family doctor for companies around the world. And money was secondary. You were in it for the intellectual satisfaction, for your reputation, for doing good, and, you made money, but that wasn't the prime objective—and that's a big theme when one reads this book.

Then I came to the United States. I eventually became a partner in Lehman Brothers. Now this was Lehman in the old days when firms were private, when it was a partnership, and it wasn't all that long ago, twenty-five years ago. My thinking was very much shaped by the fact that you were a partner in a prestigious firm; your name was everything; your reputation was everything. But your capital, your own personal capital was at risk for everything, and consequently the decisions that were taken about day-to-day operating things really, really mattered. But your reputation above all mattered.

I don't mean that everybody was a saint and that today they're all sinners. Far from it. But there was a set of ground rules that governed the way you did business that imposed a discipline that was central to the way Wall Street worked. It was the same in all the firms. And I've watched with a combination of fascination and horror at the way the world has changed, turned upside down.

RB: The next question then would be how has the world turned upside down, the financial world?

VM: Well I think, the first thing is just a complete change in the values of the people who are in the financial community in Wall Street, and in the culture. And as I said, it's not to say that the people in my era were all angels and that they're all devils today. But, having said that, there has been a huge cultural shift that has been driven by several things. The growth of the trading side of the business, the addition to the complexity with these opaque and synthetic instruments that nobody really understands, the technology-driven dimensions of the business today—all contributed to an evolving culture of going in there and trying to make as much money as you can. And where reputation, putting your name on a prospectus, is not quite the sacred thing that it was before all these publicly owned behemoths were created.

I'll give you a little example of how things have changed. An old friend of mine, I won't mention his name, used to be a partner of mine at Kuhn, Loeb, was on the Commitments Committee of Lehman Brothers—this was before the collapse. I was having lunch with him, and he was telling me that the committee has to approve all the deals they're doing every day, and the investment bankers would come in with these complex C[ollateral] D[ebt] O[bligations]s, and related products, and he would start asking questions about it, and the team would say, "Look, don't worry about it, we're in the moving business; we're not in the storage business." And he was saying this as: "Oh my god, can you believe how the world changed." In other words, once you had distributed the securities, usually within twenty-four hours, it didn't matter what happened to the bonds thereafter.

In the old days, we all thought we were in the storage business. In other words, you put your name on it and you're investors in what you finance—you say that the credit is solid because we've put our own name on it. And today that is sometimes not the case. If you can get it out there, and you can distribute it in twenty-four hours, that's what matters, because you get big fees. The culture has just changed in very profound ways.

It's also changed in the sense that the trading side of all these firms has grown disproportionately big—and most big financial institutions in one form or another are sort of massive hedge funds. Also, as a result, with the huge trading that takes place in the bond markets, in a way they're frequently trading against their own clients. So the moral responsibility, if you will—back to what I was saying about Siegmund Warburg—doing what's right for the customer, has shifted in a way that nobody understood. . . . Now it's sometimes what's right for the customer is what is profitable for the big financial house. That happened in one generation, and it has happened without significant consequences. There was not, it turned out, a huge reputational risk by putting your name on something that actually turned out to be worthless or by having a firm reach a settlement with the SEC and pay a big fine without admitting any wrongdoing.

RB: Do you have a hypothesis about why or at what time this concern with reputation has in some way been replaced with a concern to move product in the world of business?

VM: It's a very tough question. I would say it has to do with investment banking firms going public and getting rid of Glass-Steagall. A lot of little things happened. But going public, I think, moved the responsibility from the personal to the institutional level. And then what became the important thing was growth in earnings per quarter, which put a premium on whatever was the way to make the most money that quarter. That started becoming the focal point, and gradually, without realizing it, you start focusing more on that, and perhaps once or twice you shortchange a client or investor to make more money, but it's one of those things that happens imperceptibly. But I think being public and creating the quarterly pressure for earnings growth versus the proprietary sense that we all felt as owners of the business was a huge element.

I'm not suggesting turning back the clock. Of course, today, these huge firms must be public, and there are some excellent boutique firms that are public. What I'm saying is that the managements of these firms have to figure out a way to grow earnings without being imprudent from a risk or reputational standpoint and make clear to all employees that the firm's culture will never tolerate excessive financial risk or potential reputational damage to achieve more profits.

Siegmund Warburg used to say, "What's wrong with sometimes saying we had the third-best level of profits in our history?" It's a question of managing employee and shareholder expectations intelligently, remembering that in the long term a strong financial position and an excellent reputation are the foundation on which sustainable long-term growth is built.

I can't prove this, but it's a judgment—I think the media and the obsession with who the most profitable firm is, who's the richest, or who the biggest billionaire is, or who made the most money—and so creating sort of rock stars out of wealth—also had something to do with it. So whether it's television, the financial journals, the newspapers, the whole emphasis became, Who's the richest? Who's number one? You have big egos involved in this business, and they all say, "I'm going to be number one," and so they take risks they shouldn't take to increase profits. The media didn't used to obsess twenty-five years ago about all the stuff the way they do today.

RB: You talk about shifting responsibility, which I think is an important point, and one of the main ways we shift responsibility in our modern world is bureaucracy. But another is lawyers. We say, well, this may not be totally ethical, but it's legal. How much more active are legal concerns in doing deals today than they were when you began? And is that a way of shifting responsibility: "Well it's legal, *and therefore it's okay*"?

VM: I just think that's not so much the problem. You know, everybody, whether it's in my era in Wall Street or today, wants to be sure that things are legal, but the rules of the road have always been pretty clear. I think that other factors have been more important.

RB: What do you think of the rating agencies' role in this crisis?

VM: The ratings process was shown to be totally deficient. The rating agencies get paid by the issuer. The more ratings they give, the more money they make; it became a gravy train. The investment bankers put them under tremendous pressure to rate the senior tranches of these structured instruments Triple A; the agencies oblige; and preposterously you have over a thousand Triple A rated CDOs and other structured securities, many of which turned into junk. There are fewer than ten industrial companies rated Triple A in the whole United States. To get such a rating is a big deal. The problem is the conflict of interest that is built into the process with the issuers paying the rating agencies. The investors are left holding the bag for all these poor credit judgments and have suffered massive losses as a result. Unfortunately, this matter was not addressed in the financial regulatory reform bills passed last year.

RB: What about regulation? Was poor regulation at fault for this crisis?

VM: I'm not one of these people who blame the regulators and the government, although clearly there were serious regulatory lapses. But I find it ironic that the same people who say "leave it to the private sector" and "the market knows best," say, after this crisis happened, it was the government's fault. And there was this incredible statement by Alan Greenspan a few months ago, when he said: "I'm shocked that the leadership of these big financial institutions was not more serious about protecting their interests." Greenspan forgot that greed can trump good judgment and that in certain cases effective regulation can save shareholders and taxpayers from the excesses of a free enterprise system out of control.

There are two things that occurred that I think were very important. One is getting rid of Glass-Steagall, which I already mentioned. I worked my whole career on Wall Street where Glass-Steagall was the law—and one could argue, certainly with the benefit of hindsight, that it was the reason the system was working so well. It was a radical change to say we're going to get rid of Glass-Steagall. Suddenly, we took down all those barriers that separated investment banking, trading, and commercial banking. And everything just became one again. I think that was a shift that was drastic enough to be absolutely decisive when you impose on top of it all the other things that I mentioned. So Glass-Steagall was important. And the other thing, which you don't read about all that much, was getting rid of the Uptick Rule, which was a very important circuit breaker in a down market. And, again when you add all the other things that we talked about, each one is an important element in itself, but it's a combustible mixture to have all of those things.

RB: Given that some of this is based on values, a values shift, as you put it, who is responsible? Is someone responsible? Is that the right question to ask? And should people be punished, either legally or financially? It seems that from many perspectives very few people in the financial industry have suffered greatly. They may have quit but came away with huge golden parachutes and things of that sort. They immediately go back to work for other firms. One of the things that struck me is the people who were in charge of these failed companies are largely not thought to have done anything wrong. Not only morally or legally but even economically. They're being hired once again. How do you see that as someone from inside the business community? Do you wish there was more responsibility, or do you think it's been about right?

VM: You're getting to deep philosophical questions here. People should be punished if they've done something illegal. I have to say I can *completely* understand the anger of Main Street against Wall Street. When you think how many people were not just hurt but whose lives were destroyed by what happened, particularly in losing homes, unemployment— massive dislocations across the country. Then they see Wall Street— where this collapse mostly originated—and they see what you just said: the same people in the same positions. *And* in the newspapers we read every day these massive bonuses and all the rest. So one has to conclude that the people who were responsible for what happened, which has devastated individuals, the reputation of America, and the credibility of the financial markets, have gotten away with it unacceptably lightly, if you will.

It seems to me really inappropriate given the magnitude of what happened that basically you've got the same people doing the same things and still earning a lot of money. And then you add on top of that the fact that the government bailed out these major financial institutions. If the government hadn't, they would have collapsed. And so the whole moral hazard question—which is a very legitimate one—has not been addressed. The government really saves the system, and then the system basically continues more or less intact, more or less unscathed, despite the new banking regulatory reform, which, I think is pretty tepid given the magnitude of what happened.

RB: You mentioned a reputational hit to the financial system in the United States. Is that really true in the world? And have individuals suffered reputational hits, or for the most part have people been going on as if this wasn't much of a to-do? And how does this not affect people's reputation, if it doesn't?

VM: Look, I don't think it has affected adversely many people's reputations except the few who were obvious poster boys for what happened.

But by and large, people have got through unscathed. I think that it has unquestionably affected our reputation and our credibility in Asia, in countries like China, Japan, India, which are hugely important to us. It was a shock to them that our system could be so toxic, so contaminated, that major firms like Lehman Brothers could be in business one day and out of business the next day. These people have got *huge* assets of theirs invested in our financial system, and there's no question that this was a very, very sobering experience for them, because they thought that our system was the model, you know. So it's been a huge blow to our credibility, and I believe that it's going to take years—if at all—for us to restore our credibility to where it was. That's not to say that they're not going to deal with us because we're the biggest capital market. The dollar is what it is. People *have* to deal with us. But I think that they are rethinking a lot of their commitments long term. They assumed our capital markets were unassailable, and they realize, no, they're not.

RB: What's the best way, going forward, to deal with what you have identified: The upside-down shift from a private partnership, reputation-, customer-service-driven model to a public company, move the product, earn as much as you can model? Is this a lost cause? Do we try to restore it? Or is this just the future, and we have to deal with it?

VM: I'm always optimistic, but I have to say on this one, I hate to use the words "lost cause," but it's a formidable challenge to try to change the culture. And one of the reasons is the sort of tired, obsolete ideological debates that go on in Washington and New York about the free markets, and "get government off your back"—all of which creates a complete inability to think about the challenges in a strategic way, and in a way where they see *us*, the United States, as a part of a global system. There are economies developing huge investable funds around the world, and people have choices and options. And we have to stay abreast of all those changes and be competitive and show that we're worth putting the trust in *us* and in our ability to deal with these problems. I find these ideological battles, which have nothing to do with common sense, and nothing to do with the strategy of government and regulators partnering in an effective way with Wall Street to create as strong a foundation as possible. This is what it should be all about. Instead we have a rather acrimonious dialogue, which gets in the way of really sound, long-term strategic decisions that will lead to a secure and dependable banking system that can play the pivotal role it should in our continued economic prosperity.

RB: What would be the first thing you would want to do if we could change the dialogue? How would you frame it?

VM: I think the financial community has to argue something that's bigger than its own immediate self-interest. You know, you can argue, don't do anything—leave us completely alone—because then the maximum flexibility we've got, the more money we can make. And I think it's unfortunate to approach it that way.

I would start off by saying that you want a financial system that is stable, that is predictable, and that you can count on long term. And that's for *all* the constituent elements, from the individual consumers to lenders to borrowers to governments, that there's predictability and a stability to the system. And that the Wall Street community ought to figure out a way *with* government to impose a regulatory structure that achieves those objectives.

So it's not one thing, but it's a process of how you get to the right answer, where you realize or it's understood that everybody's interdependent. Because there has to be a much larger objective here than the immediate self-interest of the financial community. And I think the financial community—to its shame—has been excessively active since this whole collapse in working to blunt any effective regulation. Now it may be smart in the short term, but I think we've paid a very big price long term. The starting-off point has to be the safety and soundness of our banking system, and that has not been effectively addressed, which is astonishing given the magnitude of what happened.

RB: A last question. You obviously know a lot about South Africa. Is there anything that we could learn from South Africa as they enter, really, into the capitalist system. I mean, they've become a different country in the last fifteen years, some would say with a sort of ethical groundwork to their government. Is this something that we should and could learn from them regarding values in business and government?

VM: The first thing, South Africa during this whole collapse: The financial system was completely intact. I mean there was no financial crisis in the banking system, but there was no crisis in the banking system in Canada, and there was none in Australia. Why? Admittedly, they're smaller and less complex markets, but they had very strong and effective regulation. One could do well to look at why it is that they've got these stable systems. The objectives that I talked about—it's not a utopian thing—they actually exist in some countries, and we could learn from others.

But back to South Africa. Look there's a lot that's great about what's happened in South Africa, and there are a lot of big challenges. If I had to see an overarching thing about South Africa that we could learn from . . . , and I take this from Nelson Mandela. Here's a guy who's in prison for twenty-nine years, really lost a life, comes out with the most magnanimous, forgiving attitude, and so with the whole idea of truth, forgiveness, reconciliation, and realizing that there's a bigger goal in life than the ambitions of one individual. Well, I think that is a big lesson out of South Africa.

SEVEN

Brazil as a Model?

:: ALEXANDER R. BAZELOW

The subject of these brief remarks is the film *Twelve Hours to Midnight—How Brazil Has Responded to the Global Financial Crisis* (October 2009)—a film that premiered at "The Burden of Our Times: The Intellectual Origins of the Global Financial Crisis," the conference sponsored by the Hannah Arendt Center for Politics and the Humanities at Bard College and from which this volume emerged. The film came about after a visit to the Arendt Center by the directors, Ms. Simone Matthaei and Dr. Wolfgang Heuer, in June 2008. This visit was partly at my invitation, to speak to a group of businesspeople and community residents about a film project they were proposing. There were many reasons for my interest.

I had known through correspondence and emails with Dr. Heuer about the movement to reform capitalism in Brazil, and I was eager to learn more. By this time it was clear that a financial crisis of some unknown dimension was brewing. What was not known was the exact timing of the crisis or the extent of the damage. But this much was obvious: The crisis, once unleashed would be global in nature.

What had interested me, even before the present crisis, was this notion that capitalism could "reform itself." I wanted to know, "Was that true?" We understand that capitalism can change; it changes all the time; that much is clear. But "reform" and "change" are two different things. Change implies an alteration of "form" or "structure" without a corresponding alteration of "essence or fundamental identity." Reform, in contrast, means that the nature of "what something fundamentally is" changes. What it "is" is now something else. So can capitalism reform itself? That is the question.

This crisis that we are in has been called all kinds of things, and it is being used in all kinds of ways. It has been called "a crisis of capitalism," "a crisis of global capitalism," "a crisis of American capitalism," a global economic crisis, an emerging market crisis in the developed world, and so on. In the United States the causes have been ascribed to everything from subprime mortgages to overindebtedness caused by persistent trade deficits, indebtedness that led to an overreliance on borrowing, and finally to stock market and real estate bubbles. It has been blamed on deregulation, on persistent corruption in the political and financial spheres, and so on. And there is a grain of truth in each of these. But in fact the causes of this crisis have been around for a long time and have been building for a long time. It has been obvious to discerning people that this was going to happen. George Soros, for example, has been predicting it for over a decade.[1] The interesting question is not "Why did it happen?" but "Why did it happen *now?*"

There is a tendency to look at crises as if they are the result of forces beyond human control. Certainly, those who cause them would like us to believe that. So, as Michael de Portu has recently suggested, it is helpful to go back to the Greek word for "crisis," *krisis* (literally "decisions"),[2] to remind ourselves that behind every crisis there are human decisions, and behind those decisions are human actors. What, then, were those decisions that led to this crisis, and how do we know if the actions that have been taken thus far are enough to prevent a replay?

Yes, we have had trade deficits, and yes, we had subprime mortgages. Prior to the Clinton administration "subprime" mortgages were less than 1 percent of all mortgage originations. By the time the Clinton administration ended, they were 12 percent. At the height of the real estate bubble, in the last years of Bush, they were 40 percent. Any data used to model them would have been suspect from the beginning, because there almost were none. Prior to 2000, homeowners involved in subprime mortgages mostly had jobs and mostly could afford their homes. They simply wanted a low interest rate so they could invest the excess money elsewhere. And that meant they were very likely to pay those mortgages off. By 2005 all that changed. If I go out on the streets of Cologne[3] and I ask ten people what their income level is, and nine of them say 50,000 euros and the tenth says 5,000,000 euros, the average is 545,000 euros, but no one would say that half a million euros is a valid representation of the incomes of those people. Why? The data are contaminated by one very large number. The same can be said for the data that were used to model the behavior of subprime securities. The model was based on few data points involving atypical borrowers. In the beginning almost no one took these mortgages. By 2007, securitized mortgage debt exceeded total U.S. government debt.

That is an astounding fact, astounding. And a large number of the people who held those mortgages could not afford the homes those mortgages financed, and therefore any securities built out of those mortgages had high levels of default risk.

What else? The United States has an approximately $14.5 trillion economy.[4] Consumer spending accounts for 70 percent of total U.S. GDP, but who does that spending? Forty years ago, consumer spending was driven by the middle class. The data show it clearly. By 2008, the last year of the Bush presidency, the top 10 percent of the U.S. population had approximately half of total U.S. income and accounted for 42 percent of total consumption, about $4.2 trillion, an astounding figure.

How did our debt figures get so skewed? And how did income inequality get so lopsided? In the 1980s, many laws protecting income levels were watered down or overturned. People relied much less on savings or discretionary income to pay for purchases, because they had less money, and instead relied on debt financing. Beginning in the early '90s and with ever-increasing frequency the large banks successfully lobbied the government to change laws and to weaken regulation. This was done to such an extent that the banks were able to engage in practices on a scale that formerly would not have been imaginable. In particular, as time went on, they were left with balance sheets that had large amounts of difficult to price and difficult to evaluate securities representing long-term liabilities that were increasingly funded and financed in the short-term money markets. This left them, and the global financial system, vulnerable to low probability events, which, if they were to occur, had the potential to bring the system down. One of those events happened with the collapse of Lehman Brothers.[5] The global system then crashed. It is my belief, when one looks deeply into this, and in particular, at case histories of the securities that were at the bottom of this crisis, it is clear that many of them could never have been profitable if the full level of risk had been taken into account, under almost any scenario. They could never have been profitable, even in a million years.[6]

So now we come full circle. If capitalism is about profit, and if much of this edifice of subprime and high-risk securities could never have been profitable, then how could this have happened in a capitalist system? The answer is as simple as it is banal. It happened because it could, and the people who did this did it because they could. What we risk evolving in the United States is what the mathematician Nassim Nicholas Taleb has suggested is the worst economic system imaginable: socialism for people who have money and capitalism for people who don't.[7] This is not a system that is sustainable. It is one we will either change, or one that fate and time will change for us. And this is the origin of my interest in Brazil.

At the initial showing of *Twelve Hours to Midnight* at Bard College I said the following:

Twelve Hours to Midnight is a documentary about how a country emerges from an economic crisis and ultimately redeems itself. It shows what is possible after all the easy answers have been tried and have failed, after denial is no longer possible, after once powerful economic doctrines have lost respectability and no longer guide public policy. It is a documentary about what happens to a country when it realizes it has hit "rock bottom" and has no choice but to face traditionally repressed realities and begin the long hard road to reforming itself. In short, it is where this conference should end, rather than begin, and I think it is also a fitting tribute to Hannah Arendt, the thinker whose ideas inform and inspire it. Above all, it is the story of five men, Oded Grajew, Helio Mattar, Paulo Itacarambi, Ricardo Young, and Raymundo Magliano, who helped found the CSR (corporate social responsibility) movement and later the Instituto Ethos upon the collapse of Brazil's last military dictatorship.[8] Starting as a political movement for democratic reform, it has evolved into a powerful instrument of social change that now includes over a thousand corporations responsible for up to 33 percent of Brazil's gross domestic product. It is a movement that is finally addressing what has long been denied in Brazil, corruption of the public space, impunity in the legal system, denial of basic human rights to large sections of the population, and massive inequities in the distribution of wealth.

I had the honor, as a young man, to know Hannah Arendt; I was a student of her husband, Heinrich Blücher, and after her husband's death she asked me to assist her with the publication of his philosophical lectures; and I did that, for five years, right up until her own death. Her thinking always encompassed two aspects: one, a hard look at the world as it really is; the second, an orientation toward what is invisible in human affairs, and especially within human beings. She always did believe that as dark as things may seem to us now, there are new things coming into the world, things we have the barest intimations of but can never quite foresee. And so it is, with what has been done in Brazil and especially the beautiful film you are about to see. They are harbingers of such new things, that arrive in the darkest of times, just when we most need them.

EIGHT

An Interview with Raymundo Magliano Filho

:: CLÁUDIA PERRONE-MOISÉS

CLÁUDIA PERRONE-MOISÉS: Can you talk a little about the importance of Hannah Arendt for your life and work? In particular, are there one or two ideas that have played a particularly important role in the evolution of your own thinking and subsequent career?

RAYMUNDO MAGLIANO FILHO: I was introduced to the ideas of Hannah Arendt in a class I took with Professor Tércio Sampaio Ferraz of the School of Law at the University of São Paulo. It came about this way. By the time I had finished my studies I was already working in my father's brokerage business.[1] One day, a philosophy professor, Professor João de Scatimburgo, who was a close friend of my father's and who helped him in his brokerage firm, resolved a particularly difficult technical problem he was having in a very philosophical way. I was deeply impressed. I asked him if he could recommend some books and also a professor I could study with. He recommended Professor Tércio. For two years I studied *The Human Condition* with Professor Tércio, and in this literary way, I began to acquire the fundamental knowledge that I later applied to my personal and professional life. In my personal life, I would say there are three of Hannah Arendt's ideas that have been of particular importance to me. First is her "theory of action": that only humans have the capacity to start new things. Second is her belief in the "liberating power of forgiveness." Third is the observation that "life contains the seeds of events you can never quite foresee, but that you must take into account in any further analysis." For my professional life, I would say the idea that has been the most important is her observation that power can never be a single individual's property; rather, it lies at the basis of, and derives its legitimacy from, group action. During my tenure at the Bovespa, I always tried to make decisions in a collective manner.

CP: Where does your civic consciousness come from? Did your parents influence you in that regard, or are there others who played an equal and important role?

RM: During my formative years, civic consciousness was encouraged by my father, who was the CEO of his own brokerage firm and who always was preoccupied with public things. Later, of course, I was influenced by my study of Hannah Arendt's philosophy and by the works of the Italian philosopher Norberto Bobbio. Those studies continue to this day, and over the years I have become more and more preoccupied with the question "What constitutes a public space, and how does that relate to the greater society at large?"

CP: You have written that the "global Financial Crisis, which we are still in, has its origin in a crisis of values." Can you elaborate on that?

RM: I have a conscious belief, reinforced by the events of each day, that this crisis we are living through is not just a financial crisis but also a crisis of values. Many factors led to the collapse of the global system. First, the deregulation of financial markets and the structure of finance that allowed for the creation of very sophisticated financial products. This then empowered greedy speculators, who were able to manipulate investors, creditors, and beneficiaries. One consequence of this has been "the instrumentation of human beings" in a way that allowed them to become the instruments of this greed, and which, without a doubt, reflects a crisis of values that has infiltrated society at large. In considering whether or not a person is simply a means to advance someone else's material ends, we must apply Kant's insight, that man is an end in himself and not simply a means to someone else's end. From my viewpoint, this crisis of values is a consequence of a very particular kind of market logic that Hannah Arendt understood very well from her analysis of imperialism and the way in which it evolves in societies and which has relevance even up until this day.

CP: Brazil in particular has faced many financial crises in the past. How might you advise someone from Europe or North America who was looking for specific guidance on how to deal with this crisis in their own countries?

RM: I have worked all my life in the Brazilian stock market. I have witnessed many Brazilian economic crises whose root causes were either domestic or international. I consider this to be part of my country's history. But this crisis we are living through is global in nature, and seems to me to have deeper roots than just economics. Therefore it would be difficult for me to offer practical advice at the present moment.

CP: What role does business transparency play in encouraging ethical behavior in a polity? Also, can you talk about the ISE index, which is something you created to help companies institute transparency and ethical business practices at all levels of the enterprise?

RM: Transparency, as I learned from the political thinker Norberto Bobbio, is one of the pillars of democracy and was one of the principles I tried to apply at the stock exchange. The ISE, or "Corporate Sustainability Index," was created with the intention of enabling investors to consider the profile of companies in their investment decisions as well as to incentivize companies that have not yet signed the Global UN Compact to consider implementing the model. The Brazilian stock exchange was one of the first to adhere to the criteria, first proposed by the UN, to protect and respect workers' rights and implement environmental standards as part of normal operations. In order to deepen my understanding of the Global UN Compact and how to implement it for publicly traded companies, I made a trip to Geneva and Vienna in 2004, visiting the main UN bodies that were responsible for all matters pertaining to the covenant. In particular, I consulted Louise Arbour, UN High Commissioner for Human Rights, on projects we were implementing at the stock exchange with respect to the sustainability index. We returned to Brazil with the certainty that we had found the way forward.

CP: Of all the things you accomplished while at the stock exchange, what do you feel was the most significant and means the most to you?

RM: Of all the things I accomplished while at the stock exchange, I believe the most important was its transformation from an institution that was considered to be elitist and that lacked transparency to one that is more democratic and transparent. This meant we had to popularize the market, a goal we have achieved by virtue of the fact that there has been a significant increase in individual investors. The inclusion of women in the market has also been a great success. Women were always excluded from our financial markets, but today they have a significant participation.

I also believe that symbolically the participation of union representatives on our board of directors has been a great advance. Another important project was aimed at developing "corporate citizens" as a means of showing that the stock exchange was not just a powerful means of financing individual businesses but also had a role in facilitating concern for the "public purse" and participation in the economy of the country.

CP: What are the things that must happen to a country in order for it to realize that it has no other choice but to change?

RM: The Brazilian case is very special, and we are still in the process of improving social and economic conditions in our country; therefore I think it would be premature for me to say anything definitive. After all, no one country can be a model for all others with respect to the conditions that determine their economic and social development.

RM: Cláudia Perrone-Moisés, thank you for your time.

CP: Raymundo Magliano Filho, thank you!

NINE

Round Table

THE BURDEN OF OUR TIMES

:: RAYMOND BAKER,
:: REBECCA BERLOW,
:: JACK BLUM,
:: ZACHARY KARABEL,
:: THOMAS SCANLON,
:: TAUN N. TOAY

Over the course of two panels at the Arendt Center's fall 2009 conference, some speakers were echoing similar ideas or offering counterbalance to other comments made at the conference. I caught up with some of these individuals after the conference to continue the conversation and draw these individuals into dialogue. The following comments are from Raymond Baker, director of the Global Financial Integrity Project; Rebecca Berlow of Sandelman Partners; Jack Blum, chairman of the Tax Justice Network (USA); Zachary Karabel, president of the political science think tank River Twice Research; and Tom Scanlon, attorney adviser to the U.S. Treasury Department.—*Taun N. Toay*

TOAY: Let me begin with a broad question: How "free" is the free market?

KARABEL: Markets have never been "free" of government intervention. Markets aren't natural phenomena. They are created by rules among their participants, and that usually entails some form of government. In the United States and Europe, "free markets" would be impossible without contract law and the willingness of government to enforce it. Although there are varying degrees of government intervention—and although some intervention can inhibit rather than facilitate the free flow of goods and capital—the notion that there are free markets entirely distinct from laws and governments is a myth.

BERLOW: Proponents of free markets in the financial arena have historically advocated deregulation on the grounds that market participants are best able to assess the risks implicit in transactions and to price assets using available information. They advocated further that transactions entered into by market participants acting in accordance with their perceived interests generate positive wealth for society as a whole. In the wake of the financial crisis, deregulated markets "free" from government intervention would seem to require additional justification. Risk assessment models lagged well behind market activity, and asset prices diverged wildly from fundamental values. The social costs of the failure of proper risk and valuation tools have been great, far overshadowing the wealth effect that transactions over the period may have had on the privileged few.

The financial reform legislation, passed in the aftermath of the failure of market participants to assess, and internalize the cost of, the risks they assumed, marks a turn away from the free market ideology that sustained the deregulation of the last thirty years. The main thrusts of the legislation—supervision and recapitalization of financial institutions, consumer financial protection, capitalizing and increasing transparency of derivatives trading and establishing the Financial Stability Oversight Council (FSOC), a council consisting of financial regulators and charged with reviewing financial market stability—each separately evidences the conclusion that some intervention is required to promote sound markets, since market participants will not, or perhaps do not have the ability to, act efficiently and maximize welfare in the absence of such intervention.

Congress delegated rule-making authority to regulatory agencies to implement the legislation. These agencies are well suited to such implementation, as they work closely with the market participants they regulate and have greater expertise in implementing the reforms. They are, however, for the same reasons also subject to capture. The success of the financial reform legislation may be determined by the extent to which these agencies steer clear of both overregulating and thereby dampening growth, and underregulating and externalizing risks on the public.

TOAY: Hyman Minsky, among others, saw relaxed regulation as intrinsic to the business cycle; namely, that during prolonged upturns political pressure relaxes regulation in the name of profit. This, in turn, encourages excessive risk and borrowing, which ushers in a crash. Out of the rubble emerges regulation that is intended to address the crisis that just occurred. Do you agree that regulation is destined to relax during good times? How do these views reconcile with addressing instability in capitalism?

BLUM: I agree with Minsky's observation. However, the proposition that at some point in the future regulation will once again be relaxed is not an argument for avoiding a fix for obvious present problems. If you take the long view, no deep societal problem is ever permanently fixed. Crime has ebbed and flowed for all time; similarly, poverty has been around since the beginning of human society. My point is that the purpose of politics is to ameliorate these problems so that we can live together in reasonable peace and harmony. We need to make use of the political system and remember that its function is not the support of a particular economic system; rather it is to improve the overall welfare for the common good.

BERLOW: Professional economists and political scientists are best suited to evaluate the theoretical adequacy of Minsky's description of the cyclicality of prosperity, increased leverage, deregulation, and crisis. At a more pedestrian level, it will be interesting to watch the Fed, Basel Committee, and others determine the efficacy of countercyclical capital requirements, in the light of the recent crisis. Adopting such requirements—and creating a legal regime to ensure their implementation in times of prosperity—would be a challenge.

KARABEL: As a historical observation, Minsky and others are correct: In boom times, people stop worrying as much about the downside and focus on the seemingly endless possibilities. They pay less heed to the checks and balances of an earlier era and come to see them as impediments to even more growth. But it is also true that while historical patterns rhyme, they do not repeat. No one episode or crisis is precisely like another, and regulations are best at preventing a precise repeat of something that happened before, not at something new that will happen in the future. It is the financial equivalent of fighting the last war. We look for risk where it is familiar and therefore fail to pay adequate attention to the risk that lies ahead. Now, the focus is on leverage and derivatives, and we may prevent the next leverage and derivative crisis. But what we cannot and will not prevent is human and societal nature. We cannot and will not prevent greed, desire, hope, fear, and innovation from excesses and imbalances. Amoeba-like, it will shift form, but regulation cannot stifle those impulses and tendencies. That said, the economic waves have become gentler over the past century, even as the fear and rhetoric remain heightened. Today's crises have not upended governments, triggered wars and revolutions, or led to widespread material suffering such as starvation. So we have learned collectively to moderate the lows and avoid the worst effects of financial crises.

::

TOAY: Many aspects of the recent crisis were historically unprecedented. Which events and/or reforms do you see standing out a decade from now?

SCANLON: Many years from now, the actions by the U.S. Department of the Treasury to guarantee money market mutual funds will stand as one of the most momentous acts of the upheaval in the global financial markets during the period of 2007–8. The temporary guaranty program for participating money market mutual fund companies ("MM Guaranty Program") was unprecedented on many levels—and eventually will lead us to pause and reconsider what it means for our government to intervene to conserve institutions that are deemed "too big to fail."

The MM Guaranty Program was the emphatic signal that our nation's core financial infrastructure was in crisis and perceived to be at risk of collapsing on itself. Money is a store of value as well as a medium of exchange, and since the Banking Act of 1933 (the Glass-Steagall Act) money in the United States had consisted in two basic forms: currency (and credit) issued by the Federal Reserve and bank deposits insured by the Federal Deposit Insurance Corporation. Both instruments are money because each is backed by the full faith and credit of the government. By contrast, securities issued under the Investment Company Act of 1940 are *not* money; these instruments are securities issued by mutual funds companies, and each is backed by the assets of the underlying company. But because (1) federal law generally prohibits banks from paying interest on demand deposits and (2) customers generally desire to earn interest on the balances in their accounts, banks and mutual fund companies developed elaborate systems, such as "sweep accounts," which allow bank customers to hold both deposits (to facilitate payments) and securities (to earn interest). The finishing touch, as well as a sleight of hand, was to persuade the government to help market the securities leg of these accounts as "money market" securities in order to induce customers to skip the due diligence that they ordinarily would be expected to take before buying securities issued by a company (including an investment company). In my own view, the MM Guaranty Program proved—in a profound, political, and philosophical way—that our nation was in a crisis because, when customer-depositors/investors and citizens alike collectively lost sight of the crucial differences, both in value and purpose, between deposits and securities, the government intervened to merge the two instruments: Participating investment companies now suddenly issued lawful money.

Before 1933, our nation debated the concept and details of insuring bank deposits for *decades*; in 2008, our nation implemented the MM Guaranty Program within *weeks*. Banks were furious because precisely at the time they desperately needed funding through deposits (which is cheap) and trust by customers (which is dear), the government undercut both. In a letter to Secretary Paulson, on September 19, 2008, the American Bankers Association pointedly asked: "How will you keep corporations from taking unreasonable advantage of the lower cost of funding provided by the guaranty by moving more and more of their financing to commercial paper in these funds?" To my knowledge, Secretary Paulson never answered, but we all know the nature of a true response: The MM Guaranty Program was intended to allow—not prevent—corporations to lower their costs of funding in the commercial paper markets because, without these markets, individual depositors/investors and companies throughout our nation would lose both the value and use of their "money" in those securities.

BERLOW: It has been noted that the scale (in dollars, persons affected, duration of recovery period) of the 2008 financial crisis and the degree of contagion (from mortgage-backed securities to money market instruments, from the United States to the UK, Euro-zone, and emerging markets, from private to public debt) were unprecedented. Another aspect of the crisis that appeared unprecedented was the complexity of the financial markets at the time of the crisis. This complexity created a knowledge gap between financial institutions' senior management (including senior risk officers), on one hand, and the sales and traders on particular desks that created the profit/loss for such institutions, on the other. Perhaps an equally large knowledge gap existed between the regulators and the regulated entities. Though regulators spent multiple months per year auditing banks, broker dealers, and thrifts, the regulators on their own admission did not have a basic understanding of the financial instruments used by institutions that created an interconnected and interdependent web of risk and counterparty exposure. In the absence of this knowledge, regulators were unable to assess the risks that were tolerated intentionally or out of ignorance by senior management.

With the socialization of knowledge of the complexity of the financial markets since the crisis, it could be that the financial reform bill will be seen as a sorely belated correction that updated the regulatory landscape to take account of the internationalization of financial markets (where Basel III and U.S. capital requirements could be integrated); integration of regulators and financial markets (FSOC); and recognition of financial innovation (integrating OTC derivatives into trading, accounting, and risk systems of regulators and market participants and the need for consumer protection). In fact, in ten years, it may be that students of the financial crisis will be incredulous that the regulatory framework was so backward at the time of the crisis.

::

TOAY [ADDRESSING JACK BLUM AND RAYMOND BAKER]: You both have made your names in your work on tax evasion and regulation. In terms of magnitude, is this any more than a rich nation's problem?

BAKER: The greatest impact of tax evasion is actually on poor countries. We estimate that some $1 trillion a year of illicit money drains out of developing countries into Western economies. It comes in three forms, namely the proceeds of corruption, crime, and commercial activity. All of it is tax evading. If this money remained in developing countries, it would accelerate poverty alleviation and sustainable economic growth far more than any other instrument available.

BLUM: I agree. These tax revenues are essential to education, health care, and the building of national infrastructure. An apt example is that of Mexico. Hacienda, the Mexican treasury department, says it collects about 10–15 percent of the taxes owed to it. As a result there is little money for the government other than oil revenue. The money fleeing Mexican tax comes to the United States to be invested here. There are some in the U.S. who believe that this flow benefits the U.S. But I would argue that the Mexican failure to collect tax is directly related to Mexico's inability to control its border with the United States. Mexico's police are in large measure corrupt, and many of the people crossing the border looking for jobs might remain in a Mexico that had more social services and better government.

TOAY: But is such evasion inherent to capitalism and international financial flows?

BAKER: It certainly is not inherent. The fact is that we have built a global shadow financial system over the last fifty years or so to facilitate the movement of illicit, tax-evading money across borders. This structure comprises tax havens, secrecy jurisdictions, disguised corporations and accounts, trade mispricing used in much of global imports and exports, and money-laundering techniques that have become normalized. There is nothing inherent in capitalism that fosters this.

BLUM: Your question implies that capitalism and the free movement of capital are a given and the role of governments and the international system is simply to prop up a natural and beneficial system. If there is one thing the financial disaster of the past few years has taught us, left to its own devices, capitalism without regulation and supervision will be our ruin.

The real issue is that of sovereignty and the integrity of national government processes. As things currently stand, corporations have a privileged status that allows them to operate outside of a legal system that binds ordinary citizens. They can arbitrage national rules to avoid taxation and regulation. Wealthy individuals can also adopt the corporate form and use the system to skirt the rules.

The system allows free movement of capital, and the decision to respect corporate form over substance allows that capital to operate from any national base it finds convenient. Not surprisingly the most congenial venues are places with secrecy, no tax, and no regulation. In the name of free movement of capital we allow the money to move without identifying the ownership. There is nothing in the theory of capitalism that requires anonymity for money or that any country allow its laws to be disregarded—that is unless you believe that capitalism trumps democracy and political freedom.

TOAY: So what can be done?

BAKER: Transparency. Transparency in the global financial system is the answer. In our work we recommend five steps to make financial transparency a reality: (1) knowledge of beneficial ownership of all entities and accounts (no more disguised entities); (2) country-by-country reporting of sales, profits, and taxes paid by all multinational corporations and financial institutions (no more faking losses in some countries while showing enormous profits in tax havens); (3) automatic exchange of tax information across borders (the European Union Savings Tax Directive expanded); (4) curtailment of trade mispricing through use of reporting and monitoring mechanisms; and (5) harmonization of offenses under anti-money-laundering laws by all countries, including tax evasion as a predicate offense. Each of these steps builds on something that is already in place; so they are not radical. Each will make a decisive contribution to a more transparent world, benefiting both rich and poor countries alike.

BLUM: Some things are obvious. For example we should not respect shell corporations formed in secrecy jurisdictions as legitimate. We should insist on form over substance. We should prohibit American banks from using offshore shells for derivatives trading and from having entities in secrecy and regulatory havens. Several pieces of legislation that have been proposed by Senator Levin and Congressman Doggett would address some of the issues.

TOAY: Why care now, when the global system is so fragile? Aren't there more pressing priorities?

BLUM: It seems to me this is the moment to fix what has been a major factor in the current crisis. The maze of offshore entities at major banks and brokerage firms, the secretive offshore dealings by hedge funds, and the use of offshore entities to keep questionable liabilities off the books of banks and financial corporations made them impossible to regulate. If we want a system that can be regulated and we want to control the potential for catastrophe, this is the time to move.

BAKER: To prevent the next crisis, we must require transparency now. Nothing will be so effective. Transparency gives investors, lenders, regulators, governments, civil society organizations, and citizens knowledge of what is going on in their own spheres and around the world. With eyes wide open we will not commit financial suicide.

::

TOAY: To what extent has technology changed the landscape of capitalism?

KARABEL: The modern technology revolution of the Internet and wireless communications has transformed the flow of goods and capital. The amount of capital daily in motion dwarfs any one state or government, and the software revolution has made it possible to construct global supply chains to an extent that would have been impossible even two decades ago. The result is that a global capital system is emerging with different dynamics than any one national economy, and beyond the control of any nation.

TOAY: Is capitalism the problem or the solution?

KARABEL: For the moment, it doesn't much matter. Capitalism in its various forms is the only game in town, with billions in India, China, Brazil, and the rest of the developing world thriving as never before as a result of their embrace of a capitalism that allows for a more openly prominent role for the state than is the case in the United States. In its simplest form, capitalism is a system that rewards growth and innovation of goods and ideas with money. That money in turn allows individuals, groups, corporations, and to some degree society to meet needs and desires. Financial reward is the reward, and the system is indifferent to concepts such as the spirit, the common good, happiness, or other nonmaterial aspects of human life. For the billions of people outside the Western world, capitalism is proving more able to generate material prosperity and individual autonomy than any system has in the past, and until that ceases to be the case, capitalism will be the overwhelmingly dominant global system. It will generate problems and solutions, depending on the acumen and wisdom of the particular society.

BERLOW: It is both the problem and solution.

::

TOAY: So what can be done? If you could leave the current administration with one charge, what would it be?

BAKER: Recognize and address and resolve the linkage between the global shadow financial system and its negative impact on the 80 percent of the planet's population living in developing countries. No greater legacy could be left to our nation and to the world.

BLUM: Worry less about restoring the financial system as it was before the crack-up and focus on returning the system to the boring, relatively unprofitable basics of investing the short-term savings of the society in productive ways.

BERLOW: Leaving to experts whether boom-bust cycles are inevitable, and whether we can lessen the hardship caused by the busts, it would be useful to keep track of the results of the finance reform. Many people have become more sophisticated about financial matters and have learned that we remain ignorant of Wall Street's doings at our peril. As financial reform wends its way through the administrative rule-making process, the results of the process should be publicized, and the extent of industry capture should be subject to scrutiny. Although this will not guarantee against undue deregulation, it at least provides indispensable information to the public.

PART III

The Crisis of Economics

The Roots of the Crisis

:: S A N J A Y G . R E D D Y

Practical men, who believe themselves to be quite exempt from any intel-
lectual influences, are usually the slaves of some defunct economist. Mad-
men in authority, who hear voices in the air, are distilling their frenzy
from some academic scribbler of a few years back. I am sure that the power
of vested interests is vastly exaggerated compared with the gradual en-
croachment of ideas. Not, indeed, immediately, but after a certain inter-
val; for in the field of economic and political philosophy there are not
many who are influenced by new theories after they are twenty-five or
thirty years of age, so that the ideas which civil servants and politicians
and even agitators apply to current events are not likely to be the newest.
But, soon or late, it is ideas, not vested interests, which are dangerous for
good or evil. —JOHN MAYNARD KEYNES, THE GENERAL
THEORY OF EMPLOYMENT, INTEREST AND MONEY

The financial crisis itself has made it possible to have a new kind of conversation across the trenches of disciplines—the kind that is taking
place in this volume. I do not think it would have been possible to have
this sort of conversation five or ten years ago. There is a sense of shock
that accompanies an unexpected event of this magnitude, and a search-
ing for answers. This has rightly undermined previous disciplinary pre-
rogatives and created a more welcoming atmosphere for new approaches.

Academics in various disciplines, as well as ordinary citizens, quite
legitimately want to know what exactly happened, and how it is going to
affect their futures. We have a new level of interest in economic questions and some skepticism about the previous answers provided. Economists in particular have been scrambling to provide answers, often in a
rather *ex-post* manner. Precious few of them predicted anything like this
particular event. Very few understood the current microstructure of the

financial markets, which was so central to the unfolding of these particular events. As a result, there is a crisis of legitimacy of the field of economics just as there is a crisis of legitimacy of the banking system.

Even though this crisis has created an opening to address all sorts of important questions, nevertheless we are at a very early stage of the dialogue. There is a great deal of mutual education that has to take place in order to make it fruitful. I would like in this essay to touch on a few themes that I think are fruitful for such a transdisciplinary dialogue. How can we take advantage of this moment to reflect *together* about the political and institutional arrangements that undergird the contemporary economy? Can we not only understand better how this system has worked (or not, as the case may be) but also how it might be revised so as better to promote the ends of justice?

It is helpful to begin by taking seriously the title of this volume as a whole, *The Intellectual Origins of the Global Financial Crisis*. What are the intellectual origins of the present global financial crisis? In intellectual history it's quite common to think about the relationship between previous ideas and current ideas, as well as to explore the relationship between ideas and events, or occurrences in the world. How is the relation between ideas and facts in the world manifested? Of course, the individual actors who possess those ideas are consequential. Who were the actors in this case, and what are the ideas they possessed that led to the relevant transmission? Economists were very much at the center of this process of the provision of the intellectual rationale for the complex financial derivatives that were developed (which were the basis of the various kinds of toxic assets at the heart of the crisis) even if they played a subsidiary role in the development of the markets in which such assets were actually traded.

Toxic assets that have been at the center of this crisis were developed by "practical men, who believe themselves to be quite exempt from any intellectual influence" (to use Keynes's phrase from his seminal *General Theory of Employment, Interest, and Money*); they have also been very much supported by (not so defunct) economists. Very often the work of financial economists such as Fischer Black and Myron Scholes in the 1970s—on the pricing of options and other derivatives—is pointed to as the origin of these developments, but there is a deeper origin still. Kenneth Arrow and Gerard Debreu put at the very center of modern economic theory the idea of complete contingent claims markets. Their implied conception of a market utopia was a world in which it would be possible to write contracts involving all possible states of the world, which would specify what each of us would owe one another if one of many possible contingencies would arise. Derivatives contracts are precisely such securities. Arrow and Debreu argued that in a world of complete contingent claims markets, efficient (or Pareto optimal) outcomes would under certain conditions arise. The heaven of economists and, of course, their conclusion rested on certain premises about the rationality of the agents and their ability to foresee the future. However, these assumptions were treated as not wholly implausible. So if one wanted to lay the blame, one could do so in part on the shoulders of Arrow and Debreu.

I remember personally in graduate school talking to a then PhD student at the Harvard Business School, who is now a tenured professor at one of the foremost business schools in the United States, who was previously a banker working on a derivatives desk of a leading investment bank in New York. I had been reading some of the semipopular work of people such as Randall Dodd, one of the unsung heroes of this debate, who from the early 1990s had been pointing out the possible dangers of derivatives for systemic stability. It says much about the times that such persons were accused of understanding very little economics by the mainstream economists who saw no danger in the explosion of the derivatives markets, if they had noticed it at all. Indeed, my friend informed me that I understood very little about economics, obviously, and I must have had no idea what derivatives were if I thought that they could generate systemic instability. I was told that it was immediately obvious, from their very definition, that a derivative was a risk-reducing instrument and could not be a risk-increasing one. I'm sorry to say that this point of view was not uniquely held, and it was in fact the dogma of the time among academic economists generally and among financial economists in particular with some very rare exceptions. Even distinguished financial economists such as Robert Shiller, who is associated with the view that there can be "irrational exuberance" in financial markets, recognized that manias, crashes, and panics are endemic to all financial markets, but did not give importance to the role of derivatives in generating systemic instability. On the contrary, Schiller argued that derivatives can play an important role in providing insurance against sources of risk and instability.[1]

The recent historical experience provides an important case of economic ideas influencing the world. Other ideas also lie behind the phenomena we have observed—for instance, political ideas concerning the degree of deference that should be given to technocrats. There is a need to better understand what degree of deference should be given to proclaimed technocratic expertise in the organization of the economic system. This is a discussion that has unfortunately been avoided in the last three decades, at considerable social cost. Discussions in this volume have rightly focused on this issue, as well as the more general question of the appropriate relation between "capitalism" and the institutions of democracy, including the regulatory state. Let me therefore now focus on the question of whether "capitalism" is the root of the financial crisis, which has been posed by the organizers of this valuable volume based on an equally valuable conference.

I think the most fruitful way to approach this might be to note that "manias, crashes, and panics," to use the memorable phrase of Charles Kindleberger, are endemic in market systems. One can find historical examples of such mania, crashes, and panics going back a very long time indeed. There are very deep reasons why these manias and bubbles are endemic to market systems. At root, the source of these bubbles is the fact that financial assets have indeterminate valuations that are influenced by expectations of the future. Since valuations are at least partly based on future expectations, they are influenced by the psychology of market participants. Therein lies the problem for the "science" of economics.

Negative feedback mechanisms dampen down deviations from "equilibrium," or fundamental prices, which are experienced in financial markets at least over the short or intermediate term. For instance, higher prices for financial assets relative to the stream of returns perceived to be attached to them may lead to decreasing demand for them and thus mitigate price increases. There are also positive feedback mechanisms in financial markets, which exacerbate deviations from "equilibrium," or fundamental prices. For instance, higher prices for financial assets may lead to greater perceived wealth, which in turn leads to higher demand for such assets. Such positive feedback mechanisms can generate what are called bubbles, which involve bloating of asset prices, at least for a period.

In mainstream economics bubbles are usually wished away. Those who have studied economic theory at an advanced level will be familiar with a mathematical concept known as the transversality condition. It is usually imposed in macroeconomic models of the standard type and has the effect of simply wishing away the occurrence of bubbles. We know that a central economic reason why bubbles emerge is that it is entirely rational to hold a financial asset that one does not believe has a sound valuation (in relation to "fundamentals") if one believes that one can with considerable likelihood pass it on to someone else at a higher price. As long as there are "suckers," there is the possibility of bubbles, and indeed of rational bubbles. The transversality condition asserts that one cannot do that forever; there is some point at which one cannot find a "sucker." As long as that point is "not yet," then it's perfectly rational to participate in the bubble, although of course one does not want oneself to be left "holding the bag." It is clear that there can thus be systematic overshooting of the "fundamental" or warranted price of assets in financial markets, although it is also difficult to establish what such a price is.

What separates the recent financial crisis from the "garden variety" of manias, crashes, and panics? In referring to garden-variety manias, crashes, and panics, I am not taking the view that such crises are not important, or that they cannot have tremendously disruptive effects. Take for example the Japanese real estate bubble of the late 1980s, which when it collapsed, seemed to propel Japan into a deep depression from which it has not yet emerged. Although that was a bubble with enormous macroeconomic consequences, I would say that it was a garden-variety bubble in the sense that the value of the underlying asset, for instance a square foot of central Tokyo real estate, was known by the primary market participants, just as hundreds of years earlier the price of tulip bulbs was known by all of the participants in the infamous historical bubble of the Dutch Golden age. At any one moment in time (from month to month or week to week even if not from minute to minute), the market participants knew the market price at which the key asset traded. At a certain point in time the asset was trading at a very high market price, and then at another point in time, perhaps the very next moment, the bubble had burst and it was trading at a very low market price. However, the price was transparent to all of the participants (and, even more basically, the object was well defined). The garden-variety bubble centers on a financial asset that becomes overvalued, but the price of which is known at any one moment in time, before or after the bubble bursts.

One crucial difference between the garden-variety crises and the present crisis has been that the present crisis has, to a greater degree than previously, involved an epistemic problem. The market prices and warranted values (e.g., the stream of returns that might be expected by holding them to maturity) of the financial assets, which were traded (or, more pointedly, not traded) during the unfolding of the recent crisis—were to an extraordinary extent opaque to the market participants themselves. The radical uncertainty concerning the appropriate values to ascribe and the market valuations that would emerge if these assets were actually observed to be traded led to considerable confusion on the part of the market participants.

It is really remarkable that major financial institutions with enormous sophistication and resources with which to hire the best available experts were not able to determine what their net assets and liabilities are, despite the considerable work on accounting conventions for derivatives that preceded the crisis. The crisis has made bare that accounting involves conventions, that those conventions are based on underlying theories as to how the world works, and that those theories can be upended, in which case, rampant confusion can be sown among all concerned. There can be as a result such deep uncertainty about the values to be attached to the assets being held that trade in those assets might for a time stop! The story of how markets temporarily "froze" has many elements to it and may have yet to be fully written, although there have been recent highly illuminating contributions.[2]

The recent financial crisis has shown us that markets can go missing temporarily as a result of radical uncertainties (in turn tied to the informational complexity involved in valuing the underlying assets) and that such problems in valuation can lead to various knock-on effects, for instance by decreasing confidence in the liquidity and solvency of the major actors in the financial markets and causing a resulting decrease in economy-wide credit. This is a quantitatively different feature of the current crisis, although it has features of traditional manias, crashes, and panics. From this standpoint, advanced *financial* capitalism, which has emerged over the past forty years of financial innovation, is one of the most important roots of this crisis. The primary lesson of the crisis is that we must establish a new role for the public interest in the governance of the economic system. The public interest has in the years preceding the crisis been insufficiently respected, even if often invoked. It is appropriate here to recall the insistence of Hannah Arendt that the 'public' is not grounded merely in overlapping interests but rather in the recognition that we live together in the world, sharing it 'in common', from which recognition our sense of public responsibility must stem.[3]

ELEVEN

Where Keynes Went Wrong

:: HUNTER LEWIS

I would like to begin with a few words for the students who were attending when I first offered these remarks.

I will be focusing on John Maynard Keynes. He died in 1946—it might seem long ago. But he remains immensely influential. I would argue that he is the most influential person of the last century, with Winston Churchill, another Englishman, perhaps a close second.

Virtually all world governments today may be described as Keynesian in their approach to managing economies. In particular, almost all the responses to the Crash of 2008 have come out of Keynes's playbook. One person's ideas have never before so thoroughly dominated the world.

I will offer a critique of Keynes and of Keynesian policies. It is a negative critique. This puts me in a very small minority of anti-Keynesians. It is not that I am alone. The world's biggest and busiest economic website reflects the ideas of economist Friedrich Hayek and Hayek's teacher Ludwig von Mises, which ideas are decidedly anti-Keynesian. But even so I am in a small minority worldwide. Thus any conclusions I reach today will be highly controversial. It is important that students understand this context.

If I am offering a heretical view, ironically this might not have displeased Keynes. He described himself as a "rebel and heretic." He spoke in his *General Theory* of the brave army of rebels and heretics down through the ages, and certainly included himself. I think Keynes was quite surprised when he and his ideas were so thoroughly embraced by the establishment.

Keynes was also someone who lived in the moment. He developed policy recommendations and then theory to back them up. All his friends agreed about this. It was policy first and then theory. Keynes's last book was written during the Great Depression and reflected the conditions of that time. Would Keynes be a Keynesian today? I have my doubts. But there is no way to know for sure.

In giving my negative critique of Keynes's ideas, the ideas that run our world today, I also want to emphasize that I am not wantonly attacking this highly respected man. This is not what is called a hatchet job. I have read just about everything Keynes wrote, read it carefully, and any assertions I make are based on what Keynes himself said.

This is important. Much of what Keynes wrote was obscure. It takes some labor to follow it, and most people don't try. They rely on what others tell them. Particularly today, when we are betting trillions of dollars and the future of our country on Keynesian remedies, this cannot be acceptable. We need to read Keynes carefully and be very clear about what he said and did not say, and then argue from there.

With this as background, let's begin with a brief word about Keynes the man.

Sometimes in the afternoon as when I originally gave this talk, we could all use some personal stimulus. If John Maynard Keynes had been there in person, he certainly would supply that stimulus. He was not only the immensely influential figure I have described. He was also an electrifying personality. He always seemed to be "on." The art historian Kenneth Clark said, "He never dimmed his headlights." He could out-talk and out-debate anyone. And he knew it.

This annoyed some people. U.S. Secretary of the Treasury Henry Morgenthau described Keynes as "one of the fellows that just knows all the answers." Even friends were wary. Here's what Bertrand Russell, philosopher and mathematician, one of the smartest people of the twentieth century, said about Keynes: "When I disagreed with him, I felt I took my life into my hands. . . . I seldom emerged without feeling something of a fool."

Keynes could be utterly charming. He could also be extremely rude. Kingsley Martin, editor of the *New Statesman,* which Keynes partly owned, put it this way, in of all places an obituary notice: "His wit was shattering and his capacity for rudeness unequalled."

On one occasion, Keynes reduced a (later) Nobel Prize–winning economist and treasury colleague to tears. During a "high table" dinner at Cambridge, he turned to Isaiah Berlin, not yet famous, and asked him what he was doing. On hearing, he replied "rubbish" or words to that effect. He then turned away to the companion on his other side and said not another word. Pity for Keynes—Berlin was not only brilliant, he was witty and fun.

Keynes was full of personal contradictions. He railed at the love of money. He called it "the worm . . . gnawing at the insides of modern civilization." But he also very much wanted to be rich. He railed against investment speculation but avidly speculated himself. At one point, he was completely wiped out, and had to turn to his father, a teacher, for rescue. Two more times, he could have been wiped out, one of them 1929, which he did not expect, and the other 1937, which he did not expect either.

In the early years, Keynes held few investment positions, loaded on the leverage, and also market timed. After 1937, he gave up on the market timing. But he always kept the high concentration and especially the leverage. Very oddly, the man who called gold the "barbarous relic" often recommended buying gold as a diversifier. He ended up a millionaire in pounds, but not especially rich by today's jaundiced standards.

Keynes also liked to subvert and poke fun at what he called Victorian morals. He called himself an "immoralist." But he worked as hard and saved as diligently as any Victorian.

As I mentioned, Keynes thought of himself as a rebel and heretic. But he loved being lionized and listened to by the establishment. He may be said to have invented the role of the public policy entrepreneur. He also invented the role of the mass media intellectual and seemed to enjoy every minute of his celebrity. The media especially loved it when the Cambridge intellectual married a ballerina.

Let's stipulate that if Keynes were here, he could make a complete fool of his critics, certainly including me. But as brilliant as he was, there is something initially troubling about his ideas. They have a formulaic quality. In so many cases, he delighted in taking some piece of conventional wisdom or even of common sense and turning it on its head. So—you think that prudent saving and investing is the way to wealth. On the contrary, spending is the way to wealth. But surely one must invest in order to get rich? And how can one invest without first putting aside some savings? No, no, said Keynes. Don't be a dunderhead. Where do you get the savings if not from income? And where do you get the income if not from someone's spending? So it's really spending that drives everything.

This is something like a parlor game. Take a circular flow and interrupt it wherever you like, giving the old folks apoplexy in the process. More fun than Monopoly. But it's a parlor game that leads directly to China's 15 percent of GDP stimulus program. Meanwhile, never mind that Keynes personally was not a spender but rather a diligent saver and investor.

Let's continue a little further with Keynes's logical inversions. Perhaps you think that too much debt is imprudent, will lead to bubbles, and thence to ruin. Not at all. There is actually no such thing as too much debt. So long as humans still have needs, there should be more, not less debt. In order to afford the debt, all we have to do is keep reducing interest rates. By continually reducing interest rates, we can sustain a permanent condition of boom. Viewed this way, there is no such thing as a bubble. Or—a bubble is a boom with interest rates too high—not too low, too high.

The eventual goal should be to reduce nominal interest rates to zero. Then keep them there. In other words, credit should be completely free. For reference, see especially pages 220–21 and 336 of The General Theory. Keynes did say that it would take some time to abolish interest rates. Perhaps a generation. On that schedule, we should have reached a regime of free credit by about 1966.

Free credit is not a new idea. The French socialist Proudhon proposed it in the nineteenth century. This does not necessarily make Keynes a socialist. But Keynes embraced free credit for the long term (without, incidentally, mentioning Proudhon). Of course today we have respected Keynesians such as Gregory Mankiw and Kenneth Rogoff calling for negative interest rates, to be achieved by ramping up inflation. But even they haven't endorsed keeping nominal interest rates at zero forever.

When you read Keynes right through all his many volumes, this habit of taking the conventional wisdom and turning it on its head begins to seem a little too predictable. You think that high interest rates will persuade more people to save and thus increase savings? Nonsense. Low interest rates, not high rates, will increase savings.

However, you don't really want more savings. There is usually a glut of it. There is a glut of it even before you reduce interest rates. And as we have seen, reducing interest rates is a good thing to do. The way to deal with this perennial savings glut is for the government to print new money. Keynes says that this new money is also "savings." It is just as "genuine" as traditional savings. But by adding this new savings to the old savings, you can cure the problem of a savings glut. Got it?

Please note that Alan Greenspan, Ben Bernanke, and Paul Krugman have each echoed this recently. They also say that there is a global savings glut. The correct response has been to print more of what Keynes called "genuine savings." Of course we don't call it "genuine savings" anymore. We now call it liquidity or quantitative easing or some other handy euphemism. It still seems highly paradoxical to try to solve an alleged savings glut problem by printing more money to add to the available cash.

We are focusing on Keynes at this moment because the world is applying his ideas on such a giant scale. In this country, Democrats are Keynesians, but so are Republicans. Same in the UK for Labour and the Tories. As previously noted, few actually read Keynes, but nevertheless it seems that everyone is a Keynesian. Why not—everyone else seems to be a Keynesian. This might be said to define an intellectual bubble, a bubble supporting all the other bubbles. But intellectual bubbles, like others, may become largest just before they pop.

The policies of George W. Bush and Barack Obama have come directly out of Keynes's playbook. Consequently they have that paradoxical, stand common sense on its head, flavor. For example, we are told that: The Crash of '08 was caused by too much debt. We will therefore solve it by adding more debt.

Yes, we do derive economic growth from debt. But the more you borrow the less growth you get. For the decade ending 1959, we got 73 cents in new GDP growth for every dollar we borrowed. That has steadily declined as the debt has grown. For the seven years ending with the Crash of '08, it was only 19 cents. At some point, we will find that the return on debt is totally negative. And the United States may meanwhile lose its credit in the wider world.

It is true that the United States does not seem in imminent danger of losing its credit. It is an ironic fact that the International Monetary Fund relies on the two great borrowing countries, the U.S. and Japan, for most of the money that it then lends to countries in distress. In other words, the U.S. borrows and then relends this money to the IMF, which in turn lends it further, often with no realistic hope of repayment.

Much of the borrowing the U.S. does is from world central banks. Where does this money come from? It is printed. Of course the U.S. itself currently prints some of the money used to buy its own treasury bonds. In other words, it sells to itself. The U.S. also prints money and uses it to buy U.S. mortgages back from foreign central banks that want to sell them. The foreign central banks then, by prior agreement, rechannel this money into U.S. treasury bonds. So directly or indirectly the U.S. is printing quite a bit of the money currently needed to support the U.S.'s credit—not, it would seem, a sustainable situation.

This idea of borrowing our way out of debt isn't the only paradox that is currently guiding our affairs. To take another example, our government concludes that some firms are "too big to fail." We therefore insist on merging them and making them bigger. Result: We get more and more "too big to fail" firms. Sheila Bair, the head of our FDIC, which stands behind bank deposits, thinks that we need to abandon "too big to fail" before it devours us. But nobody else in government seems to agree with her.

Paradoxicalism is an entirely bipartisan affair. George W. Bush got right into the swing of it. He told us, "I have abandoned free market principles to save the free market system." Barack Obama has his own paradoxes. For example, he said that his first budget was taking us from "an era of borrow and spend" to an era of "save and invest." Never mind that it is all deficits into the future. Similarly, to reduce medical expenses, we must increase medical expenses. I thought it particularly interesting that he saw spending as a good way to increase demand generally. But it wouldn't increase demand and therefore prices in health care.

We have become so accustomed to this paradoxical language we just take it for granted. If the Keynesian paradox of thrift and all the other Keynesian paradoxes are so widely accepted, they must surely be right. After all, Keynes explained why all this is true. If anyone doubts, just read Keynes.

But there is a problem here. Keynes did not prove his propositions. He did not even try to prove them. He claimed in a letter to the governor of the Bank of England, Montague Norman, that his ideas were a "mathematical certainty." But that was just a crude bluff. There are very few chains of closely reasoned logic in Keynes, mathematical or verbal. There is almost no interest in evidence. In the whole of *The General Theory*, there are only two pages devoted to empirical evidence. And one of the two studies cited is dismissed as "improbable."

Keynes was more of an intuitionist than a logician or empiricist. He threw out intuitions, really hunches, and expected people to grasp their truth directly, without the need for tedious step-by-step argument or evidence. He explicitly said that economics consisted of one person's intuitive brain speaking to another's.

There is nothing wrong with hunches. But can we really bet the future of the world on them? And it is a bit disconcerting how vague Keynesians are, even today. Respected Keynesian economists, people such as Christina Romer in the White House, Robert Shiller, and Paul Krugman, when asked how much stimulus is needed, say things like "more than you think" or "It must be done on a big enough scale." And how long should stimulus be applied? "For a year or two." Or even "For a long time in the future." Why so nonspecific? Because we are betting our chips on hunches.

We sometimes hear that Keynesian remedies were proven by their success in getting us out of the Depression. That's what I was taught in school and my children are still being taught. This is of course a complicated question. My own view is that the United States printed too much money in the 1920s. This blew up a bubble that popped, precipitating the stock market crash. Prices began to fall precipitously. President Hoover then made the error of getting commitments from businessmen not to lower wages. It was not that Hoover was "hands off" as is often alleged. He was very active, and his interventions were misguided.

Holding up wages while prices were falling was a crucial error. It is a formula for massive business bankruptcy. If a business's revenues are falling, costs must fall or bankruptcy must follow. Since businesses were told that they should not reduce wages, under threat of federal action against them, they had no choice but to adopt the next best way to get costs down: a strategy of massive layoffs. The ironic result was that those lucky enough not to be fired enjoyed the equivalent of a raise: Their wages could buy more and more as prices fell. Meanwhile those laid off lost everything. If prices and wages had fallen together, no one would have suffered; no one would have had to be laid off; because real purchasing power of wages would have remained the same. It would have still involved some pain, because the number of hours worked would have fallen too. But there would have been no breadlines and mass suffering.

When Roosevelt became president, he continued many of Hoover's policies, including an explicit policy of keeping wages up. Indeed he incorporated it into law through the National Recovery Act. Keynes was not a fan of the NRA in general, but he did say that he favored the policy of keeping wages at pre-Depression levels.

Keynes was also not exactly the Keynesian that we assume he was during the Depression. A close reading of his writings and speeches reveals that he did not favor stimulus after the 1929 Crash. He thought that lower interest rates would fix everything. He also recommended an end to stimulus in Britain in 1937. Keynesianism in the 1930s was not the fully developed formula of print money, lower rates, bail out, and stimulate that we saw in 2008.

Was President Roosevelt a Keynesian? Yes and no. Raymond Moley told us that Roosevelt was never known to read anything "serious." We can be pretty sure he never read Keynes. The two did meet once for less than an hour. Accounts of the meeting differ. The president told Felix Frankfurter, a friend of Keynes, that he was impressed. He seems to have told others the opposite. So we don't know.

Roosevelt's policies may be described as broadly Keynesian. But we also need to remember that these policies did not pull us out of the Depression. Only World War II did that. Some Keynesians respond that World War II provided the massive stimulus that was needed all along. But comparing peacetime and wartime economies is comparing apples and oranges. It is generally agreed that this amount of stimulus in peacetime would have blown prices through the roof. Wartime price controls worked fairly well precisely because we were at war. Also because the economy had a few clear and simple goals, not true in peacetime.

Have Keynesian policies worked since? Most agree that they did not work in the late 1960s and 1970s and instead contributed to the Great Inflation of that era. Nor did they work for Japan after its crash. Twenty years later, Japan is still struggling. As is often remarked, the Japanese did not liquidate the mistakes of the past. The zombie loans, banks, and companies lived on and on. By contrast, the avoidance of Keynesian policies in East Asia in the late 1990s seemed to work very well. The East Asians did liquidate, and recovery was fairly swift. This was like the U.S. Depression of 1920 when we also liquidated, and the economy recovered in only a year and a half. Today in America we have relatively little liquidation and lots of zombie loans, banks, and companies. We seem to be definitely on the Japanese path.

Let's return to some of Keynes's most famous ideas. Some of them have clearly been disproven. He said that stimulus spending would produce a gusher of new taxes. It would pay for itself and not increase the debt to GDP ratio. Tell that to Japan. Paul Krugman now says that stimulus should pay for 40 percent of itself.

Keynes also said that his multiplier, the ratio of stimulus to employment or economic growth, would be as much as twelve times and no less than three or four. Since then no one has been able to demonstrate a multiplier higher than one. It may often be closer to zero. I don't think that money borrowed from abroad should give us a multiplier today of zero, but the results remain to be seen.

Keynes's most famous idea, that economic slumps are not self-correcting, was disproven by a Keynesian disciple, Franco Modigliani, even before Keynes's death. Yet President Obama still echoed it in 2009.

He told us that without stimulus the economy might fall past the point of return.

Another well-known Keynesian idea, that you can't have inflation when the economy has excess capacity, has had its ups and downs. During the 1970s stagflation, it fell out of favor. But it has come back and is guiding Fed policy today. The trouble is that we can't really measure capacity. In any case, average capacity isn't what matters. What matters is the capacity of each sector and how these sectors interact with each other. History does make clear that inflation can coexist with excess average capacity.

Some of Keynes's mistakes are very odd. For example, he stated that an investment in the stock market was "sterile" because the cash did not go into new plant and equipment and the like. He evidently forgot that the seller of the stock gets cash and that cash doesn't disappear. To me the oddest slip of all is his argument that long-term investing on Wall Street is impossible because everyone is a short-term speculator. That's backward. The potential return on long-term investing should go up, not down, if everyone else is doing the reverse.

Keynes famously said that the private economy was run on "animal spirits." By contrast, government makes decisions based "on long views and collective wisdom." In an unguarded moment, Keynes also said that politicians were "utter boobies." But leaving that aside, why are public officials immune from animal spirits themselves? There is a further paradox. If Wall Street is a death star of financial and political corruption, why will a marriage of Wall Street and Washington not corrupt Washington? Surely it is no coincidence that the flow of campaign contributions from Wall Street to Washington increased throughout the bubble eras and spiked after the crash.

This feature of today's economy worries me a great deal. I think that Keynes himself would have been appalled by the kind of crony capitalism that his ideas have helped spawn. When he said the politicians should lead the economy, I think he was thinking of the politicians listening to him and doing what he said. He did not mean that there should be this torrent of campaign money flowing to Washington because Washington is making so many crucial economic decisions. People do worry that the Treasury Secretary, according to his own logs, is talking to Goldman Sachs almost daily. But has anyone noticed that Goldman in the fall of '08 acquired the right to borrow at virtually zero interest unlimited dollars from the Federal Reserve, dollars that have been conjured out of thin air.

Goldman repaid the TARP loans with much fanfare. But why is it still allowed to borrow newly printed money from the Fed at giveaway rates?

Crony capitalism is still in its infancy in the United States. In China the government simply tells the banks to get the loans out the door and they do. Chinese loans have grown almost 40 percent this year, and this has contributed to the new bubble that is forming there by deliberate government policy. The Russian government has adopted a similar approach. Prime Minister Putin told his bankers this summer that they would get more loans out the door, hang the quality of the loans, or they would get no summer vacations. So far as I know, they did get the vacations. And, of course, if one of the reckless borrowers gets in trouble, he or she can just go to the government, which will instruct the bank to forgo repayment. Is this the kind of world that we are creating for ourselves in the United States as well?

This threat of crony capitalism is bad enough. But if one were to try to pinpoint a single problem with Keynesianism, it is what it does to prices. The Soviet Union collapsed because it wouldn't allow prices to tell the truth about the economy. But the essence of Keynesianism is price manipulation. Especially the big prices like interest rates and currencies. We keep making the same mistake. Secretary Paulson's original TARP plan didn't work because real mortgage prices had been obliterated. Geithner's follow-up plan just tried to manipulate mortgage prices further. At a minimum we need real price discovery in interest rates, mortgages, and currencies, and we also need to reverse the steady government reduction in required bank reserves, and instead make them much bigger.

The bottom line I am offering here is that Keynes is the emperor without any clothes. His ideas may be helping the elite get richer. They are first in line to borrow the cheap money. But these ideas are impoverishing the masses, including the people clinging to life on a dollar a day.

For the moment, world governments are congratulating themselves on having weathered the Crisis of '08. They enjoy what passes for financial calm, but an eerie calm. None of the imbalances and distortions that precipitated the crisis have actually been addressed. The governments' printing presses are still furiously running off American, European, Japanese, and Chinese currency—the cheap currency that got Wall Street "drunk" in the first place. Borrowing and spending are up, not down. Total debt continues to grow faster than income. Speculation thrives. Patient, "good citizen" savers are, as usual, granted the merest pittance of interest. Global vendor finance still prevails, with China still the dominant seller/lender, the same role that the United States played in the 1920s. The same group of people who created the dot-com and housing bubbles by and large remain in charge.

Much debate currently swirls around whether the Federal Reserve's massive rescue effort will ignite inflation or whether the real risk is not inflation at all, but deflation. Very few commentators entertain the possibility that what lies immediately ahead is neither inflation nor deflation but more bubbles. But we would miss the lesson of the last fifteen years if we fail to understand that excess credit creation and controlled low interest rates can lead to inflation of assets, that is, bubbles, just as easily as inflation of consumer prices.

Keynes saw himself, along with Lytton Strachey and other Bloomsbury friends, as a great debunker of Victorian values. If you reread the great Victorian novels, there are many morality tales, not least about debt. In these pages, easy credit and debt are described as addictive and dangerous, the seducer and undoer of vulnerable human beings, especially young people.

Is it possible that the Victorians were right? That Keynes, for all his brilliance, was morally blind? Are we living through a Victorian novel with ourselves as the heedless victims of greed and folly? If so, there may still be time for a Victorian happy ending, but only if we, as a society, are willing to give up our illusions and stop borrowing faster than we earn.

If this is right, it will not be enough to say, paraphrasing Saint Augustine, give me virtue, but not yet. If I understand them correctly, it is this Augustinian stance that Warren Buffet and George Soros seem to be recommending. I do not personally think it is realistic. I believe instead that if we are to start saving and investing, rather than borrowing and spending, we must start now, without further delay. This is what the Victorians told us, and I think it is time to heed them.

TWELVE

Managed Money, the "Great Recession," and Beyond

:: DIMITRI B. PAPADIMITRIOU

The worst economic crisis since the 1930s afflicting most developed economies began in 2007 and is still not over. Financial and economic statistics in the United States and around the globe represent a troubling state of affairs. The United States and many other nations' expansionary aims in fiscal policy (through relaxed taxation) and monetary policy (through low interest rates) have been insufficient to restore economic health. To be sure, the emerging market economies of Brazil, Russia, India, and China (the so-called BRICs) and a few others seem to have weathered the storm much better and recovered, showing significant growth rates. In America, however, the housing market has yet to stabilize, and despite the historically unprecedented measures of the Fed and the Treasury that have led to increased liquidity, banks are still reluctant to renegotiate mortgages or lend from their growing cash coffers.

Since 2007, more than $10 trillion of homeowners' equity has vanished. Almost half of all mortgages are "underwater," as debt exceeds the home's original value, generating skyrocketing defaults and foreclosures. Unemployment remains very high, hovering over 9 percent in America and in many countries in Europe exceeding 12 percent. Consumers have decreased spending, are paying down debt or increasing savings, and, in general, they show a lot of pessimism for the future. Nonfinancial corporations are not investing, but keeping sizable amounts of cash. The pessimistic economic landscape notwithstanding, the official word from the business cycle arbiter, the National Bureau of Economic Research, has declared the 2007–9 recession over as of June 2009. Economic growth in America and Europe is very much below potential and not sufficient to end labor layoffs, much less robust enough to absorb new labor entering the market. Exactly how this jobless recovery will become job-full still remains an enigma.

Although the subprime mortgage market was what precipitated the financial crisis, largely due to financial deregulation, it cannot be assumed that it was the sole culprit. Many economists fault the unbalanced trade positions that led to global imbalances among nations by which the United States became the largest debtor country. This debt was largely financed by foreign nations, allowing the United States to enjoy artificially low interest rates.[1] As I will argue later, the deeper cause, however, should be attributed to the flaws in the constitution of the current financial structure.

In the current economic system, Keynesian economics has gained renewed currency, so much so that only those absolutely committed to free and unfettered markets argue against government intervention. However, John Maynard Keynes's *General Theory* does not offer a satisfactory treatment of financial instability. In Keynes's theory, as in those of Ludwig von Mises and Friedrich Hayek, financial movements are dependent on the fluctuations in the real side of an economy and are not necessarily due to financial causes.[2]

What Keynes recognized, however, was the instability of market processes. It was Hyman Minsky who convincingly updated Keynes and understood that finance was the cause of instabilities in a capitalist system that have repercussions in the real economy and manifest themselves in a financial crisis. Minsky insisted that continuous stability was not possible even with apt policy because behavior tends to lead to speculative booms. For this reason, Minsky rejected any notion of "fine-tuning," even if policy did manage to achieve transitory stability that would set off processes to reintroduce instability. Hence, "the policy problem is to devise institutional structures and measures that attenuate the thrust to inflation, unemployment, and slower improvements in the standard of living without increasing the likelihood of a deep depression."[3] Indeed, Minsky's fundamental question was whether a downturn similar to the Great Depression might happen again and what was required to prevent it. He concluded that what was necessary was a framework of strong financial regulation and supervision by the central bank, and instituting ceilings and floors that would prevent debt deflation from happening again. However, in an economy with continuous financial innovation, success could not be permanent, and government policy would have to continually adjust and adapt to changing circumstances.

The Rise of Money-Manager Capitalism

As Minsky argued in 1996, postwar capitalism has evolved from "commercial capitalism" to "industrial capitalism" to "paternalistic, managerial and welfare state capitalism" to "money manager capitalism." Minsky defined money-manager capitalism as the new stage in the United States "in which the proximate owners of a vast proportion of financial instruments are mutual and pension funds. The total return on the portfolio is the only criterion used for judging the performance of the managers of these funds, which translates into an emphasis upon the bottom line in the management of business organizations." Within money-manager capitalism there is a higher level of uncertainty because of the dominant role played by mutual funds, high leverage and pension funds hungry for higher returns that systematically underprice risk.[4] The financial system within which managed money interacts has moved toward increasing levels of instability that finally reached the danger zone of a systemic risk and pushed it to its collapse in 2008.

Many commentators and market analysts have suggested that 2008 was a "Minsky moment," precisely describing what Minsky had in mind when he warned that rapid debt deflation might happen again. For Minsky, the transformation of the economy over the postwar period from robust to fragile states would lead to financial crises. And so in the past three decades, we have experienced the savings and loan crisis, the leveraged buyout junk bond failure, three stock market crashes in 1987, 2000, and 2008, the Long Term Capital Management meltdown, and the current global financial crisis with the incipient "Great Recession" we are still enduring. These are examples of crises set off by managed money with a large appetite for excessive risks that operates outside traditional banking and is to a large extent unregulated and unsupervised.

Responding to the demand from managed money for instruments with high returns, Wall Street's financial engineers developed complex and model-dependent methods to value financial instruments. High prices could be placed on these financial products with the accord of the credit-rating agencies that underpriced risk. Arguably, financial markets entered a wave of innovation with no historical precedent. Financial instruments embraced every possible domain of investing, including the inflated real estate markets that boomed with mortgage-backed securitization that made house ownership available to households previously excluded; real estate prices grew faster than ever and enabled homeowners to "cash out" equity as they borrowed against appreciated values in order to increase their spending. All of this was facilitated by the relatively low interest rate policy maintained by the Federal Reserve with the belief that better monetary policy would constrain inflation. Despite the Federal Reserve's tardy response to stop this process by raising interest rates, gains in real estate values continued unabated. The relaxation of lending standards allowed borrowers to keep on borrowing and lenders to push loans. Rather than imposing stricter lending rules, the Fed kept tinkering with interest rates. By summer 2007 problems began to appear in many of the mortgage-backed securities, and eventually markets seized up when demand for such products collapsed.

The Fed, then, started lowering interest rates, but losses continued to accumulate and spread beyond banks as market after market experienced liquidity problems. Lower interest rates did not do the trick, as the real problem was elsewhere. Financial institutions and investors in mortgaged-backed securities were highly leveraged, and the financial products they were holding had become illiquid. Fear emerged in the face of the stark reality of the impending massive collapse of the Ponzi structure they had created.

When real estate markets cooled, U.S. and foreign speculators moved to other profit opportunities. Speculation on physical commodities was next, boosting storage facilities to their limits to sell later at higher prices. Soon, the turn was to the commodities futures markets, with managed money buying paper commodities not to speculate, but to hold as an inflation hedge in a diversified portfolio. The global collapse in commodities prices and hedge funds followed soon thereafter.[5] In a finance-guided economy, together with the ease of investing made possible by the advancements in information and instant-execution technology, financial innovation knows no boundaries.

Banks, Securitization, and the Current Financial Crisis

In principle, all mortgages can be packaged into a variety of risk classes, with differential pricing to cover risk. Investors could choose the desired risk-return trade-off. Thrifts and other regulated financial institutions would earn fee income for loan origination, for assessing risk, and for servicing the mortgages. Financial engineering would create collateralized debt obligations (CDOs), slicing and dicing the mortgages to suit the need of investors. All this could be achieved with securitization. Securitization reflected two developments in the financial markets: the decline of traditional banking and the globalization of the financial world.

First was the decline of traditional banking (narrowly defined as financial institutions that accept deposits and make loans) in favor of "markets." This development, itself, was encouraged by the experiment in monetarism (1979–82) that decimated the regulated portion of the sector in favor of the relatively unregulated "markets," but it was also spurred by continual erosion of the portion of the financial sphere that had been ceded by the rules and regulations of traditional banking. As Minsky showed in his essay "Securitization," the growth of competition on both sides of banking business—checkable deposits at nonbank financial institutions that could pay market interest rates and the rise of the commercial paper market that allowed firms to bypass commercial banks—squeezed the profitability of banking.[6] By contrast, financial markets can operate with much lower spreads precisely because they are exempt from required reserves, capital requirements, and much of the costs of relationship banking. At the same time, financial markets became freer from New Deal regulations that had made them safer. Not only did this mean that an ever-larger portion of the financial sector was free of most regulations but that competition from "markets" forced policymakers to relax regulations on banks.

By the time of the real estate boom that eventually led to the current subprime mortgage crisis, there was no longer any essential difference between a "commercial bank" and an "investment bank." The whole housing sector that had been made very safe by the New Deal reforms had been transformed into a huge global casino, rendering the United States a Ponzi nation. The New Deal reforms related to home finance had been spurred by a common belief that short-term mortgages, typically with large balloon payments, had contributed to the Great Depression; ironically, the "innovations" in home mortgage finance leading up to the speculative boom largely re-created those conditions. Financial institutions responded to each tight money episode by innovating, creating new practices and instruments—making the supply of credit ever more expansive. Furthermore, the Fed and Congress gradually removed constraints; ultimately the Glass-Steagall Act that had separated commercial and investment banking was repealed in 1999, allowing commercial banks to engage in a wider range of practices so that they could better compete with their relatively unregulated Wall Street competitors.

Deregulation and legal recognition of new practices were not, by themselves, sufficient to bring on the current global financial crisis. If these innovations had led to excessively risky behavior that generated huge losses, financial institutions would have been reluctant to retain them, and this can be documented by the absence of depressions during the postwar period. To be sure, recessions occur regularly, but they are constrained; while financial crises arise from time to time, the fallout is also contained. This is owing in part to the various reforms that date back to the days of the New Deal but also to the countercyclical movement of the "Big Government" budget, to lender of last resort activity of the "Big Bank" (the Fed), and to periodic bailouts arranged by it in concert with the U.S. Treasury or Congress. Thus, by preventing "It" from happening again, new practices and instruments were validated. Putting it differently, the upside exuberance observed in each bubble is just the end result of long-term policy-induced, and in turn policy-validated, profit-seeking financial innovations that stretched liquidity and enabled prices of real estate and of equity to reach unjustified and unsustainable levels.

Over this period, growth of managed money competed with traditional banks and provided an alternative source of funds in competition with bank loans. Initially, bank funding had an advantage over market sources of funding because banks could diversify risks across a large number of borrowers with different income sources. Further, banks had access to insured deposits as well as to Fed lender of last resort intervention, ensuring they could issue liabilities without facing much chance of a run. However, by the early 1970s, firms were already turning in large numbers to the commercial paper market for short-term borrowing. An early 1970s crisis in the commercial paper market led to the practice of obtaining backup lines of credit with banks. On the one hand, banks then could earn fee income for provision of the backup facilities, but on the other, this practice reduced their competitive advantage in direct funding of business.[7] Another market innovation allowed for diversification of risk by issuing securities collateralized by pooling loans. Taken together, such innovations reduced the advantages that banks had previously held.

Over time, new instruments continually eroded the bank share of assets and liabilities—which fell by half between the 1950s and the 1990s: The securities market share of private nonfinancial debt rose from 27 percent in 1980 to 55 percent in 2008.[8] Banks were forced to become more market oriented. They would settle for a smaller share of the financial system, and servicing Wall Street firms would replace some of the relationship banking they had lost.

To restore profitability, banks began to earn fee income for loan origination, and by moving mortgage and other loans off their balance sheets, they could escape reserve and capital requirements. They could, however, continue to service the loans and earn additional fees. Investment banks would purchase and pool these loans, then sell them as securities to investors. Investment banks would pay rating agencies to bless the securities and hire economists to develop models demonstrating that interest earnings would more than compensate for the assumed risks. Risk raters and economic modelers would certify that prospective defaults on the underlying assets would be low enough to justify the investment-grade rating required by insurance and pension funds. These developments appeared to offer an alternative to relationship banking. There was no need to develop relationships with individual borrowers to assess credit worthiness because loan pools diversified risks, raters evaluated the risks of the overall pools, and insurers offered credit default swaps (protection) against possible losses. To replace lost income, banks began to take direct positions in these loan pools, the securities, and the insurers. They also provided backup liquidity guarantees to those involved in packaging and selling securities, and even gave money-back guarantees to holders of securities if the underlying loans went bad, and thus banks were exposed to default risk of borrowers they had not properly assessed.

The second development was that securitization was part and parcel of the globalization of finance, since it created financial securities that were international. German investors with no direct access to America's homeowners could buy mortgage-backed securities originating in U.S. real estate markets. Packaged securities with risk weightings assigned by respected rating agencies were appealing to global investors trying to achieve the desired proportion of dollar-denominated assets. Securitization is a "market-oriented" financial practice in contrast to "bank-based" transactions where activities are financed by loans held on bank balance sheets against deposits of the banking system. Securitization has also been called the "originate and distribute" model, which accurately captures a distinguishing feature of the process: The institution that arranges the financing of activities does not hold the loan. Lots of presumptions about these instruments and practices have been cleared up by the crisis, including the belief that securitization shifted risks off bank balance sheets, that securitization allowed for diversification of risks while efficiently allowing investors to achieve the proper risk-return trade-off, and that securitization put risk into the portfolios of those best able to handle it.

In the aftermath of the 2000 equity market crash, investors looked elsewhere for sources of profits. Low interest rate policy by Alan Greenspan's Fed meant that traditional money markets could not offer adequate returns. Investors sought higher risks, and mortgage originators offered subprime mortgages and other "affordability products" with ever-lower underwriting standards. Brokers were richly rewarded for inducing borrowers to accept unfavorable terms, which increased the value of the securities. New and risky types of mortgages—hybrid Adjustable Rate Mortgages (ARMs, called "2/28" and "3/27") that offered low teaser rates for two or three years, with very high reset rates—were pushed, even by Fed Chairman Greenspan.

Although the troubled instruments and institutions varied, many of today's problems can be traced back to securitization. Although seemingly innocuous, securitization led to a dizzying array of extremely complex instruments. Throughout the financial world, "mark to model" or even "mark to myth" substituted for "mark to market" accounting because markets could not value the instruments. Thus, by 2007 we faced a systemic problem resulting from the notion that markets can properly assess risk based on complex, backward-looking models; that markets can hedge and shift risk to those best able to bear it; and that market forces will discipline decision making. Alas, each of these presumptions proved to be woefully incorrect. The models were constructed based on data generated during an unusually stable period in which losses were small, and required that the structure of the financial system remain constant. But as Minsky argued, relative stability will necessarily encourage behavior that changes the financial structure (he used the terms "hedge," "speculative," and "Ponzi" to describe the transformation). This evolution, in turn, rendered the models increasingly useless even as they were used on a grander scale to justify falling interest rate spreads, implying that virtually no defaults would ever occur. Further, as is now recognized, the models could not account for growing interrelations among debtors increasing the systemic risk that insolvency by some would generate a snowball of defaults. This was another process that Minsky always emphasized and one that is enhanced by the kind of leveraging that became common as margins of safety were reduced. Further, as we now know, neither risk was properly hedged nor was it necessarily shifted. Much of it came back directly to banks through buyback guarantees, backup credit facilities, and bank purchases of securities.

Finally, markets did not discipline behavior but instead encouraged ever-riskier activities. For example, the increased competition coming from managed money narrowed interest rate spreads, but because fund managers were in a desperate search for high returns they were forced to ignore risk where it was underpriced. Competition forced them to take excessive risk given returns. Many did not even pretend to understand the instruments they were buying, as they were content to either rely on credit-rating agencies or to simply follow the leader down the inevitable path to destruction.

Final Comments: A Return to Keynesianism

The financial bailout plan enacted by the U.S. Congress gave an opportunity to consolidate control of the U.S. financial system in the hands of a few large (Wall Street) banks. As the evidence has shown, relieving banks of some of their bad assets, or injecting some equity into them, has not thus far increased their willingness to lend. Since the U.S. economy is still enduring the "Great Recession," this is not a good time to lend. After a dozen years of virtually unrelenting spending by the private sector, households and firms are already too heavily indebted. They are instead deleveraging by paying off debt and do not want to borrow more. Government should not rely on, much less encourage, more borrowing by the private sector to pull the economy out of this downturn.

There are also other policy alternatives that merit serious consideration. The Fed has opened its discount window to far more institutions and has more than once used quantitative easing to increase economic activity in the light of the limited use of expansionary fiscal policy. However, more needs to be done: The Fed should remove all collateral requirements and lend without limit, and the FDIC should eliminate any caps on its deposit insurance to include all deposits in member banks, in order to protect large deposits held by businesses.

What still requires immediate attention is to arrest the unprecedented number of foreclosures for households whose mortgages are underwater and for homeowners who are unable to keep up with their mortgage payments. Helping homeowners would entail a combination of either reducing the principal outstanding and restructuring the debt or allowing them to stay in their homes paying market value rent until the time they could resume mortgage payments. Furthermore, for homeowners whose current mortgage payments exceed one-third of their household income, relief can be achieved by offering a 5 percent fixed-rate thirty-year mortgage. This plan will require that both the U.S. Treasury and the financial institutions holding the mortgages share its cost.

The strong calls to exit from expansionary fiscal policy are much too early. For the United States and many countries in Europe austerity measures should be delayed and instead more fiscal stimulus implemented (tax cuts and spending increases) that would raise aggregate demand and bring the U.S. and other economies out of the economic crisis. In the United States, a new and large fiscal stimulus package is an absolute necessity, despite the government deficit hysteria from anti-Keynesian writers and Tea Party followers. Other proposals as part of a fiscal stimulus have been suggested, including "lowering the price of consuming" by suspending sales taxes, with the federal government covering the state and local revenue losses or implementing a temporary suspension of the collection of payroll taxes, with the Treasury directly making all Social Security payments at least until the economy recovers. This will put more income into the hands of households while lowering the employment costs for firms, fueling spending and employment. There are also government expenditures that can be directed toward the neglected physical and human infrastructure similar to the programs put into effect under President Roosevelt's New Deal legislation.[9]

Can the government afford this huge price tag? The answer is yes, absolutely—and it will be a bargain whatever the cost, if it enables us to avoid the Great Recession continuing with the devastating economic and social effects of high levels of unemployment.

THIRTEEN

Turning the Economy into a Casino

:: DAVID B. MATIAS
:: SOPHIA V. BURRESS

The events of 2008 are unprecedented in the history of civilization. Never before have so many people been affected so dramatically and has so much economic wealth been destroyed in a matter of weeks, days, and even minutes. Yet today, years after these events, we still have an incomplete understanding of the causes and an even lesser understanding of the impact. The underlying currents of neglect and greed, amoral—if not immoral—bankers, and political corruption are easy targets in the aftermath of the collapse. It seems as if culpability is so widespread and runs so deep that placing blame on specific entities only opens one up to criticism.

The premise of this essay is that an insightful analysis of the crash recognizes the tectonic, almost glacier-like, changes in society. We attempt to explain these events to the best of our ability using both the realms of political and economic theory. No one realm can handle the intricacies of the situation: combined, they begin to explain the interplay that created a third realm of modern finance and its agent, the financial services industry.

At the heart of the financial industry's growth since World War II is the belief that our value to society is found in our bank accounts. This growth has its origins in the failure of our politicians to effectively limit and control the unbridled and ultimately destructive growth of finance. In the context of the transition to a consumerist society in which we consume three dollars for every four dollars of production, the symbiotic growth of consumerism and financialization provided for extraordinary asset inflation and economic collapse.

The Financial Society

At the root of the financial crisis is the unprecedented rise of the financial services industry. In the years leading up to the crash, the financial services sector was viewed as a core example of private institutions providing public value. Because the financial services industry was contributing more than 20 percent to the annual GDP, its value was perceived to be vitally important to the economy. This premise, however, is deeply flawed. Although the absolute value of the financial industry is large, the creation of societal value is small.

Some services of the financial industry are necessary to the real economy, but many are ancillary and ultimately deadweight. Michael Hudson, a distinguished professor at the University of Missouri at Kansas City, wrote in 2004, "Today's economy is best seen as a financial bubble. . . . Credit—and hence, debt—is being created to inflate the bubble rather than to finance direct capital formation. In this respect the banking and financial systems have become dysfunctional."[1] This dynamic—the unchecked growth in the financial sector—is the fundamental shift that exemplifies how the economy has entered into a completely untenable state.

Depository banks are integral to the healthy working of an economy and can balance the twin goals of capital return (generating revenue for stakeholders) and public good. Commercial banks are needed to facilitate capital creation (the building of tangible assets using capital and labor) and to eliminate economic frictions. They allow individuals and entrepreneurs to place illiquid assets up for collateral in exchange for necessary funds, for example providing lines of credit to small businesses. The basic functions of accepting demand deposits and lending at interest allow the economy to grow.

Today, and especially during the past decade, the financial sector searched for profits by issuing debt for already existing assets. When a loan is issued for existing capital, it does not add to the capital base of the economy. In the case of a mortgage loan for an existing house, it is especially clear that the transaction is "net-zero" from a societal perspective. The exchange of the asset from one person to another leaves the real economy unchanged; it is only a transfer, although the individual seller experiences a financial gain and the buyer a commensurate loss. It is true that the seller can use that money to invest in new capital (or maintain existing capital), but this was often not the case. Often the seller saw that money as income, not capital return, and promptly increased consumption. Mason Gaffney, in *After the Crash*,[2] outlines the myriad ways that investment is diverted away from productive capital during real estate bubbles, even when sellers do not immediately increase consumption.

Another equally important dynamic is that financial institutions tend to "save" the majority of their income—that is, interest payments are reinvested into new loans. These investments, again, are not generally invested in new capital formation, but rather debt structures. Because of the ability to utilize excessive leverage, the financial sector can grow much more quickly than the rest of the economy. The financial industry's progression is not innocuous; it is only possible because of those interest payments that siphon income from the borrower. The unsustainable advance in the financial industry is thus met with an economy that has a weakening capacity to support it.

The financial industry, composed of "finance, insurance, and real estate" (as amalgamated by the Nation Income and Product Accounts) and known by the acronym FIRE, has experienced unprecedented and continual growth at the expense of real production (i.e., manufacturing). In terms of contribution to GDP, FIRE has grown from 10 percent in 1950 to over 20 percent today, while manufacturing has declined from 25 percent to only 11 percent as of 2010. This statistic, however, conceals many important points. One is that the growth in the industry has not been accompanied by a commensurate increase in employment. Another is that the relatively small numbers of employees receive unparalleled compensation.

Compensation in the entire FIRE sector has outpaced wages for the rest of the economy by almost a doubling. Breaking down the sectors within industry shows that the two activities that have experienced the majority of the gains are securities trading and fund management—both of which employ few people (less than 1 percent of all employees) and increasingly do little more than transfer wealth. Since 1987 the growth rates for real wages for employees in securities trading and fund management have been more than 3 percent, while all the other industries have experienced an average real wage growth rate of a paltry 1 percent. In real numbers, employees in the two sectors make an average of $196,000, more than triple the average in other industries of $63,000. These statistics are more anecdotal than rigorous, but they convey the fundamental trend that is apparent in the U.S. economy. That is, we are an economy increasingly based on financial services that advances the wealth of a few while the rest struggle to cover the rising costs of living.

The Consumer Society

At the same time as the financial industry was coming to dominate the U.S. economy, consumer spending became the engine of that economy. This coincidence is neither accidental nor innocent. Bush's invocation after 9/11 to "support the economy" and *Time* magazine's spin, "just go shopping," were the most blatant statements of what has become a mainstay of the American consciousness. The willingness to accept the debt, not only mortgages and auto loans but also unsecured debt such as credit cards, was necessary to build the unsustainable pyramid. Consumption as a percentage of GDP has grown from 63 percent in 1960 to 73 percent in 2010. While our manufacturing sector moved offshore and our export power diminished, we used domestic consumption to push the economy forward.

Mortgage debt, further fueling consumption, was at the heart of the financial crash. Hannah Arendt in 1950 wrote of the 1870s financial turbulence: "For the first time . . . uncontrollable investments in distant countries threatened to transform large strata of society into gamblers, to change the whole capitalist economy from a system of production into a system of financial speculation, and to replace the profits of production with profits in commissions." Change "in distant countries" to "in the mortgage market," and her statement is more prescient than most.

The mortgage bubble, and the financial sector in general, required the support of the consumerist economy. The willingness of the average person to use his or her home as a bank account was an underlying factor in the growth of the bubble. Although it is necessary to consider the fact that education costs and inadequate safety nets for retirement necessitated some people to draw down on their real estate equity, it was just as common for housing income to pay for vacations, additions, and extravagant consumption. The mass consciousness feeds and is fed by media perceptions of wealth. Seeing their wages decline in real terms, individuals needed to use the rising value of their house if they were to respond to the pressure to consume. The financial industry both fed this perception and used the inclination to its advantage.

An insidious example of the financial industry's feeding consumerism is the manipulation of 401(k) retirement programs. Building on the back of a well-intended tax benefit, financial service firms promote these plans as the key to a well-funded retirement. Through the hype and buzz that an aggressively designed plan would realize these goals, firms promoted a raft of products (from mutual funds to variable annuity contracts) that provided a steady stream of profit to the firms while exposing future retirees to inappropriate risks. Financial service firms skimmed 2–5 percent from these assets *each year* in the form of fees, some disclosed and some hidden, as permitted by then-current regulation. Despite the high costs of providing "appropriate" vehicles to investors, at least one trillion dollars of retirement funds were permanently erased by the financial crisis.

The damage from this dynamic is far-reaching. With a manufactured perception that retirement could be secured through these accounts, workers felt free to deploy disposable income into consumption. And with rising income tax rates looming into the next decade, the tax advantages could simply dissipate. Again, consumption has been prioritized over the public good with the aid of government policies and regulations.

The Asset Bubble

None of this could have happened without the real estate bubble and the mortgage market. The story of mortgage proliferation in the years leading up to 2007 has been told many times by many authors. Essentially, low interest rates and rising home prices enticed many buyers and sellers into the market. Mortgages are a fairly risky asset because the bank is making itself dependent on the earning ability of one person or family for the next thirty years. Moreover, houses are physical assets that people make into their home. They are clunky, hard to sell, easily damaged, sometimes unattractive, and most of all, subject to the whims of the capricious real estate market. For this reason banks tend to be very cautious in their loans. Prime loans are by definition leveraged by no more than 5:1. With an 80 percent loan-to-value, the ability to foreclose and auction the house theoretically provides a cushion so that the bank does not lose money in the event of borrower default.

Over the past twenty years financial investors have been translating this very tangible asset into a tradable security. However, the mortgage market is peculiar due to the length of the loan and illiquidity of the asset. Banks found it profitable to originate loans and then sell them off in bundles in order to get a lump-sum payment. This insulated them from the long payback period associated with ten- to thirty-year mortgage loans and provided the capital necessary to originate even more loans. The financial industry, today more than ever, is predicated on the immediate nature of its profits—such securities can now be traded in a matter of minutes.

Further, the distinction between the house and the land is paramount to understanding the asset bubble. When the price of a house increases, it elicits new supply, bringing the price back toward an equilibrium level. Increases in the price of land have no equilibrating adjustment. Because land is never produced, its price is based solely on the current interest rate and future expectations of appreciation. When interest rates are low and growth expectations are high, the price of land increases untenably. The low interest rates instituted by the Federal Reserve after the dot-com crash had a major effect on asset prices, in effect inflating a housing bubble to replace the internet bubble.

This small differential between expected growth on real estate assets (myopic investor expectations) and low interest rates from loose monetary policy justified the ever-growing asset valuations through the financial calculus of the day. Yet actual risks were poorly understood, and pragmatic growth was rarely incorporated into the math. With this lack of understanding, the mortgage rating agencies assigned AAA ratings to many mortgage products, allowing the products to be sold and held as risk-less securities. Adding further volatility to an already tenuous structure, insurance contracts were written on these mortgage products to protect investors against unforeseen losses. Credit default swaps (CDS), a completely unregulated market, were harnessed by banks and speculators alike to protect them against the possibility of losses on these products, to the tune of trillions of dollars in nominal contract values.

The failure of AIG during the crash brought this dynamic and dysfunction to the fore. As an insurance company, they were one of the largest issuers of CDS on subprime mortgage products with over 500 billion dollars worth of contracts issued in 2007. As a financial institution, they entered into the unregulated market of securities lending to feed the growing demand for stock shorting. With the financial collateral from their stock-lending activities (upwards of $80 billion going into 2008), they purchased AAA-rated subprime mortgage products to further increase their profits with little regard for the risks. When the collapse ensued, the lethal mix of activities left a $150 billion hole in their balance sheet.

Leading up to 2008, government abdicated its role as guardian and allowed excessive leverage and speculation masked as financial innovation and market efficiencies. Financial institutions soared when real estate was appreciating, even when the appreciation was fueled by the financial industry itself. When the economy stalled and the banks failed, government stepped in to protect the institutions and the jobs of those institutions that were at the heart of the crisis. Profits, compensation, and employment in the financial industry are returning to pre-2008 levels. The actors who guided institutions into the crisis received their outsized remuneration and in most cases kept their jobs. Meanwhile, the real economy continues to falter. Acting as a drain on the rest of the economy, the financial services industry continues to parade behind the mask of essential services. The divergence between the health of modern finance and the average worker indicates otherwise.

Public Good

The story of American capitalism begins with Adam Smith, the adopted father of liberal economics, who coined the term "invisible hand." In that euphemism he meant to describe how the interactions of many isolated individuals could lead to an unplanned harmony of interests. In Smith's use, the public good is the synchronization of activities so that labor can find employment and citizens can fulfill their basic needs. He imagined a bustling marketplace where the interactions of competing self-interested agents automatically created a stable equilibrium of prices within the current supply-and-demand constraints.

In the United States today we commonly hear politicians argue for the efficiency of the "free market," where Adam Smith's "invisible hand" has free rein to create a balanced coordination among individuals. It was one of the main themes Federal Reserve Chairman Alan Greenspan used in his battle for deregulation during the 1990s. Inefficiency and economic stagnation were proclaimed to be the greatest threats of government regulation, and the free market was lauded as the highest good. What was good for capitalism was good for everyone.

Only the first among many economists to articulate the vision that individuals acting in isolation will create a larger order, Smith writes, "By pursuing his own interest [an individual] frequently promotes that of the society more effectually than when he really intends to promote it."[3] Misinterpreting Smith's original intention, the "invisible hand" was embraced by our society. Supported by the government (mainly expressed through our tax code) and exemplified by various financial innovations of the 1970s, '80s, and '90s (such as stock options for company executives), greed became culturally accepted.

Hannah Arendt was deeply skeptical of the liberal concept that private interests could promote a public good. When this happens, she writes in *The Origins of Totalitarianism*, "Public life takes on the deceptive aspect of a total of private interests, as though these interests could create a new quality through sheer addition."[4] For Arendt, the doctrine of an invisible hand is a "communistic fiction"—society as a whole is imagined to have one overarching interest. In reality, the individual desires of many do not mutate into a singular desire of society. The crux of the dispute goes to the heart of the crash. Policies that enabled or promoted the growth of the financial services industry, often at the expense of the rest of the economy, were instituted as if the magic of capitalism would cure the conflicting interests. Government viewed its role as a facilitator of "economic growth" and hoped for the best.

In reality individual interest most often manifested itself as an unmitigated desire to consume. The financial sector took advantage of the opportunity initially and promoted it eventually. The addition of these private interests created a calamity of unequaled proportions. Hannah Arendt, observing the rise of a consumer society in 1958, worried about the subversive but growing trend toward consumerism. She worried that as we became a society of laborers focused on our jobs and our incomes, the activities of labor and consumption would encompass the greater part of our world. For the sake of "making a living," the laborer labors. Consumption, the fruit of labor, follows. In a process that can never be contained or limited, this is the natural cycle of what Arendt calls biological, or the animal part of human life. What consumerism means, Arendt writes in *The Human Condition*, is that "the spare time of the *animal laborans* is never spent in anything but consumption, and the more time left to him, the greedier and more craving his appetites."[5]

Arendt's conclusion is that with consumerist society comes the loss of political freedom and the idea of a public good. Because consumption is unlimited and has no natural endpoint, it devours all spare time. All other activities that once were held valuable in human life—religion, the life of the mind, and public-spirited community action—come to be seen as merely wasted time and lost opportunities for consumption. In a laboring society, Arendt writes, the unending and infinite need to consume threatens to overwhelm all other values and life-styles. Consumption is inexorable and unending. As a result, the idea of a public good beyond and apart from the consuming interests of private individuals becomes ever more rare and difficult to ascertain.

Over the past decades we actively practiced schizophrenic policies promoting both free markets and intervention. The financial services industry sought ever-weaker regulations to foster ever more lending and consumption. We repealed Glass-Steagall while providing tax incentives to hedge funds. We encouraged personal enrichment of financial services employees yet bailed out the institutions when they failed. The list goes on. The economy became a casino with the financial services industry owning the house: "You win, I win—You lose, I win." Combined with the shift to excessive consumerism and the financialization of society, we created a bloated national balance sheet around the shrinking core of the real economy. As the economy hollowed out, failure and collapse were only a matter of time. Let us hope there are lessons learned for the next generation.

PART IV

The Origins of the Financial Crisis from Nationalism to Neoliberalism

FOURTEEN

Capitalism

NEITHER PROBLEM NOR SOLUTION—BUT
TEMPORARY VICTIM OF THE FINANCIAL CRISIS

:: LIAH GREENFELD

I want to respond to the provocative question raised by the editors with regard to the recent financial crisis: "Is capitalism the problem or the solution?" It is neither the problem nor the solution. Instead, capitalism is the temporary victim—in academic discussion, in the United States and some European countries. It is held to be responsible by those who don't know whom to blame. If we are looking for the origin, or the solution, to the financial crisis, we should turn from capitalism to nationalism. Nationalism, not capitalism, is both the creator of the problem and the provider of the solution.

What is capitalism? The term *capitalism* nowadays most commonly designates the modern economic process, as distinguished from traditional economies by its orientation toward and capacity to sustain growth. The principle of capitalism is, as formulated by Marx in *Capital*, "Money > Commodity > More Money," or by Max Weber, "profit and forever renewed profit."

So understood as the power of wealth to beget more wealth, capitalism emerged in sixteenth-century England, which set the example of sustained economic growth for the world. Before England spawned the first modern capitalist economy, economic activity throughout the world was oriented to subsistence. If people accumulated wealth, they did this to live, rather than living to accumulate wealth. As rational economic agents, they worked hard and saved until they felt that they had enough for whatever condition they felt to be comfortable. And when they reached this stage of comfort, they stopped working hard and began to spend their savings.

Of course, the great majority never accumulated wealth at all. Even in better times they had just enough to survive and in the very best days they had enough to raise children, but they had nothing to save. Subsistence economies were cut to size by the "Malthusian scissors." When such economies grew, people produced more children who survived to maturity, so the population grew too; however, the growing population consumed the surplus and ate into the very stock of the economy. As a result, the economy contracted, the population decreased, and the cycle began again.

So it went until the time in England when this traditional orientation toward economic activity was replaced by a very different one—one in which wealth and ever-increasing wealth became the end and human beings the dedicated means to achieve it. The English experiment in capitalism stood on its head the central principle of rational behavior: the pursuit of pleasure and the avoidance of pain. This new orientation was, as Max Weber stressed in his famous attempt to explain it, fundamentally irrational. In fact, as he wrote, the presumed foundation of the capitalist economic ethic—"the earning of more and more money, combined with a strict avoidance of all spontaneous enjoyment of life is completely devoid of any eudemonistic, not to say hedonistic, pleasure. It is thought of so purely as an end in itself, that from the point of view of the happiness of, or the utility to the single individual, it appears entirely transcendental and absolutely irrational. . . . Economic acquisition is no longer subordinated to man as the means of satisfaction of his material needs. This reversal of what we should call the natural relationship, so irrational from a naïve point of view, is, evidently, as definitive and leading a principle of capitalism as it is foreign to all peoples not under the sway of its particular influence."[1] That capitalist behavior is so unlike rational behavior means that it could only be accounted for by the emergence of a new system of values, values that make the accumulation of wealth into a good in its own right and not simply as a means for the achievement of another good, such as life. Capitalist accumulation of wealth, Weber writes, now comes to attach directly to a new supreme and self-standing good rather than being the necessary means to the achievement of the latter.

Weber's book *The Protestant Ethic and the Spirit of Capitalism* was, until recently, the only account of why capitalism emerged when and where it did. Unfortunately, Weber's thesis, that the transformation of values accompanying the Protestant revolution made possible the capitalist valuation of wealth as a good in itself, has not been borne out by empirical evidence.

Following the lead of Weber's logic, I have argued, in my book *The Spirit of Capitalism*,[2] that the new system of values that inspired the reorientation of economic activity toward ever-expanding growth has its origin not in Calvinist Protestantism but in another contemporary development: nationalism. The new capitalist ethic did not result from the change in the religious Christian worldview. Rather, capitalist values have their true foundation in the replacement of a religious worldview by a dramatically different secular image of reality.

Focused on this experiential (empirical) world—a world that it endows with ultimate meaning—nationalism has at its core an image of social reality whose fundamental building blocks are nations—sovereign communities of essentially equal members. The inherent egalitarianism of nationalism and the view of a community of living members as the bearer of supreme authority necessarily elevate the status of every member of the nation. In a nation, all citizens are endowed with the dignity of an elite. As the source of individual dignity lies in one's membership in the nation, it comes to be profoundly associated with the dignity of the nation. In a nationalist period, one's personal dignity necessarily reflects one's nation's position in relation to other nations or international prestige.

Prestige is a relative value that fluctuates with the prestige of the relevant others. The national population in each case is strongly committed to maintaining the prestige of its nation. This makes nationalism a competitive ideology. Any particular nation is likely to choose that sphere of life as an area of competition where it has the best chance to succeed. In every area of national competition (economy, military, education, etc.), the competition is constant—a race with a moving finish line. When a nation decides to compete in the field of economic activity, the result is its reorientation toward the accumulation of ever-increasing wealth and, given that the competitors are capable by definition, economies of sustained growth or capitalism.

My point is that competitive national exertion is what explains the persistence of capitalist activity. As Weber successfully argued, the dedication of an individual life to the accumulation of wealth rather than the other way around is, from the individual point of view, an irrational behavior. But, this irrational behavior is rationalized by nationalism. The accumulation of ever-increasing wealth—the seemingly endless growth—

actually serves an end: the end of national prestige and therefore the dignity of the individual in economically competitive nations.

Nationalism emerged in England in the early sixteenth century and for about two centuries England was the only *nation* in the world, that is, the only society organized on the basis of the inclusive and, for that reason, competitive national image of social reality. It is not surprising that the English *national* economy was the first economy to become competitive, to reorient itself toward growth. Moreover, although the English saw competition everywhere, England remained without any serious competitors for two centuries—because no other economy was as yet nationally, that is, competitively, motivated. It is also not surprising, therefore, that the English, and then the British, economy emerged as the world's preeminent economy and maintained this position well into the twentieth century. The explanation for England's economic power lies in its nationalist competitive motivation, a spur that propelled England to its exalted place. Nationalism, and not any particular advantage in regard to the material ingredients of a strong economy, was the original force that shot England into its capitalist future—for it should be remembered that before it embarked on its road to economic dominance, England enjoyed no such advantages, and its economy, as compared with those of its neighbors in the Netherlands, France, and Spain, was backward and weak.

We must take seriously this too-long overlooked fact: Capitalism was born in England within a generation or two of the emergence of English nationalism, in the middle of the sixteenth century. The emergence of a nationalism-inspired capitalism was signaled by the renaming, in 1564, of the Company of Merchants Adventurers as the Merchants Adventurers of England. The time lapse between the emergence of nationalism and the take-off into sustained economic growth happens to be one or two generations in length in other nations that opted to compete in the economic arena. The first four countries that did so were France, Germany, the United States, and Japan.

Because of its early identification with England, and the identification of England with liberal politics, post-eighteenth-century capitalism—especially as defined by Karl Marx—became associated with political and economic liberalism. The prevailing theory has been that economic liberalism, free trade, free competition, and free markets were necessary for capitalism. Additionally, political liberalism was viewed as a condition for economic liberalism. But the identification of economies of growth—the pursuit of forever renewed profit—with political liberalism is contradicted by at least three out of the four cases of economies entering the race after England: France, Germany, and Japan. During respective periods of great economic growth, each of these countries featured completely authoritarian politics and did not allow free markets to function. Even the economic regimes of England and the United States—both considered politically liberal environments—could be by no means characterized as "liberal" by the economic definition used today. England was the mother of mercantilism, an economic policy consistently inveighed against by Adam Smith in *The Wealth of Nations*. Protectionism was characteristic of England until the late half of the nineteenth century (that is, three centuries into its capitalist history) and similar anti-"capitalist" (antiliberal economics; anti-laissez-faire) policies continued in the United States until after War World II.

The present understanding of capitalism is plagued by numerous misconceptions. Seeing globalization as inherent in capitalism as such is one of them. Globalization is commonly understood in the United States as the increasing integration of the societies of the world into one global community, or "the global village," to use the most accepted metaphor. This integration may be interpreted narrowly as, specifically, an economic integration—the extension of mutually beneficial economic interdependence and the inclusion of an ever-widening circle of societies in one common economic system. Especially in the United States, however, the capitalist economy is considered the foundation of liberal democratic institutions and political culture. The belief that the nature of the economy is tightly connected to the nature of politics expresses an idea of "globalization" interpreted broadly, one connoting the increasing integration of the societies of the globe not only in an economic but also in a political and cultural sense. In this broad, and more common, sense the claim of globalization is obviously false. It is contradicted systematically by everything we see in the empirical life.

But even in the narrow sense of growing economic integration, the claim of globalization outside the European Union is not supported by strong evidence. The concept presupposes a steady trend, a constantly increasing integration of previously independent economies into one common, ultimately global, framework, therefore, an ever-freer flow of capital and labor between previously self-sufficient parts, an ever-larger share of foreign trade in every previously inward-oriented constituent. But there is no such steady trend. In fact, we reached the peak of such interconnectedness of world economies about a century ago and have been oscillating between the pre- and post-World War I levels of interconnectedness ever since.

There is no better example in economic history as to how "globalization"—the *forced* integration of straggling independent economies into a common system by the strong—actually proceeds than that of the "opening to trade" of Tokugawa Japan in the second half of the nineteenth century. For a quarter of a millennium that island country kept itself isolated from the rest of the world. Its government was openly authoritarian (as everywhere else with the exception of England in the beginning of the period—the 1590s—and everywhere with a few exceptions at its end—the 1850s), but it did not intrude in anybody else's affairs, molest foreigners, or bend them to its will; it simply did not allow them in. The country's economy was subsistence oriented, like most of the economies at the time, and nobody in Japan thought that their economy should grow. Then suddenly, in the middle of the nineteenth century, Japan's isolation became a problem for the American whaling industry. For this particular industry to continue growing, the American whaling fleet needed a place to refuel in the part of the Pacific where Japan was located. And so, with some shelling of a coastal city, Japan (which at the time had no firearms and could only defend itself with swords), against its will, was opened to trade.

The intruders, however, came bearing gifts: They introduced nationalism to Japan. The alacrity with which Japan adopted this new, secular, and competitive view of reality was nothing less than astonishing. By the end of the 1850s, national identity was already growing in Japan. As nationalism was presented to the Japanese in an economic package, their nationalism was focused on the economy from the outset. They were moved, in other words, by the spirit of capitalism.

Within a generation, the little country regrouped itself on new principles. By the early decades of the twentieth century, Japan—already a formidable military power with a record of victories over China and Russia—had the fifth strongest world economy after Britain, the United States, Germany, and France. Ironically, Japan's reorientation to international competition and economic growth as a result of its forced opening was the first sign of "globalization" in a very different sense from the one the term usually carries. Capitalism is indeed tightly connected to this particular version of globalization. Globalization in this sense refers to connecting in a competitive relationship vastly different civilizations. These civilizations, notably, do not become integrated into one system.

Instead, they retain their separate and mutually incomprehensible modes of thinking and feeling, but they become relevant to each other and vie for world dominance.

Up to the opening of Japan, the civilization referred to as European, Western, and Judeo-Christian had been enclosed within itself. Its boundaries were defined by the cognitive framework of monotheism and, closely related to it, a logic based on the principle of no contradiction, established 3 and 2.5 millennia ago, respectively. With the emergence of nationalism and competition between nations in this civilization, it came into contact with India and to a very limited extent China, but it did not conceive of them as different civilizations. It conceived of them as *lower* cultures within the same civilization.

Until the twentieth century (and with a striking but lonely exception of Japan until the twentieth-first century) international competition—whether economic, military, or cultural—was limited to a small number of European or European-derived nations. What made Japan's reaction to the West so remarkable was that despite the brutal unceremoniousness of its forced opening to the so-called world economy, it did not repay the West with envy and resentment, the common currencies between the nations within Western civilization. The Japanese perceived no identity between their country and the powers that tried to humiliate them and never developed a sense of inferiority to them. Of course, they recognized the comparative disadvantages that allowed Western powers to violate Japan's sovereignty. In 1853, the West had science, technology, and industrial wealth—all of which Japan lacked. The obvious thing was to acquire similar science, technology, and industrial wealth. The motto Japan adopted was: "Eastern ethics, Western learning." They learned fast and proved that where there is a will there is a way.

Japan is small and poor in resources; the only thing it has had in abundance is motivation. Until very recently it was the second largest economy in the world, trailing only the vast and naturally rich United States. But by the end of the twentieth century, nationalism caught up with China and India. Together, these two colossi contain more than two and a half billion people. They have never lacked anything but motivation between the two of them to dominate the world both economically and militarily. The *Economist,* as you know, predicts that China will be the largest economy of the world by 2020. After five hundred years of competitive economic development—of capitalism—virtually without competitors, the West is finally meeting its match. This is what explains the confusion and panic that made us—Americans—imagine a glitch in the mostly Western financial system (which happened, basically, because of our overevaluation of mathematics and model-building economics) as a crisis comparable in its consequences to the effects of totalitarian regimes in Germany and Russia, which murdered people by the millions and caused suffering on the vastest of scales.

Please, stop worrying, or worry about something else. What explains the panic is the sudden and unexpected-for-us emergence of Asia as claimant for the leadership in the economic race fueled by nationalism. So the West won't be the dominant force in the world anymore. It will bow to China, India, and Japan. The United States will become an equivalent of Switzerland without banks and will be producing cuckoo clocks and milk chocolates for Chinese consumption. Is it that bad? It is only status we are losing after all, not our lives.

FIFTEEN

Retrieving Chance

NEOLIBERALISM, FINANCE CAPITALISM, AND
THE ANTINOMIES OF GOVERNMENTAL REASON

:: ROBYN MARASCO

Let me begin with a reference to that familiar speech from a fictional icon of American cinema, Mr. Gordon Gekko, played by Michael Douglas in Oliver Stone's 1987 film, *Wall Street*. The infamous scene, no doubt screened for scores of first-year MBA students over the past two decades, features Gekko addressing a group of shareholders in the Teldar Corporation, a paper company he intends to "liberate" from its management executives—"bureaucrats with their steak lunches, their hunting and fishing trips, their corporate jets and golden parachutes." The shareholders, Gekko insists, are the real owners of Teldar, those with an actual stake in the company. And Gekko pleads with them to reclaim what is rightfully theirs, to take Teldar back from the cronies who are calling the shots, by, ironically, delivering the paper company over to his corporate raid and readjustment. He concludes the speech with what are now among the most memorable lines in the history of American cinema. Here is Gekko:

> Greed—for lack of a better word—is good.
> Greed is right.
> Greed works.
> Greed clarifies, cuts through, and captures the essence of the evolutionary spirit.
> Greed, in all of its forms—greed for life, for money, for love, knowledge—has marked the upward surge of mankind.
> And greed—you mark my words—will not only save Teldar Paper, but that other malfunctioning corporation called the USA.

Gordon Gekko, the archetype of American corporate excess in the 1980s, could also be said to embody the spirit of capitalism in a period of dramatic monetarization. I will come back to this point about money—as I think it is crucial in discerning the ideology of finance capitalism and mapping the neoliberal apparatus of government—but first let us pause on the most striking feature of the "greed is good" motto.

What this motto suggests is not precisely the erosion of countervailing passions and virtues (charity, love, prudence, humility) in late modernity but the elevation of greed into a moral value in itself. What it reveals is the end of an eighteenth-century vision of bourgeois morality, in which the conflict between greed and its opposing moral sentiments constituted the scenes of sociability and commerce. On Wall Street, greed is the only moral sentiment—utilitarian, functional, simple, and progressive or redemptive. It is aligned with technical efficiency, evolutionary confidence, and corporate power. And if Gekko remains as compelling a figuration of Wall Street as he was in 1987 (the sequel to *Wall Street*, entitled *Money Never Sleeps*, was a success at the box office, especially in its first week, eventually bringing in over $130 million worldwide, despite tepid reception from many critics), then I would suggest that we err in treating the triumph of greed as the consequence of a general loss of values, as if it cannot form the groundwork of an ethical system. Greed contains a genuine polemic against nihilism, and Gekko's sermonizing, albeit self-serving, points to the abstract value harbored in the virtue we mistake for sin.

Moralizing against greed is no match for realist recognition that what is often called greed—greed for life, greed for love, and greed for knowledge—is constitutive of human striving, what Spinoza called *conatus*, what Schopenhauer names the will to life, what Nietzsche terms the will to power. Greed is, indeed, good, if by it we mean a dynamic and energizing force that resists satisfaction in any particular object.

But when we speak of greed today, we do not usually mean this general striving for more life; greed, more typically, names an unquenchable desire that has attached itself to a particular object, usually money. Does this attachment not mark a certain fetishism, a curious perversion of the will to power? This important question was put to me by another participant at the Bard conference, and I cannot dispute its basic premise. What I would say in response is that it is a mistake simply to declare mammon a false deity and think that is enough to deny it worshippers. And even when it does indicate a fetish-relation toward objects in the world, greed also registers an elemental human striving that rebels against all cheap satisfaction. A world without greed is not simply a fanciful reverie, one that treats human beings as they ought to be in abstraction from how they really are; it is a world rendered stagnant and lifeless, unrecognizable for the absence of a creative principle.

To take the world as it really is remains the first task of critical theory; that our world is populated by greedy people is no cause for moralism or pessimistic despair. Rather, it is a reality that begs for historical analysis, social critique, and honest admission that no one is left untouched by the structure of desire on which late capitalism feeds. The question put to us—*Is the Financial Crisis Rooted Simply in Unavoidable Human Greed, or Is It Specific to a Loss of Values Endemic to Our Time and Place?*—sets up what, I believe, is a false dichotomy. Might we say that greed is *both* unavoidable *and* endemic to our time and place, at once an inescapable feature of the human condition and historically specific in its iterations—in the form it takes, its chosen objects, its expression, and its effects? Further, might we admit that there is nothing "simple" about "unavoidable human greed," that its complexity inheres in the way particular social forms simultaneously unleash and harness that basic human striving? It is not greed for money and wealth that produces socioeconomic inequalities. Rather, it is a society structured by the principle of socioeconomic inequality that unleashes a particular form of greed that chases after money.

Allow me a few remarks on our specific time and place, for it will allow me to speak with greater precision about the roots of the current financial crisis—and why I think greed alone will not explain the recklessness, the "creative destruction," by which finance capitalism has flourished for the past several decades. What is needed in analyzing the "intellectual foundations" of the current financial crisis is that vexed and vexing term, *neoliberalism*. As an economic doctrine, born of the demise of the gold standard, the introduction of a fiat monetary system, and the shift in capital's center of gravity from commodity production to financial circulation, neoliberalism names the dematerialization and deregulation of capitalist accumulation and the radical reconfiguration of the partnership between the economy and the state. With neoliberalism comes the privatization of public services and state enterprises, the financialization and deterritorialization of capital, the erosion of trade unionism and exaltation of entrepreneurialism, and the steady reorganization of everyday life according to the logics, principles, and assumptions of competitive market behavior. Neoliberalism is also, therefore, a political rationality, a mode of governance—one that models citizenship after the image of *homo oeconomicus* and distributes rights, recognition, and entitlements according to one's position in a field of market relations, not one's membership in a political community or one's belonging to a common world with others.

Neoliberalism assumes a world governed by complexity, contingency, and chaos, retaining from classical liberalism the conviction that competition is the ideal instrument by which order can be given to the disorder of human behavior.[1] But if Adam Smith sought to animate the moral sentiments against the antisocial vices of the modern commercial spirit (greed and luxury, for instance), the chief menace to the neoliberal capitalist economy is not greed but *chance*. The entwinement of neoliberalism with statistics and probabilistic reasoning, expertise and technical knowledge, and the powers of government (not quite reducible to the powers of the state) points to both the disruptive force of chance and to the forces deployed to tame it. Neoliberal government trades in calculable risks and mobilizes powers and technologies of risk management through its dispersal across populations. My sense is that a critique of neoliberalism, as an apparatus of government, a rationality of conduct, and a complex of powers and material interests, might well begin with chance.

I want to distinguish this claim, concerning the central problem that chance poses for neoliberal government, from what I see as an ideology of chance taking hold in contemporary political and economic discourse, particularly in the aftermath of the financial crisis. The ideological purchase of chance is perhaps nowhere more striking than in recent references to the so-called Black Swan event—that event that is unforeseen, unpredictable, with high impact, and itself the effect of randomness. Entering the Western philosophical lexicon in the eighteenth century, following the discovery of black swans off the west coast of Australia by Dutch explorer, Willem de Vlamingh, the black swan has been a permanent fixture in the history of logic, most famously in the writings of John Stuart Mill.[2] And it has been revived and simplified for our era by Nassim Nicholas Taleb, who made the black swan into the subject of a *New York Times* best seller and hit the financial news circuit as a self-appointed guru of chance.[3] The economic historian Niall Ferguson has invoked it, with explicit reference to Taleb, in commentary on the 2007 Virginia Tech massacre, which left thirty-three people dead, and in analyzing the current financial crisis, which has left millions unemployed and the entire political-economic apparatus at heightened risk. The mantra might be summed up: *We simply do not know!*

Taleb has applied the malleable appellation of black swan to just about everything we call newsworthy and hurls it mainly at professional economists, the Fed, and Ivy Leaguers to expose all that they do not know about how the world works. To his credit, Taleb casts a spotlight on the failures of social scientists to make good on their promise to explain, much less foresee, the most significant of political and economic phenomena of our times, a procedure tinged with the resentment we might expect in a world ruled by experts and initiates. If we need a reminder that luck is often mistaken for skill, that human beings impose meaning on processes that are largely random, and that various indeterminacies thwart predictive instruments, so be it. But black swan theory also shrouds late capitalism in the mist of chance, as if our economic crisis has no structural origins, as if its causes are pure accident and its effects are simply random, as if ours is somehow not an economic *system*, as if the *unknown unknowns* cancel out all that that we do know and can predict about ravishes of neoliberal political economy. It also—and here's the rub—reinforces that system as *historical fate*, inscrutable and indeterminate, built for disaster and therein revealing itself as *destiny*.

We ought not presume, though, that a "ruthless critique" of the ideology of chance, which fortifies more or less regulated markets and market rationality with the armor of necessity, involves a rejection or a repudiation of the aleatory dimension of political life. Indeed, revaluation may be most vital at precisely those moments when an idea assumes ideological form. In the spirit of such revaluation, I propose five theses—polemical in style, but provisional and conjectural in substance—on neoliberalism, finance capitalism, and the current crisis:

Thesis 1: *Neoliberalism is a strategic mode of managing, distributing, and circulating risk across populations.* As I have suggested, its watchword is not greed, but chance. Neoliberalism brings to the fore what could be called the aleatory dimension of social and political life, what Foucault identified as the beginning of government—or, more precisely, the governmentalization of the state and society.

In a set of lectures delivered in 1978 and published under the title *Security, Territory, and Population,* Foucault details how the discourses of classical political economy and the modern security apparatus emerge in response to the political and economic problem of chance. He argues that "economic government" first took hold in classical political economy as part of an antimercantilist strategy of taming the impact and effects of the aleatory event—grain scarcity, in particular. This strategy involved, first, the transformation of chance into a matter of calculable risk and, second, the "government" of risk through its (uneven) circulation and (unequal) distribution across populations. It was antimercantilist in that "good government" did not strive for the elimination of chance but instead took the aleatory event as the occasion to clarify the "effective reality" with which powers must adapt and contend. And in contrast to "the disciplinary police of grain . . . [which] focuses essentially on action on the market or on the space of the market and what surrounds it," this new strategy, which called for the free circulation of grain and the end to the prohibition on hoarding, was "centrifugal" and laissez-faire, not meaning that everything was left alone, but rather that things were allowed to happen. The techniques of economic government and the apparatuses of security, says Foucault, "have the constant tendency to expand. . . . New elements are constantly being integrated: production, psychology, behavior, the ways of doing things of producers, buyers, consumers, importers and exporters, and the world market."[4]

The differences between a liberal program of economic government in the seventeenth century and the neoliberal regime that dominates today are significant, and I will return to some of these differences in a moment. What Foucault's genealogy reveals are the historical conditions for the emergence of an apparatus of government that aims neither to ensure the safety of the prince nor to protect the sovereignty of the people, but to maximize the security of populations. Governmentality, a coinage indispensable for mapping the extension of economic rationality to sites of social interaction once thought separate from the market and what surrounds it, links the physiocratic movement of the seventeenth century with neoliberal political economy in the contemporary period.

That some of the most innovative economic thinking is happening in the emerging field of "behavioral economics" lends support to Foucault's general thesis, for here researchers draw from psychological and cognitive sciences to enhance the analysis of market mechanisms. For those introduced to behavioralism via the social sciences, through the so-called behavioral revolution of the 1950s, the term is somewhat confusing, for behavioralism in economics and finance signifies something quite different, in its historical genesis and theoretical assumptions, from behavioralism in political science. As is well known, behavioralism in political science refers to the importation of the positivistic methods of natural science into the social sciences, and emphasizes empirical research and allegedly value-free analysis, toward the end of uncovering the laws that govern political behavior. The behavioral revolution in political science set the stage for the emergence of rational choice theory and formal modeling in the discipline, efforts to consolidate its status as an authentic (albeit "soft") science.

By contrast, behavioral economics—which emerged long after economics secured standing as the "dismal science"—is something of a counter-hegemonic discourse, *contesting* the assumptions of rationality that undergird the quantitative analysis of markets and economies. As political scientists remain locked in debates over the status of rational-choice theory and the alleged obsolescence of normative political philosophy, behavioralists in economics and finance are showing the extent to which rationality has always functioned as normative concept. Social-scientific predictions drawn from the assumption of rationality appear akin to fortune-telling on the basis of the categorical imperative.

An entire literature in behavioral finance emerges in response to the so-called random-walk hypothesis, which posits that the price of a stock is as subject to chance as the flip of a coin, the assumption that there is no correlation between the past, present, and future of stock prices. To the layperson, this would seem a radically disordered market, but for the "random-walk" proponents it suggests a market in which prices are, at every moment, the rational reflection of all of available information.

Behavioralists have argued, against the random-walk hypothesis, that there are tendencies and impulses—not themselves purely rational—that govern the overall trajectory of stock prices. They pose questions about mispricing (a phenomenon that is literally unthinkable according to the efficient-market hypothesis), cognitive biases and illusions, and about the various anomalies in market returns.

That market forces are not entirely random (and certainly not purely rational), that we can track patterns of wins and losses according to past winners and losers, that habits, fears, desires, and impulses of various kinds run interference against the smooth operation of reason might come as a shock to rationalist economists, though this suggests just how far free-market ideology had traveled in the postwar period from classical economic thought. Adam Smith was one among several figures of the Scottish Enlightenment to take seriously the social significance of the passions and the impact of sentiments and emotions on human behavior. And alongside Ricardo's conviction that the laws of economics follow precise mathematical formulae, we find a countertradition that proceeds from the irreducible gap between formal models and actual behaviors.

Notwithstanding this largely forgotten intellectual lineage, behaviorialism is now poised to move from vanguard to hegemon in a field embattled by the recent financial crisis. George Akerlof and Robert Shiller, leading figures in behavioral economics, invoke John Maynard Keynes and what they regard as his unrivaled attempt to integrate psychology and economic theory. They point to our so-called animal spirits in tracking market behavior, arguing that markets quite regularly fail to operate by the cool calculus of reason. Akerlof and Schiller suggest that attention to human psychology yields a radically different view of the capitalist economy and its instabilities, one that cautions against blind faith in the predictive powers of mathematical calculations. It is not that behavioralists are averse to quantitative analysis or even prediction; indeed, though they contest the supremacy of rationality in economic behavior, the challenge for behavioral researchers remains that of *modeling* these "animal spirits."

Although a welcome alternative to the orthodox rationalism that dominated the fields of economics and finance for much of the postwar period, the behaviorial revolution does not signify quite as profound a shift as its champions claim. They remain tethered to the assumptions of rationality, even as they underscore what it cannot explain, evident in their attention to "anomalies" in pricing and returns. After all, a phenomenon only appears as an anomaly if we accept rationality and efficiency as the norm. Like rationalists, behavioralists are generally silent on the radical disruptions of chance, still conflating the aleatory quality of social and political life with the economic question of risk assessment and management. Whereas the efficient-market theorists presume that there is a rationality inherent in randomness, behavioralists appeal to our cognitive biases—and the social contagion of affect and feeling—to show that market mechanisms are neither random nor rational. But our "animal spirits" cannot explain away the aleatory quality of economic life; indeed, it seems they are invoked to allow economists to sidestep the problem of chance altogether.

Thesis 2: *Neoliberalism is a rationality of conduct that reproduces financial capitalism and the security state.* What this means is that we will have to treat neoliberalism as a mode of governing subjects that extends well beyond the penetration of instrumental reason into all domains of life. This is how the political theorist Wendy Brown theorizes neoliberalism, and her account draws heavily from both Foucault and, less explicitly, Max Weber and post-Weberian social theory. I agree with much in Brown's treatment of neoliberalism, particularly her insistence that neoliberalism marks the erosion of liberal democracy and her caution against a Left melancholia that would attach itself to liberalism, leaving radical political vision crippled by an arrested mourning for the loss of something never entirely loved. Where I depart from Brown—or, more precisely, where I would add to her analysis—concerns the definition of economic rationality and its specific iteration in an age of financialization. It is my view that the mode of reasoning we might identify with the industrial capitalist factory owner, for instance, is quite distinct from the mode of reasoning characteristic of the hedge-fund manager, the investment banker, and the Wall Street speculator.[5] Although Max Weber's account of modern rationalization will take us up to a point—and it surely does—the particularities of contemporary capitalism (capital in a highly speculative and heavily securitized form) and the state (a complex of powers that targets the security of populations through the uneven circulation of risk across populations) seem significant to the specific rationality that has taken hold in the present.

The critique of instrumental reason, such as that developed by first-generation Frankfurt School critical theorists, has long rested on the assumption that, although capitalism has a history and ideologies are dynamic and responsive to changes in the material structure, instrumental reason is itself an unchanging form. It may be more or less dominant in a given society or a specific time in history, but instrumental reason is without an *internal* dynamism: It refers in the eighteenth century to the same *way of reasoning* in the twenty-first, namely the reduction of quality into quantity, the view of means always in relation to calculable ends, the analysis of costs and benefits in monetarized measurements, and so on.

But financial capitalism today is motored by a highly speculative rationality that thwarts and defies human calculation, even as it relies so heavily on the will to quantify. To grasp the interdependence of neoliberalism and market forces, we will have to specify the paradoxical form of "irrational rationality" at stake in the intensification of a speculative-financial system rooted in credit and debt. Of course, for the Frankfurt School critical theorists, bourgeois rationality always contained something horribly irrational within it, which is precisely why they viewed the

Holocaust not as a lapse from Enlightenment into barbarism but as the catastrophic confirmation of the "unreason" harbored in instrumental reason. But, in the wake of the recent economic crisis, critical theory might refine and develop the critique of instrumental reason by analyzing its specific contours in relation to the financialization and dematerialization of capital.

The recent financial crisis bears witness to the tragic irony of governmentalization, namely that with the management of risk through its circulation and distribution comes also the intensification of systemic risk, of generalized vulnerability to the chance events that befall peoples and populations. By this I do not refer to what has come to be called simply "moral hazard"—namely, that individuals, when insulated from the consequences of risky behavior, will act less carefully and cautiously than they would if fully exposed to risk. Moral hazard, while inescapable wherever there is information asymmetry, collective insurance, and risk transference or displacement, has been cited as one of the main problems with the Troubled Asset Relief Program (TARP) and bailouts more generally. Whether "too big to fail" or "too interconnected to fail," our major financial institutions have every incentive to engage in high-risk trading and lending practices, assured that any profits will remain their own, while any loses will be incurred by the American taxpayers. Privatized gain and socialized losses is a formula for heightened moral hazard.

Yet I think there is something else at stake in the intensification of systemic risk. Martin Wolf, from the *Financial Times*, puts it this way:

> The combination of state insurance (which protects creditors) with limited liability (which protects shareholders) creates a financial doomsday machine. What happens is best thought of as "rational carelessness." Its most dangerous effect comes via the extremes of the credit cycle. Most perilous of all is the compulsion upon the authorities to blow another set of credit bubbles, to forestall the devastating impact of the implosion of the last ones. In the end, what happens to finance is not what matters most but what finance does to the wider economy.[6]

This idea of "rational carelessness" is not quite the same as moral hazard, for it is the *generalized* effect of *both* state insurance protection and limited liability for shareholders, in which *both* creditors and shareholders have incentive to assume as much risk as possible, with potentially catastrophic results for the wider economy. Put another way, it is an arrangement in which moral hazard exists on all sides and is system-wide. This situation yields not just rational risk-taking, but a marked carelessness about these risks. Add to this the speculative frenzy that has taken hold on Wall Street, and Wolf's doomsday scenario seems entirely credible, for what we have is a system of organized gambling in which all wagers are protected against loss. Here we catch a glimpse of the curious perversion of economic rationality in the neoliberal period.

Thesis 3: *Neoliberalism is the ideology of the new leisure class.* It is an ideology in which social worth is measured, not by work, industry, and diligence, but by credentials, "insider" expertise, savvy, and the expansion of social networks. It corresponds to an economic system in which actual commodity production gives way to fictitious valuation—value that is finally (and we can only wish Karl Marx could be here to see it) unhinged from both utility *and* relations of exchange. I would say we are at a substantial remove from the spirit of capitalism as Max Weber delineated it in *The Protestant Ethic*, though I wonder if Weber did not overstate the asceticism of the nascent bourgeoisie and exaggerate the real importance of the work ethic, sermonized to the working classes much more than it was lived by the owning classes. Further, the locus of contemporary capital accumulation is not with commodities but with money itself; the classic Marxian formula (M-C-M, money begets commodity which, in turn, begets money) has been outstripped by money exchanged for money, M-M, or what Marx describes in the third volume of *Das Kapital* as interest-bearing capital, capitalism in "its most superficial and fetishized form"—in its "finished" form. "[Thus] it becomes a property of money to generate value and yield interest, much as it is an attribute of pear-trees to bear pears."[7] It is a form of capital that dissolves the classic postulate of bourgeois economics, that profits are tied to producing and selling commodities. The surplus-value created by money appears to inhere in money itself, an autogenerative profit supply.

Take, for example, the story of Paolo Pellegrini, who made billions of dollars for the hedge fund Paulson & Co. and a hefty sum for himself by betting against the housing market. Just a few years prior, Pellegrini was unemployed, living in a one-bedroom apartment in Westchester, and struggling to maintain a floundering career in finance. By a stroke of good fortune, hedge-fund manager John Paulson reluctantly took him on board and assigned him the task of figuring out how to wager against subprime mortgages. According to the *Wall Street Journal*, Pellegrini is "an unnamed but key character in the government's lawsuit against Goldman Sachs

Group Inc.," for while neither Pellegrini nor Paulson has been accused of impropriety, the government alleges that Goldman deceived investors by selling mortgage securities created by Paulson & Co. without disclosing their origins. Just a few years later, and $175 million richer, Pellegrini now manages his own hedge fund, vacations with his new wife in the West Indies, and traded his one-bedroom apartment for a palatial abode on the Upper West Side.

Make your money work—this is the mantra of finance capitalism, one that holds out the utopian promise of the end of work, in which profits are available to anyone with a little know-how, some extra cash, and a willingness to exploit "inefficiencies" in the market.

Thesis 4: *The crisis in finance capitalism has not resulted in a corresponding crisis in neoliberalism.* Indeed, we find that the near collapse of financial capitalism has led, ironically, to the intensification of neoliberal governmentality. This is because ideology, power, and knowledge do not simply reflect material conditions; they also serve to organize and stabilize those conditions. Further, and more concretely, the neoliberal emphasis on expertise and specialized knowledge means that the existing ideational landscape is reproduced, even strengthened, in moments of crisis.

Professional economists, most of whom failed to anticipate (or even imagine the possibility of) a severe systemic collapse, became our trusted sources of guidance and expert knowledge in the wake of the financial crisis. And many of them had been trained in university departments where certain orthodoxies about the free market go unquestioned, where training remains limited to quantitative analysis and formal modeling, and the range of permissible economic ideas remains relative narrow. Indeed, the revival of Keynesian economics after the crisis suggests something of the dearth of economic theory, for it remains the only real rival to neoclassical economics, not because it is the only imaginable alternative, but because professional economists had not given much attention in recent decades to developing these alternatives.

Thesis 5: *We are all gamblers now.*

Walter Benjamin, in a section of the *Arcades Project* that deals with modern gambling, claims the following: "The wager is a means of conferring shock-value on events, of loosening them from the contexts of experience. It is not by accident that people bet on the results of elections, on the outbreak of war, and so on. For the bourgeoisie, in particular, political affairs easily take the form of events on a gaming table. This is not so much the case for the proletarian. He is better positioned to recognize constants in the political process."[8]

Let us not be sidetracked by the question of whether the proletariat can, in fact, penetrate the ideology of pure randomness, can recognize "constants" in political life, by which I take Benjamin to mean "structures." Let us think instead about how political affairs have come to seem like events on a gaming table, about how the "scientific" study of politics has fallen completely under the spell of "game theory," about how finance capitalism (its most speculative and, therefore, riskiest form) and neoliberalism (a mode of governing risk through its circulation and distribution) shape and contour the "constants" that mark our political processes. It hardly seems a matter of "chance" that the impact of the financial crisis— home foreclosures, unemployment, bankruptcy—falls disproportionately on the poor, the working classes, immigrants, and people of color.

By the claim that we are all gamblers now, I mean not only that we are compelled, by various forces, to buy into the logic and practice of financialization—and here we might think of the near-complete substitution of 401(k) retirement plans for traditional pensions. I mean, further, that political subjectivity assumes, to an ever-greater extent, the form of the gambler. It is for this reason that Hannah Arendt's close friend Walter Benjamin remains as relevant as ever for political thinking (even if Arendt, in her own reflections on Benjamin's life and legacy, underestimates his subtlety and sophistication as a political thinker). For it was Benjamin who treated the gambler as a figuration of modern life and of the distinctive pathos of bourgeois society. Benjamin's gambler, like the prostitute and the opium-eater, registers the decay of experience in modernity—the loss of experience, as well as the various attempts at the recovery of experience. Taking seriously the play of chance as a crucial dimension of contemporary political economy, which the present crisis demands, might also allow for a more robust account of politics and the construction of "the political" in late modernity.

SIXTEEN

The End of Neoliberalism?

:: MIGUEL DE BEISTEGUI

In this essay I want to ask several questions and examine one way of framing the discussion regarding the possible intellectual origins of the current crisis. Those questions and my attempt to frame recent economic events are all a way of asking the following: To what extent is the set of facts that led to the quasi collapse of the financial system and its rescue by governments a crisis? And, if it is a crisis, what sort of crisis is it?

In order to answer those questions we need to know what counts as a crisis. My first question, then, is: What makes a crisis a crisis? Now to that question, I simply want to answer by saying that a crisis is a specific kind of event—by that I mean a historical, political, and social shift such that we would be able to say that, perhaps after that moment, after that point, things never were the same again. In that respect, I am not sure that the events of the financial crisis of last year amount to a crisis.

We heard repeatedly in the six months following the crisis that it was an event. The crisis, we were told, consisted in the near collapse of the world economy, occasioned, as many of the essays in this volume show, by cheap available money, deregulation, and the shadow financial system. Those are all in many ways causes of the financial crisis. But in trying to speak about the *origins* of that crisis we should make a distinction between causes and origins. For some, especially on the Left, the origin of the crisis is none other than capitalism itself. The crisis, then, would be that of capitalism itself and signal its possible end. I'd like to be a bit more precise, and less categorical, and argue that the crisis of capitalism we are going through is a crisis of a particular form of liberal capitalism, one that we call "neoliberalism."

This takes me to my second question: To what extent is the crisis itself and the way in which it was managed something that signaled the end, or the impossibility, of neoliberal capitalism? By impossibility I mean that it could not possibly continue to go on. Or, on the contrary, is the crisis, and especially the way it was managed, entirely compatible with neoliberalism? Can the specific political and economic framework of the current world order, which I characterize as neoliberalism, absorb the current shock, or is the shock such that neoliberalism needs *radically* to be called into question? I will go on to define neoliberalism in a moment. But before I do, let me voice my skepticism regarding the claim of the crisis or the end of neoliberalism. First of all, neoliberalism was actually born as a response to the financial crisis in 1929 and attributed to a failure of classical liberalism. So what might emerge as a result of this current crisis could be something like a radicalization of neoliberalism, or a "neo-neoliberalism." The second reason, to which I shall return, is that the bailout of the banking system is entirely compatible with the very principles of the neoliberal political economy.

My third question is: Ought the answer to the financial crisis be an economical answer? Is the crisis to be solved, ultimately, just by reintroducing the regulation of cheap money? Is it just a matter of intervening in the market or for the market? And if the crisis resides in the excesses of global financial capitalism, is what is needed something like a moralizing of markets? Must we reintroduce the moral standpoint back into capitalism today? Less greed, it might be thought, leads to fewer problems.

Now those two claims—that the crisis calls for economic and moral answers—are intimately linked. Let me address them both together by saying that the situation and the problem we are facing, and so the way to confront it, is neither an economical nor a moral one but a political question—specifically a question of political economy. By that, I mean the following: The moral standpoint, as well as the purely technical-economical standpoint, won't allow us to engage critically and sufficiently with the underlying *political* and *philosophical* assumptions of neoliberalism. Neoliberalism is first and foremost a political doctrine.

The financial crisis, then, should be seen as an opportunity to raise the question of the relation between economics and politics today, and especially between the market and the state. That relation today is a relation of limits. There is a history of that relation, which goes back to the eighteenth century: It is the history of how the market emerged as a limit to the exercise of what, following Foucault, I shall call "governmental reason," and how, progressively, the state itself fell under the scrutiny and undisputed authority of the market. It is that history that I would like to sketch now, albeit very briefly. I would like to do that by turning to some of the things Michel Foucault says in one lecture course in particular, "The Birth of Biopolitics" of 1979.

The lecture is extremely interesting, in and of itself, because of what it says regarding the development of neoliberal economics. It is also interesting because of the date it was given. Nineteen-seventy-nine is, of course, the year of Margaret Thatcher's election in Britain, a year before Reagan's election in the United States. Foucault's selection of this lecture topic basically says that in order to understand where the world is going today we need to take absolutely seriously the school of neoliberal economics. By that he meant German ordoliberalism, but also and especially the Vienna and Chicago school of economics. Foucault's lecture course is also fascinating because it happened at a time when, especially in France, absolutely no one was taking the neoliberals seriously.

I want to sketch the history of the relation between market and state by turning first to liberalism in order to mark a few key differences that allow us to distinguish between neoliberalism and liberalism. The way in which Foucault presents this history is by saying that in the seventeenth and the eighteenth centuries a certain type of question emerges, and the question is the following: How can limits be imposed on the exercise of public power? To be more specific, how can public power—the state or the sovereign—impose limits on itself? Before the emergence of that question there were, of course, limits on the state, but they were limits external to the use of power. Of course, other states could limit a state's power. The rule of law was also considered one such limit. But the important point Foucault makes is that the market emerged as a solution to the second question, that is, the question regarding the *self*-limitation of public power. In other words, the market emerged as a solution to the problem concerning the *internal* limit of public power. That answer, the market answer, is a very pragmatic answer, which sees those limits not as de jure but as de facto. The principle that establishes those limits is itself pragmatic. It is a question of simply knowing what is desirable or reasonable and what is not, when it would make sense and when not to interfere with private action according to a goal that is utilitarian, that is to say, defined in terms of usefulness or happiness for the majority of a population.

The emergence of the liberal view of the market, then, takes place in the broader context of the following questions: How useful is governmental interference? How far should it go, and at what point does it become harmful? And how should governmental interference be limited?

For the liberal utilitarian tradition, interest—understood as self-interest—emerges as the actual and the most effective limit of governmental reason. Interest is no longer understood to be the interest of the state alone—that is to say, of its power, its wealth, and even its population, as in the Renaissance, for example. Interest was then a category that applied to the state only: *interesse di stato* and *ragione di stato*, or state reason, were synonymous. With the birth of liberalism, interest becomes the interest of the individual. Liberalism also creates this figure of the individual, intimately bound up with the notion of interest, the pursuit of personal gain and desires. As a result, the problem of government in liberal societies becomes one of knowing how best to govern interested individuals. A state does not govern individuals as it would govern subjects or even citizens. The answer to the question of liberal governance is that the liberal state governs through self-interest.

Self-interest is the way to govern individuals through their irrepressible search for pleasure, their freedom, and their desire. Freedom is not the actual goal, but it is the means of good government. Governmental reason is required to follow the complex game of individual interest of social utility and economic profit, of the balance of the market, and the regime of public power. What government does in this new configuration and this new context is to manage competing interests. It is the principle of utility that allows it to distinguish between the necessary and desirable action, on the one hand, and useless and harmful action, on the other hand. The material, the aim, and the end of liberal government constitute the field of interests as a whole. It is a government through, for, and of interests.

Equally, as a result of utility as the measure of good governance, the market is seen as the place where this maximization, this realization, of happiness or pleasure takes place. The market is the mode of organization of the collective that allows for such maximization. It is the vehicle of that principle of maximization. In the economic domain, the state has little to do to stimulate utility or to provoke the actions that will increase happiness. The state is unnecessary for the simple reason that individuals seek to increase their happiness naturally and spontaneously. The market therefore, so long as it is not interfered with directly, is a spontaneous producer of satisfaction, and a natural vehicle for increase of pleasure. That is the liberal belief I am describing.

The efficiency of the market in producing happiness is the reason why government intervention is to be kept to a bare minimum. That does not mean that the state does not play a decisive role in creating and maintaining the necessary conditions for the optimal functioning of the market. More generally, the state regulates the market to increase the well-being of the majority. In that respect the rule of law is a key, if not the most important mechanism, of a liberal government. The task of the liberal government is to combine individual interests with the general interest through a system of laws that are coercions that each individual integrates in the calculation that he or she makes of the risks involved in transgressing them.

To the extent that the law is always a constraint—a limitation of one's freedom—liberalism imagines law as a necessary evil, a cost one pays for the ordered pursuit of individual interests. From the point of view of individual happiness the legislator must use the law moderately.

So the question of how to govern—what Foucault calls the question of governmentality—is the following: Inasmuch as market systems of production and exchange operate according to spontaneous mechanisms, how active must the state be to ensure the functioning of the market? Under what circumstances, with which aims and objectives, and with which means is the state to interfere in individual market activities to guarantee the free pursuit of individual interest? It is not a matter of asserting that the state must do nothing; rather it is a matter of allowing its actions to be led by the sole criterion of utility. This means that liberal governance proceeds by weighing the advantages and inconveniences that its intervention is most likely to produce. This is the situation, very briefly described, of liberalism.

Let me now turn to neoliberalism and try to point to key differences with liberalism itself. I will mention three. The first one has to do with the relation between the state and the market. The relation itself changes. We saw how for liberalism the market was the principle of limitation of the state. This is what I meant when I said that that the history of that relation is the history of a limit. The market defined the limit beyond which the state would not interfere. Now, in the context of neoliberal thought, the market becomes the regulative principle of the state itself. The market becomes the principle of the criterion for good government. So it is no longer a matter of accepting market freedom as defined and monitored by the state, but it is a matter of bringing the state under the surveillance of the market itself. It is the market that comes to be seen as the principle, the form, and the model of state itself. This is how the president of the United States comes to be known as the CEO of the United

States. If anything, it is the state that is now seen as a limit, in a sense an obstacle, to the spreading of market efficiency and rationality. In other word, the old Renaissance Italian *ragione di stato* has become *ragione di mercato*—the liberal reason of state has become the neoliberal market-state reason.

There is in principle no limit to how far the market can go in a neoliberal society inasmuch as there are no ills associated with the market. There is no domain that de jure, as it were by right, would fall outside its jurisdiction and into that of the state. Once the market insinuates itself into the very apparatus of governance itself, we can ask the question that I asked in relation to liberalism again: Does this mean now that there is no role for government, that the state has become altogether redundant? Now, many declarations and many actions and many gestures undertaken by neoliberal economists such as F. A. Hayek and Milton Friedman, for example, or politicians such as Thatcher, Reagan, and, more recently, George W. Bush, would suggest just that. Less government, less interference, neoliberal economists and politicians all claim, is the path to freedom. Thus neoliberal politics embarked on massive projects of privatization—from health care to education and even, as we saw in the Iraq War, security and defense.

But the weakening, lessening, and privatizing of government are only in appearance. In fact, the role of government in neoliberalism remains considerable—and is in fact greater—than in liberalism. Government is essential to the success of neoliberal economics. It is all a matter of knowing what that role is, of defining what sort of things government is allowed to interfere with, or the level at which it is allowed to operate. If and where it intervenes, and it does intervene massively, it is not on the market itself, not, that is, on the *mechanisms* of the market—the assumption being that markets are self-regulating systems that tend toward their own equilibrium. Rather, the neoliberal state intervenes on the *conditions* of the market. Not directly on prices, for example, or on strategic objectives, but indirectly, on factors that may influence and shape the market, such as technologies, education, demographics, health, and security; or, as we saw in October 2008, on financial markets themselves through a massive injection of cash. In short, the neoliberal state intervenes on the conditions normally referred to as social. So the role of government is now to facilitate as much as it can the expansion of markets, to remove the obstacles—often seen as state- or society-generated—that are in the way of such an expansion. In other words, the role of government is to maximize market rationality. Whereas liberal governance seeks to maximize the free and individual pursuit of interests, neoliberal government works to maximize market forces. That is the first major difference I want to highlight.

The second difference in neoliberalism is this: There is a shift in what we could call the epistemological status of the market, from exchange and consumption—the classical conception of a liberal market—to competition. According to the liberal view, the market appeared as something that followed and needed to follow "natural," that is, spontaneous, mechanisms—spontaneous to the point that they could only be denatured if interfered with. What are those spontaneous mechanisms? The mechanisms of exchange—basically, offer and demand. And this is the sense in which the market became a place of truth—those natural mechanisms, if and when left to their own devices, allowed for the emergence of a price that was characterized as "natural," "good," or "normal." If, according to Foucault, it is still known as the "fair" price, it is no longer in relation to an implicit sense of justice. Rather, the price is now thought to reflect the *value* of the product—a value defined by the relation between the cost of production and the extent of demand. This is how the market appears as revealing something like a truth. Inasmuch as they follow the natural mechanisms of the market, prices began to be seen as a measure of truth, which will allow us to distinguish the correct or true governmental practices from the false. The market introduces truth in government: A good government is no longer one that meets the demands of justice, but also, and above all, those of truth.

With neoliberalism, *competition* becomes the defining feature of the market. Where there is competition, it is argued, there is efficiency, rationality, and, ultimately, satisfaction for the greatest number. What is sought through the market, and the ways in which governments protect them, is the dynamics of competition, as opposed to the inertia of monopoly and planned economy. This, of course, is only the theory; in reality things do not work in that way.

The object of government intervention, if you will, especially through the law, is the maintenance of a competitive or unequal environment from which, it is thought, individual freedom and wealth will unfold. To an extent, competition is incompatible with redistribution, with equality. We see a major opposition between distributive justice and the justice that makes sure that the highest competitive environment is at work. At its most radical, this view leads to what is known as social Darwinism. In any case, it is no longer a matter of governing *because* of the market and the situations of inequality it can generate, but it is a matter of governing *for* the market. Neoliberalism requires both this maximalist conception and practice of governmentality, for which the role of government is to accompany, support, facilitate, and encourage the market economy, and this absolutely minimalist conception of the state. So: a maximalist conception of government and a minimalist conception of the state.

The third and final difference I would like to emphasize, and which follows from the first two, concerns the reality of the subject, which liberalism understood to be the individual. In the neoliberal context, the subject become a different kind of *homo oeconomicus*. The *homo oeconomicus* is no longer the partner of an exchange, inscribed in a problematic of needs, on which a utility is founded, and which leads to the process of exchange. He or she is no longer defined by a system of exchange, value, or even consumption—at least understood in the traditional sense—that is, as the agent that exchanges money for goods. Rather, he or she has become an *entrepreneur*.

The entrepreneur is the type that corresponds to a neoliberal society that is no longer defined in terms of exchange and value, but in terms of competition. The enterprise itself is no longer limited to the sphere of the firm. The aim is to allow each and every one of us, every subject, to recognize that one is no longer first and foremost a citizen, or even an individual, but an entrepreneur, albeit of oneself, of one's own home, private property, family, body, and mind.

What is crucial, in that respect, is the way in which the figure of the worker—so central to nineteenth- and twentieth-century politics, philosophy, and political economy whether of the Right or the Left, whether for Karl Marx, for example, or Ernst Jünger—and the figure of the proletarian have been replaced by that of the entrepreneur. The worker is no longer defined by his or her labor force but by his or her skills. Now the worker is characterized in terms of his or her added value, or, as it has been referred to by Theodore Schultz and Gary Becker, as his or her "human capital." This is in a way the stroke of genius of neoliberalism and neoliberal capitalism, namely to have led us to believe that we are all capitalists. We all have or are some capital for which we are responsible and ultimately accountable. The capital in question need not be material or financial; it is both innate, intellectual, physical, and genetic capital, which is acquired through education, training, and work. Education, health, family, and community ties are all capital; they have all been capitalized.

We are all investors and entrepreneurs, albeit of ourselves, and we need to behave as such, that is, responsibly.

In that respect, neoliberalism has also generated a form of market morality, which posits individuals as responsible for themselves and themselves alone as a direct result of those individuals being construed as entirely autonomous and free individuals—autonomous in their ability to deliberate rationally about costs and benefits, and free in their ability to make informed decisions and choices. Neoliberalism needs those uneducated, poor workers, who bought all those toxic mortgages, to be seen as entrepreneurs and minicapitalists. We are all rational agents, involved in cost and benefit deliberation. We are all equal before the laws of capitalism. Capital now defines the very *being* of the human being; it has become the essence of human nature.

Now let me conclude this very brief sketch of the history of the relation between market and state, market and governmentality, and the subsumption of government under market rationality by saying that so long as markets, especially financial markets, as the vehicle for the expansion of that limit are allowed to operate in that way or at that level, so long as that nature of that relation is not called into question—the nature of the relation between market, government, and state is not called into question—bubbles will continue to grow, crises will continue to emerge, but none of them singly or even taken together will amount to crisis in a fundamental sense. That is, as a historical event. What is needed then is a rearticulation of the relation between economics and politics. What is required is a new political economy.

SEVENTEEN

Short-Term Thinking

:: OLIVIA CUSTER

I would like to start by considering a couple of the accounts of the origin of the financial crisis that have been offered to us in the public sphere. First, let us listen to Alan Greenspan testifying to Congress in October 2008:

> We are in the midst of a once-in-a century credit tsunami. . . . Those of us who have looked to the self-interest of lending institutions to protect shareholder's equity (myself especially) are in a state of shocked disbelief. Such counterparty surveillance is a central pillar of our financial markets' state of balance. If it fails, as occurred this year, market stability is undermined.

There would be much to say about the scene of the testimony, but let me just focus on what Greenspan takes himself to be saying. The problem, he says, is that there was not enough self-interest. The model on which policy was based presumed that, although the *intention* of the banks might not have been to increase shareholder equity, that would be the effect of their actions. This presumption is, of course, a variant of Adam Smith's idea that the rational pursuit of self-interest fortuitously promotes the interests of others via the mechanism of the markets.

Conceiving of lending institutions as market agents who would lend only in such a way as to promote their own interests, Greenspan assumes that their rationale must be such as to have, as an unintended consequence, the protection of the reasonable market conditions that allow their continued existence. Greenspan's story, then, is that contrary to what the model predicted, banks did not act as rational investors; lending institutions did not protect their self-interest, at least not enough, and thus shareholder equity suffered.

In his testimony Greenspan is speaking as an expert economist and explaining that in a certain sense events have shown lending institutions to be less competent experts than the model, which he supposed to exist. Notice that although Greenspan is apparently facing a situation in which he might have had to revise the idea that unintended consequences of market plays are in the interests of the market, he instead finds a way to recycle the idea; the "flaw" in the model is minimized even as it is recognized. In his shocked disbelief at the disconnect between what his model predicted and the "real world," he finds a way to salvage his belief in the model by explaining the discrepancy not as a fault with the model, but as a fault of reality. Greenspan salvages the principle that the rational pursuit of self-interest leads to collective progress the only way he can: by attributing the problem to insufficiently rational pursuit of self-interest of lending institutions. The model is recycled to produce a diagnosis that the problem was an insufficiently rational pursuit of self-interest.

Let me turn now to a second analysis, the one President Obama offered in his Inaugural Address to the American people:

> Our economy is badly weakened, a consequence of greed and irresponsibility on the part of some, but also our collective failure to make hard choices and prepare the nation for a new age.

Here again the crisis is cast in terms of a failure. It is not altogether clear in this formulation whether the "collective failure" to "prepare for a new age" is being cast as a failure of expertise in the difficult realm of economic choices for society as a whole or whether it is included, by extension, in the explicitly moral failure that "greed and irresponsibility" mark. However, in remarks about the bank bonuses that were provoking a discussion about the collective choices that might be appropriate for a new age, Obama clarified what he had in mind as the collective failure.

> People are rightly outraged about these particular bonuses. But just as outrageous is the culture that these bonuses are a symptom of, that have existed for far too long—a situation where excess greed, excess compensation, excess risk-taking have all made us vulnerable and left us holding the bag.

Obama seems to offer a second diagnosis of the origin of the crisis: Our economy is badly weakened; we are all vulnerable; and this is due to a "culture," a culture of excess, a culture of excessive greed and risk-taking. We are right to be outraged by the excessive greed of some, says the highest elected American citizen, but we must also worry that we have all been participating in the greedy rush.

There are undeniably differences between these two explanations, and indeed they might be taken to stake out the endpoints of the range of explanations of the crisis that have become popular in the public sphere. Greenspan's analysis is apparently of a technical nature; Obama's relies on a cultural analysis and embraces a moral language. The first asserts that the source of market instability is not enough self-interest, while the second says it is too much greed.

These two very short sketches of explanations of the origins of the financial crisis serve at least to roughly map some important oppositions that have organized many of the debates about the origin of the crisis: The problem is moral, or is it technical? The cause of the crisis is greed, or is it not enough greed? Rules of the market are themselves at fault, or insufficient rules of the market are at fault. Having underlined these differences, I would like to try to be attentive to where and how Obama's and Greenspan's discourses converge. I suggest we attend to the way their shared assumptions may be operating to limit the debates in such a way as effectively to avoid challenges to the basic status quo, to the ever less contested unfolding of neoliberal logic as the only rationality for political and economic choices.

Consider this explanation, again Obama's, of how we all came to be in such a "vulnerable" position. How did a culture of "excess greed" lead to crisis? It was, he explained, an era where too often, short-term gains were prized over long-term prosperity; where we failed to look beyond the next payment, the next quarter, or the next election. A surplus became an excuse to transfer wealth to the wealthy instead of an opportunity to invest in our future. Regulations were gutted for the sake of a quick profit at the expense of a healthy market. People bought homes they knew they couldn't afford from banks, and lenders who pushed those bad loans anyway. And all the while, critical debates and difficult decisions were put off for some other time on some other day.

"Short-term gains were prized over long-term prosperity." "Quick profit at the expense of a healthy market." This analysis identifies as the origin of the problem a certain myopia, a failure to see "long term," to value the long term, or indeed to calculate in the long term. The lesson drawn by this analysis is that the problem was a failure to prize what should have been prized, namely "long-term prosperity." What emerges is that Obama's denunciation of greed is the denunciation of a particular kind of greed, namely that greed that is unsustainable in the long run. I put it to you that the phrase "excessive greed" should then be read not just as a pleonasm which lends rhetorical emphasis, but as a phrase which reveals an implicit distinction between two kinds of greed, the excessive and the nonexcessive (which would be understood as acceptable, or even commendable). Of course I am not suggesting that "greed" ever has positive moral connotations; what I am suggesting is that the phrase "excessive greed" gives us insight into the economic model that sustains Obama's analysis and that this model condemns greed where it is excessive; it does not condemn the pursuit of self-interest on a reasonable scale. In fact, quite to the contrary. And this is why in some sense Obama's "excessive greed" analysis is, despite possible appearances to the contrary, the *same* as Greenspan's "not enough self-interest" analysis. Both of them consider the crisis to be a problem because it threatens overall prosperity (or the market that is supposed to provide that prosperity), and both of them are attributing this situation to a failure of market agents to act reasonably. Obama, as much as Greenspan, is deploring the existence of "some" who are not good economic agents insofar as they fail to pursue their self-interest well enough for it to promote the general interest in the long term. When Obama denounces excessive greed, or Greenspan professes disbelief at the lending institutions' failure to protect the equity of shareholders, they are both identifying the source of the financial crisis in a miscalculation. We have two versions of the idea that economic agents "failed" because they failed to do the proper calculation of their long-term self-interest. These are two analyses that say the financial crisis is due to a failure to integrate conditions of sustainability into the calculation of self-interest.

Now I don't mean to feign surprise that these two should agree, since of course I chose them to illustrate a certain consensus on how we are to understand the events of last fall in the U.S. credit market. I did not choose these two because I think they represent radically different approaches to the situation at hand. On the contrary, the point here would be to underline that what are too often *represented* as alternatives are actually different packaging of very similar analyses.

My claim here would be that, although it might seem that a context in which both "excessive greed" and "not enough self-interest" are described as possible causes of the crisis is a context in which there is a wide-ranging debate, a slightly closer look reveals that these explanations all conspire to keep off the limits questions about the suppositions both these positions share. For instance, if there is no way out of a consensus that the problem we face arose not because of the ways "the market" works, but because it malfunctioned, the regulations that will be the "answer" to the crisis will be regulations that ensure more of the same in the future, no matter how convincing (or indeed convinced) lawmakers may be when they will claim that the regulations are designed so that "it" does not happen again. We may well end up with regulations designed to promote the sustainability of the market, but, leaving aside the question of whether they can be effective, this will also have been a way of circumventing a genuine debate as to the political choices available. Regulations will be welcomed as the panacea for a range of opposing reasons (some will see them as a means to temper the brutality of the market, others as a strategy to support the market mechanisms that are supposed to save us); self-congratulations on having made hard collective choices for the new era will no doubt resonate, but there is every reason to fear that questions about the very basic allegiance to liberal, or neoliberal, principles will have been effectively kept out of the debate. And there is no reason to hope that the collective choice will have been anything other than to wait for the next iteration of a crisis that will leave everyone in shocked disbelief, wondering whether we will even have an economy on Monday.

Again, I am, of course, not surprised that there is an underlying agreement between Greenspan and Obama. I have simply wanted to draw attention to the way their divergences can be cast as representative of the range of analyses of the origins of the crisis that dominate public discussion, but, that, when this happens, the divergences serve to mask the shared assumptions. I take it to be one of our tasks here to explore the underlying assumptions of public debates on these questions, and I would like therefore to draw attention to another common feature of their discourses.

Let me introduce it with a very simple observation: Both Obama and Greenspan claim first that the problem, and therefore the solution, is connected to getting out of "short-term thinking" and, second, that *they* have recognized this. These analyses (Greenspan's, Obama's, or the many variations of these themes we have heard) effectively claim to be doing the "hard thinking" that goes with hard choices; they claim to be pushing toward a critique of what came before, and they claim that it is precisely by thinking "more long term" that they are doing so. You may think here I am belaboring the obvious. You may wonder why I underline that Greenspan and Obama, weighing in on the question of the origin of the crisis in order to construct a response to the crisis, tend to situate their analyses as part of an effort to step back and look at the big picture. Indeed, you might ask who would object to the idea that the gravity of the situation today requires long-term vision? But this is precisely where the worry I am trying to share with you comes in.

I would like us at least to reflect on the fact that "short-term thinking is the enemy/culprit" has become a cliché. When Greenspan and Obama's speeches ask for support, and claim credibility, on the grounds that they can fix the problems brought on by short-term thinking with solutions derived from long-term thinking, when they insist that what are needed are regulations to ensure that the market functions in the long term, is there a risk that all calls for "long-term thinking" play into the hands of the status quo? Is there a risk that at this point every call to "look at the big picture" will be heard as the kind of call that reinforces the stranglehold of a certain politics that I think "we" have a commitment to loosening? Of course, in our attempts to make sense of the financial crisis, to understand the burden of our times, to determine the possibilities for tomorrow, it seems silly to say we should not be thinking long term. We would not be participating in this volume and the conference on which it is based unless we thought it important to develop a long-term/big-picture understanding of the situation. That, on one level, the invitation to think is also a summons to rise above myopic short-term analysis is quite the way it should be. Yet I want to suggest that, however obvious it is that we must think long term (think in the long term and especially think the long way even though we have to do it under the pressure of the emotions and the political urgency), there is perhaps also a danger in giving ourselves over to the task of thinking long term, if it comes at the expense of focusing on the short term. My fear is that, in the current context, we may unwittingly be conceding too much when we join the chorus calling for "long-term thinking."

If we are opposed to the dynamic of an analysis that would effectively suppress debates about underlying political choices for the future even as it claims to be taking into account the hard choices, we are going to need to be very careful, on the one hand, to highlight the disagreements about the long term and, on the other hand, not to forget that it may be just as important concurrently to be highlighting disagreements about "short-term thinking." Indeed—and now perhaps I am shifting to questions of strategy—I am not convinced that opposition to neoliberal logic can come solely through appealing to the *opposite* of short-term thinking. If we do want to fight for the possibility of some alternatives to the neoliberalism that has created the world in which such crises as the one we confront today occur, we need to consider the possibility that this fight might take place precisely in the realm of the short term. To put it very crudely, although we must, of course, be working to formulate and promote understanding of the long-term logic of neoliberalism and the political alternatives, we need to consider that if we are lulled into thinking *only* about the long term, we may miss the fight.

As Miguel de Beistegui and Robyn Marasco argue in this volume, the marks of neoliberalism include "short-term thinking" and, in particular, a trend to ever shorter time frames for measuring efficiency. The "new" rationality is marked by, supported by, and productive of, results that come in the form of numbers. And what counts, and is counted, is counted faster and faster. The increasing speed of operations and the decreasing units of time measurement taken to be relevant are generally recognized as "facts," but I tend to think that these facts are often recognized without their consequences being taken into account. I think it is crucial (and difficult) to take note that the insistence on the short term is not just a "speeding" up of what used to happen. The global circulation of capital is no longer the same thing when it is $2.2 billion a minute. Management techniques are not the same when what is important is not the next decade but the next quarter (and this is all the more true when a "quarter" starts to seem like a quaint measurement in times when a weekend has become long enough to make or unmake worlds/economies). Although there is often some concession to the idea that at some point a quantitative change becomes a qualitative one, I am not sure that idea is taken seriously enough. When the shift to the short term is denounced as myopic or lauded as the means to greater precision, the qualitative aspect of the change is minimized. I take it that instead we need to consider both *what* is being managed and *how* it is being managed; indeed, we need to ask what it is to "manage," what the goals of management are, *and* what they take to be their objects. All these can be affected by the move to short-term result measurement in ways more profound than a mere change of focus. When we conceive of the difference between aiming at short-term profits or long-term prosperity as analogous to the difference between a short-sighted person and someone with 20/20 vision playing the same game, we risk blinding ourselves. I would suggest that instead we must recognize that these two players are not playing the same game. Unless we take this into account, our analyses of what is going on may themselves be suffering from a "flaw" that will come back to haunt us.

There are many people more qualified than I am to describe how and where such changes in the game brought about by shifts to shorter-term management play out in the financial sector. What I want to do is merely insist that there must be such changes and that important political choices are being made through such changes.

To clarify what I am suggesting we track, I would like to give you an example from another context. Here are some facts reported in a recent book documenting how France is handling immigration issues. In the last few years, there has been a push to import management techniques from the private sector into the French police force. New demands for measurable improvements in efficiency were made, and these had to be formulated in terms of numbered goals. The measure chosen was in a sense an old one, namely the rate at which reported crimes are solved. Pressure was put on the police to (im)prove their performance; the rise in this rate would be the measure of that. Ostensibly the pressure for results was a great success since the rate at which crimes are solved indeed increased quite spectacularly.

A look into the numbers, however, reveals what sustains this "success" and shows how far from neutral the operation of measurement is. What changed the overall rate of success in apprehending criminals in the case of the French police is *not* uniform progress but a significant change in the crimes the police force pursued. Indeed, the rate at which crimes such as violent assaults or burglaries are solved made no progress whatsoever; there was, however, a huge increase in the absolute number of certain types of crime (immigration violations, drug possession, traffic violations, and *outrage à agent*). These rather different kinds of crimes and violations share one feature: The time it takes to find the culprit is, by definition, zero. These crimes are "solved" as soon as they are reported. Thus to "get results" the police force has, over just a few years, changed its focus. The demand for short-term results has resulted in a new understanding of what it is be efficient at defending the French population from "insecurity." This is where the choice of interpretation comes in: The French government would defend the position that this criminality is being revealed as it never was before, that the demand for results produces visibility.

I would side with those who see here a certain criminality being *produced* as the reality that the police manage. I use this example to illustrate the proposition that the short-term logic/ethic/politics we have been referring to in our discussions of the characteristics of our societies and economies is not just a new perspective on the world; rather, in a much stronger sense, it determines *what can take on reality*. Or perhaps we should just say that it determines the reality we live in. It determines not just how we manage, but what it is we manage. If this is the case, then it seems to me important that debates about the long-term alternatives for our polis do not prevent us from attending to the way those debates may be shifted, or even sometimes rendered moot, by new realities being produced in the short term, by the short-term practices that are operating now.

My hypothesis then would be that resisting may require learning to think short-term as we consider the possible political responses to what we take to be the causes of the specific forms of oppression and disenfranchisement characteristic of this crisis. It may well be that, if we are going to think politically in a sense of that term that Arendt would recognize, we are going to have to allow for less separation between the political and the economic than she would have liked. We may have to allow that a properly political response, although it may be impossible if one conflates the political and the economic, will also be impossible if we do not recognize that today's political choices may only be articulated in response to, but also to some extent in the language of, the dominant economic logic. Under such conditions, political responses to the current crisis/situation may have to take on the "short-termism" of neoliberal logic neither as a regrettable myopia nor as a sign of insensitivity to moral values higher than mere economic ones but as the perspective that shapes our reality.

In this sense, inventing an alternative will not be inventing an alternative *to* short-term logic so much as inventing an alternative *within* short-term logic. In these circumstances, I fear that adopting the apparently innocuous premise that "the problem has been short-term thinking and therefore the solution requires long-term thinking" may prevent us from paying sufficient attention to the necessity of inventing a "*non*-neoliberal short-term thinking" locally.

I would like to end with an attempt to answer a question posed by an audience member during the conference at which these remarks were first given. After a discussion about Weber, a member of the audience asked: "Who might be, for our thinking here, the equivalent of the capitalist entrepreneur for Weber's thinking?" I very much like the suggestion that we provoke our own analysis of this financial crisis by asking after a paradigmatic figure who might help us apprehend the ethic of the times. But rather than choosing one of the names that have been in the newspapers recently, I would like to nominate Saccard, the protagonist of Emile Zola's novel *Money*.

To justify this suggestion, let me say a few words about the book. Given the laws of the genre, we know from the beginning that this will be a novel about the rise and fall of the protagonist and that it will be a minute analysis of the social dynamics that depend on money—the need for it, the desire for it, the lack of it, and the submission to its logic. As the novel opens, Saccard, who has just lost a fortune, is stinging from the shame of being studiously ignored at the restaurant where the stock-market world lunches. He vows he will "become someone" again, and the novel is thus set up as the story of his project for the Universal Bank, since that is the name of the financial institution he establishes to recover his lost dignity/wealth. The project becomes a reality, and reestablishes Saccard in the Parisian world of his time. His ascent from ignominy is measured, and indeed established, by the rise over the next three years of the share price of the Universal Bank from 50 to1,000, then 2,000 and even 3,000 francs before the crash at the end of the novel leaves the shares worth perhaps just a little more than the paper on which they were printed. This can, of course, be read as a novel about collective madness, irrational exuberance, reckless greed, and the inevitable comeuppance. But I submit that we have a choice in our reading: We can choose to be a "we" who sees in the novel a moral tale about loss of values leading to disaster and the irresponsible pursuit of money, or we can consider the novel to be teaching us something else. That something else would be, to put it very briefly, how the rationality of short-term credit, when it is the rationality that organizes social and economic relations, may force us to reconsider the very way we evaluate responsibility.

This novel can, as I said, be taken to confirm a rather smug condemnation of those who fall for the lure of financial gain, either in moral terms ("they were greedy") or on the grounds that those who invested failed to see that in the long term it was unsustainable ("how could they not see it was a pyramid scheme?"). It can then be read as a cautionary tale about speculative bubbles.

It can, however, also be read as a remarkably precise description of the options available in a world dominated by speculative logic. Indeed I think the success of the novel derives precisely from the way it documents, and uses, the tension between two narratives as to the responsible attitude toward money, and more precisely toward that very particular sort of "money" involved in speculation on the stock market. We know from the beginning of this novel *what* must happen; all the pleasure of reading is in seeing *how* it happens, in tracking the dynamic of a bubble, in watching the inevitable play out. We experience the whole story being carried by an irresistible logic *while knowing*, from our vantage points as readers, that the irresistible logic should be resisted. Each time a character makes the decision to invest his or her faith/savings in the Universal Bank, we know that it will turn out to be disastrous in the long run. But far from comforting a clichéd moralizing schadenfreude at the ruin of those who hoped to manage their lives by buying shares, this novel seems to me to challenge its readers to confront the underlying causes of the devastation that the (predictable) collapse of the investment scheme leaves in its wake. It accomplishes this by making Saccard a figure who defies easy judgments, especially when it comes to the question of responsibility (or lack thereof). This figure does not so much hover between extreme lucidity and blind delusion as show that that very distinction has perhaps been surviving on subprime credit. He forces on us an at least dim awareness of, and perhaps too an explicit confrontation with, the ways in which we alternately distinguish and conflate market rationality and rationality in general.

We know that Saccard begins with nothing except the certainty that if he can convince a few people to convince themselves that his bank can lead to tremendous profits, then the accumulation of riches can snowball. At every step Saccard is very clear that his mission is to create the conditions for the rise in share price that will bring new investors and a new rise in share price: He is explicit in relying on the principle that, if he can just prime the pump, and protect the bank from any extraneous shocks, there should be an infinitely virtuous circle to the top. Saccard's world is that of a market in which prices have a weak correlation with the external reality of tangible production but a very strong correlation with the story that can be told about those possible productions or investment schemes. As both the novel and its protagonist know, and confirm, the market is a market of expectations, or rather of expectations about expectations. Saccard understands very clearly that his job as a manager is to manage expectations, and that managing investment schemes is a means to that goal rather than vice versa. Building confidence in his bank is what he does. Of course, insofar as we rely on cultural clichés about greed and work, we can say from the start that such a project has its priorities backwards, that it should build real projects rather than expectations, that it is doomed and therefore irresponsible (or irresponsible and therefore doomed). But, as I said before, I think that this novel forces us to push a little further than a simple condemnation of those who succumb to the tempting dream of easy money.

What Zola describes, with the same precision as he describes the streets of Paris, the language of different social milieus, or the daily routines of the stock market, is a world in which the choice is not whether or not you gamble for your future, but only when, how, how much, and on what. We may want to condemn playing the stock market as irresponsible gambling, but we are forced by this novel to contemplate what it might mean when this sort of gambling is the only game in town for those who want to take responsibility for their future. Some do it lightheartedly, others with a feeling they are being led to the gallows, but little by little everyone buys into the Universal Bank. We know they shouldn't, yet at the same time we are forced to think about the conventions that produce the vantage point from which we would condemn them as irresponsible: In so many cases it becomes clear, not just to them but also to us, that *not* investing would, in their circumstances, be even more irresponsible.

Those who have an (antiquated) attachment to the distinction between real and fake money, those who insist that making money by charging interest is unchristian and dishonorable, enter the game because they are forced to face the reality that it is their only hope. Although some catch investment fever, some characters are reluctantly drawn into the investment scheme because it is the only option on offer. For instance, for the parents who know that their daughter's only chance in life depends on a dowry they cannot scrape together from their work however hard they try, this investment is not just the only option for hope, it is also—and this is why Zola's novel seems to me so provocative—the only option for responsibility: Try as they might, external circumstances conspire, in all their banality, to make it impossible for these characters to live up to their responsibilities to themselves, as responsible to the future, without investing in shares of the Universal Bank. And Saccard is such an interesting figure precisely because he defies easy categorization: Is he hostage to an illusion, or hostage only to reality? When, after the ultimate debacle, he does not repent or recognize that it was all a bad idea but instead thinks the only problem was an unlucky and unpredictable problem of timing and considers that his only option is to try again, some readers may be tempted to see in him a figure of a man hopelessly corrupted and blinded by ambition and greed. I think it is just as possible, and indeed necessary, to consider the perspective from which his conclusion about his model is neither irrational nor irresponsible but simply the only lucid way to resist an irresponsible resentment against the ways of the world.

It seems to me that Saccard's world bears more than a passing resemblance to the world shaped by the culture and politics of the financial crisis. Readers may ascribe the crash of the Universal Bank either to greed or to bad financial planning; they may think that Saccard should renounce either his aspiration to wealth or the idea that a price is only determined by the level of investor confidence that can be stoked. But Saccard himself does not have the luxury of indulging in such renunciations. He can only try again; the only option, if he wants to be someone, is to play the system even if that means risking going from one crash to the next. One of the many questions this novel raises is whether pretending that in our world there is an alternative to going from bubble to bubble is an illusion we cannot afford either. This of course does not mean we must submit to the laws of the stock market as if to laws of nature. On the contrary, we must struggle to discern, or create, alternatives to that sort of fatalism that is but another endorsement of the politics that led to this financial crisis. Zola's Saccard might just be a good paradigmatic figure to push our analyses of today's "ethic," as we struggle to "understand and resist," as Roger Berkowitz, citing Arendt, put it in his introduction.

EIGHTEEN

Can There Be a People's Commons?

THE SIGNIFICANCE OF ROSA LUXEMBURG'S
ACCUMULATION OF CAPITAL

:: DRUCILLA CORNELL

In *The Origins of Totalitarianism*, Hannah Arendt argues that imperialism, as it arose in the late nineteenth century, had its immediate economic origin in the depression of the 1860s and 1870s. As the economic motor of production and accumulation slowed down in Europe, the imperialists realized that the "motor of accumulation" had to be kept in motion. If that accumulation could not come from inside the nation, it had to be sought elsewhere, which led to the imperialist search for new countries with new markets to be opened to capitalist supply and demand. To keep the process of accumulation going, it was necessary to plunder others and extend the capitalist economy to the entirety of the earth. Imperialism, Arendt saw, was no accident, but was an inner law of the capitalist economic system.

In making her observation about the close connection between imperialism and capitalist accumulation, Arendt cites multiple times from Rosa Luxemburg's *The Accumulation of Capital*. Praising Luxemburg's "brilliant insight into the political structure of imperialism," Arendt embraces Luxemburg's thesis, that capitalism depends on the imperialist domination of a noncapitalist world and "non-capitalist social strata."[1] Building on Luxemburg, Arendt rightly sees that capitalism demands an unlimited course of accumulation that must have or produce an equally unlimited supply of noncapitalist people. It is this instability of capitalism that underlies imperialism and that binds capitalism to a cycle of crises and violence.

In this essay I explore further Luxemburg's extraordinary work *The Accumulation of Capital* to show how political violence, including the outright plundering of non-European peoples, is not only one part of the history of capitalism—the period of primitive accumulation—nor is it only a stage in capitalist development as argued by V. I. Lenin. For Luxemburg, the violent conquest of noncapitalist peoples and social systems inheres in the very drive to accumulate so-called wealth at the core of the capitalist system. To quote Luxemburg:

> Force, fraud, oppression, looting are openly displayed without any attempt at concealment, and it requires an effort to discover within this tangle of political violence and contests of power the stern laws of the economic process. Bourgeois liberal theory takes into account only the former aspect: "the realm of peaceful competition," the marvels of technology and pure commodity exchange; it separates it strictly from the other aspect: the realm of capital's blustering violence which is regarded as more or less incidental to foreign policy and quite independent of the economic sphere of capital.[2]

As we will see, Luxemburg powerfully argues for the inevitability of imperialism as long as capitalism exists, arguing very much against some recent thinkers who hold that we have passed beyond imperialist dominance. Her argument certainly has implications on the international level and should be brought to bear on any rich thinking about the future of cosmopolitanism and human rights discourse. But in this essay I want to focus primarily on the relevance of her argument that asserts the impossibility—yes, impossibility—of decolonization (and in the case of South Africa, the dismantling of apartheid)—without some kind of social democracy, or, more radically, democratic socialism.

The beginning of this transformation is the undoing of what Marx called the antagonistic relations of distribution inherent in capitalism. Luxemburg eloquently describes the dream of undoing these relations.

> In a socialist economy this must be completely different! The private employer will disappear. Then no longer is production aimed at the enrichment of one individual, but at delivering to the public at large the means of satisfying all its needs. Accordingly the factories, works and

the agricultural enterprises must be reorganized according to a new way of looking at things.[3]

More specifically, I will examine the continuing struggle for a distribution of basic resources in the name of people's self-governance and an ethical notion of democracy as conducted by on-the-ground movements in South Africa that are challenging the ANC's (African National Congress) neoliberal policies. But I will do so within a reinterpretation of Rosa Luxemburg's fundamental insight that capitalism both demands an outside to it and tears apart any social relation that is noncapitalistic. One way of thinking about the on-the-ground movements against dispossession of resources is that they are fighting for a people's outside, a commons that is irreducible to capitalist relations, in the name of indigenous ideals such as uBuntu, an activist ethical virtue of reciprocal obligation and support.

Let us begin with a review of Luxemburg's basic argument. Luxemburg argues that the fundamental contradiction of capitalism lies in the tension between unlimited expansive capacity of the productive forces and the limited capacity of social consumption. Since capitalist production rests on the extraction of surplus value, it is impossible for the workers to obtain enough value in the form of wages to buy back the surplus product. The same is true for capitalists, who must invest ever-larger amounts of surplus value in the productive process in order to compete for capital accumulation. It is simply impossible, Luxemburg argues, for workers and capitalists in a single capitalist society to realize the mass of surplus value.

So how does capitalism realize surplus value? The capitalist must find strata of buyers in the precapitalist world, in what Luxemburg calls either natural or peasant economies. The struggle against natural economies has, according to Luxemburg, three goals: (1) to achieve the so-called liberation of labor power, which actually means the capacity to coerce it into service, as in the persistence of unfree black labor in South Africa during the entire period of colonization; (2) to gain control over all natural resources; and (3) to introduce a commodity economy, and to separate trade and agriculture. We will return shortly to see why Luxemburg argues that these so-called achievements of imperialist transformation of natural economies can stave off temporarily the crisis of underconsumption inherent in a closed capitalist society.

Disagreeing with Marx (based at least on a strong interpretation of *Capital*, volume 2), Luxemburg argues that his famous formula for the reproduction of capital, $c + v + s = p$, could not actually explain the accumulation of surplus value. For the sake of simplicity, Marx in volume 2 assumed a simple capitalist society composed solely of workers and capitalists, from which all foreign trade was excluded. This assumption flowed from Marx's argument that the mass of surplus value is realized not only by personal consumption but by the continuous expansion of constant capital, especially in the form of new machinery and technology, which Marx refers to as Department I. His point was that the entirety of surplus value earmarked for capital accumulation need not yield an equivalent in monetary form—thus it was possible, Marx held, for a great deal of surplus value to be realized directly without having to take the form of money or the transformation into consumer commodities (Department II) to be purchased by living people. The political consequences for the reformist Marxists of Luxemburg's time was that it was at least theoretically possible for capital to resolve its accumulation problem, and therefore there was no inevitability of the collapse of capitalism. Luxemburg strongly disagreed. Instead, she argued that Marx had made a fundamental error in his formula precisely because he used a closed society of workers and capitalists, and wrongly argued that surplus value could be directly realized within a closed capitalist society.

There have been critics of Luxemburg's reading of Marx in volume 2 who have urged that Marx's diagrams of expanded production are not meant to refer to actually existing capitalist reality; rather they are abstractions meant to show that even if one assumes away the realization of surplus value—which obsesses Rosa Luxemburg—the capitalist system still finds objective limits in the *production* of surplus value. Although I agree in a broad sense with these critics, to be fair to Luxemburg, she contends that Marx actually disagrees with himself, returning to the inevitable crisis of underconsumption in capitalist antagonistic relations of distribution in volume 3. Thus, her central argument can be defended despite her misreading of Marx, for, as we have seen, her central thesis is that the crisis inherent in the drive for the accumulation of capital allows capitalism to survive only through the invasion of primitive economies.

Hers is a scorching account of the brutality of such invasions, including the role of both Afrikaners and the British in conquering the majority population in what has come to be known as South Africa. The Afrikaners, whom she identifies as having a peasant economy, did everything they could to kill off (using those words deliberately) the natural economy of the majority black population. This battle went on for hundreds of years, certainly through the establishment of grand apartheid. Again there have been critics, and I agree with them, of Luxemburg's actual description of a natural economy—but her primary point is that political violence had to dismantle social systems that opposed either the peasant economy of the Afrikaners or the advanced capitalist economy of the British.

With the discovery of the gold and diamond mines in the 1880s and the resulting desperate need for cheap labor, the British then killed off both the peasant economy of the Afrikaners and the lingering natural economy of the black population. Again, even if Luxemburg's categorization of these economies is not rich or precise enough, her portrayal of the violence against the black population is devastatingly accurate.

> In fact, peasant economy and great capitalist colonial policy were here competing for the Hottentots and Kaffirs, that is to say for their land and their labour power. Both competitors had precisely the same aim: to subject, expel or destroy the coloured peoples, to appropriate their land and press them into service by the abolition of their social organizations.[4]

For Luxemburg, opposition to the invasion inherent in capitalist expansion can only yield liberation struggles, for "from the point of view of the primitive societies involved, it is a matter of life or death; for them there can be no other attitude than opposition and fight to the finish—complete exhaustion and extinction."[5]

Luxemburg's argument as to how capitalism staves off the crisis of underconsumption runs something like this. As soon as a primitive economy has been broken into by force, cheap mass-produced consumption goods replace the old simple commodities of the peasant or natural economies and communities, so that a market is provided for ever-increasing outputs from the industries of Department II in the old centers of capitalism—without raising the standard of life for the workers who consume these commodities. The ever-growing capacity of the export industries requires that the products of Department I be maintained at home and, when they cannot be effectively put to work, expanded into the new conquered territories—hence large undertakings such as railways appear on conquered lands. This kind of investment is financed from surplus extracted on the spot as well as by loans from the European capitalist countries. The inducement to invest comes from the production of commodities and cheap labor unobtainable at home.

Apart from profits earned on capital actually reinvested in the new territories, great capital gains are made simply through the conquest and possession of the land and all natural resources. Cheap labor—in the case of South Africa, unfree labor—is provided under conditions of super-exploitation defended by the myth that black workers did not need even a wage suitable to the reproduction of their labor power; they were supplied with the ability to survive, so the myth ran, by their own plots of land in the so-called Bantustans that were officially established by apartheid. Thus, the process of building up outlets for both Departments I and II solves the problems of overproduction and underconsumption and thus, for at least a time, preserves the capitalist relations of production. The problem for Luxemburg is that capitalism destroys the very outside upon which it feeds. Capitalism has to draw all other social relations into its accumulation process—and thus, ultimately there can be no outside upon which to feed its endless drive for profit and capital accumulation. (Technological optimists still hope, perhaps, that expansion will drive into outer space—but it takes more than a science-fiction imagination to believe that planetary colonization, if even possible, would, under capitalist relations, be anything other than a repetition of superexploitation of whatever poor souls are drafted into mining the planets for new resources.)

Luxemburg's outside was precapitalist relations. We have seen that in South Africa noncapitalist relations of labor continued to exist for many years, contrary to the arguments of some radical economists, such as Harold Wolpe, that capitalism itself would ultimately break down apartheid. Ultimately, of course, the "outside" of unfree black labor, supported by the violence of the state, allowed for a process of internal superexploitation that provided for a seemingly noncapitalist relation to survive for a long time. Was apartheid ultimately inefficient? Perhaps so, in the long term, but only because on the other side of this violent invasion was constant rebellion against it.

Other more recent writing on South Africa using Luxemburg's categories has argued that the ANC's utter capitulation to what economist David Harvey has called "accumulation by dispossession" is a continual process in the new South Africa. I have to agree with the economist Massimo De Angelis, however, that Harvey's phrase is somewhat misleading, since in Luxemburg's sense accumulation *is* dispossession, and therefore there is no historical period of primitive accumulation that is overcome once and for all. Capitalism must find new relations to "capitalize on," or it will fail to accumulate. De Angelis, among others, has argued that the antihegemonic struggles against the ANC and their attempts to turn all the means of life into capital, from water to education, may stimulate people's struggles to create a commons that is outside capitalist relations. This commons has been described by the shanty-dwellers movement as a politics of living communism. To quote S'Bu Zikode:

> So comrades, today I appeal to you that what we need to do is to conquer this capitalist system because each second you turn your head the capitalist system is there. We face electricity cut-offs, water disconnections, evictions and so on because we cannot afford to pay.[6]

If we think about democracy as an ethical as well as an institutional concept, then we can see how democracy is inherent in the demand for the socialization of the basic means of life, as they should be held in common. First, decisions about how electricity is to be distributed must be part of a democratic decision-making process. It is the people who must decide how they are to live, and if these questions of economy are taken off the democratic agenda, then there is no meaningful self-governance. It is important to note here that the ethical aspect of democracy is often associated both with uBuntu and with the people, in that it is through direct participatory mechanisms that crucial decisions about resources are to be made. Inherent in the notion that it is the people who must make these decisions together is a respect for the individual as having an equal voice with everyone else—and in that sense (as the shanty-dwellers often emphasize), the government must be held accountable in the name of a democracy that respects the dignity of everyone.

Mandela famously decreed that the neoliberal economic policy was nonnegotiable; it was not a matter of political discussion. On a simple level, this took individual dignity off the table, since dignity demands a stronger democracy that takes no question of economic organization off the agenda of democratic decision making. But if, as the shanty-dwellers suggest, the people's movements against the ANC are not simply struggling to hold the government accountable (although of course they include that demand), if they are much more radically setting themselves up as coproducers of an alternative outside—our outside, the people's outside—then that would allow for the possibility of the effective maintenance of noncapitalist relations against the current government's drive to dispossess the masses of the people of precisely this. Thus in a sense Zikode's living communism might be seen as a deeper form of democracy, one that not only involves decision making but also organizes the mass of the people as coproducers of a common outside . . . which is "ours." This is not socialism as traditionally understood through state ownership. This is living communism, in the sense that a socialist or communist ethic lives and breathes in the space outside capitalist relations; it is not born of the death of capitalism, but rises up as a fully grown reaction to it.

NINETEEN

An Economic Epilogue

:: TAUN N. TOAY

For many, the Great Recession was characterized by a series of acronyms, marked by intentionally opaque jargon: ABSs—asset-backed securities; CDOs—collateralized debt obligations; and the now infamous CDSs—credit default swaps. Even for industry insiders, these structured products were "innovations" in finance. A more efficient means of risk sharing had been born, or so it was argued, and further testament to the superiority of *American* (read "jungle") capitalism.

Although the buildup to the recession characterized structured products (a euphemistic catchall term for the aforementioned acronyms) as a means to facilitate efficiency, the crash painted such products in a far different light. At best, structured products were complex instruments to extract high fees from clients in exchange for risk spreading; at worst, structured products were the ingenious instruments of criminals, drunk on greed and statistical software. In either case, they were not what they appeared—at least if you valued the input of rating agencies.

There are many ways to interpret the downturn and resulting chaos. Many point to Bear Sterns as the seed of instability or the failure of Lehman as the straw that broke the camel's back. What was clearly at hand was a "Minsky Moment," the term Paul McCulley of PIMCO coined to describe the catalysis of crisis.

Detailed in the Papadimitriou piece, Hyman Minsky was a Keynesian scholar who has enjoyed postmortem recognition for his work on financial instability. Minsky's core premise was surprising simple: Firms fall into one of three classifications depending on the balance sheet of the firm—hedge firms, speculative firms, and, finally, Ponzi firms. The more firms at the latter end of the spectrum, the greater the financial fragility and a higher probability that an economic shock can send the system into chaos. To paraphrase Warren Buffett's amusing analogy, "It is only after the tide goes out that you can see who was swimming naked." The receding water was the Minsky Moment, and we were all left on a largely nude beach. The Minsky connection is more than merely tangential, as his ideas on fragility were largely the natural continuation of Keynes, Keleckski, and—especially—Kaldor. Although the latter two are not household names for many, neither is Hannah Arendt, who occupied the initial thematic section in this volume.

Both Minsky and Arendt posed questions that surpassed the mechanisms of capitalism and inquired into the very core of the concept. Minsky may have asked, "Are crises inherent to capitalism?" Arendt may have inquired, "Does capitalism institutionalize power and violence?" Both would have likely shared the question, "Are these dangers mere propensities or inherent in the system?" Such questions, albeit not verbatim, were characteristic of both thinkers' deeper views of capitalism. The deeper view was the aim of this volume. From the intellectual origins of the crisis to the nature of capitalism to the vanquished values that veiled the recent crisis, the question asked of the scholars and financiers who contributed to this volume was how we ended up where we are today.

For economists, the crisis offered both a blazon of the shortfalls in the "dismal science," especially as applied to modeling and forecasts, *and* an opportunity to revisit the nature of the assumptions in our *science*.

The idea that there exists a species, *homo oeconomicus*, that operates according to predictable axioms, is partially responsible for the events of the last recession. In a world of this idealized economic individual, touted are the maxims of neoliberalism, that is, free markets, deficit aversion, privatization, and the idea that government is incapable of enforcing values on markets. It is as though markets have emerged as amoral arenas in this brave new world.

From Berkowitz's initial mention that *homo oeconomicus* has replaced *homo sapiens* to Weber's questions over man as a "maximizer" to Strong and Kohn's applications of Arendt's "imperialism" to the modern financial crisis, it is clear that the ground has shifted. This shift was neither rapid nor recent. It is somewhat unique, however, that the current crisis has called into question the nature of capitalism itself. Is the neoliberal capitalism we have built in America a system that delivers wealth or instability? Discussions that frame such issues in the context of Marx, Weber, Keynes, Minsky, and Arendt are somewhat commonplace in academic circles today. How such questions reverberate in Main Street and Wall Street is still very much in flux. The focus of Callahan, the round-table participants, and the interviewees (notably Mai) is on values, which highlights the need to widen the conversation.

Part of what emerges from the discussions in this volume is the question of whether values have left economics or, more aptly, whether economics has divorced itself from values. Great strides were made over the course of the nineteenth century to align economics to physics. Agents exist in vacuums, with everything else constant, *ceteris paribus*. This may have marked the retreat of values from economics and with it, the absence of the human aspect of this social science. How far we have fallen from Adam Smith's economic man.

Many selectively quote from the *Wealth of Nations* (*WN*) to advance neoliberal ideas, yet few reference as selectively Smith's companion writing, *A Theory of Moral Sentiments* (*TMS*). Reading later volumes of *TMS*, one is struck by how centrally the needs for social constraints and altruism emerge in the work. For Smith, economics is not the clash of beasts over scarce resources; rather it is the interaction of moral citizens, taking what they can, *provided* that plenty is left for others.

Compassion, pity, and above all empathy (or "sympathy" for Adam Smith) are the moral sentiments that are crucial to the "disposition of the self toward the maintenance of the public . . . good, identifiable with the political association, polis or republica itself."[1] Virtuous citizens who are self-sacrificing, humble, and independent and who naturally amass wealth—but desire no luxury—are the beacons of light in a prosperous society where the citizens put the public welfare ahead of their own. And although these individuals are key components of a virtuous society, Smith acknowledges that most people are "of imperfect virtue . . . [and] act in ways, that while not virtuous, nevertheless lead to results analogous to those that would have been achieved if individuals had in fact been acting with perfect virtue."[2] It is in this realm that a reader can see the continuity between Smith's *Theory of Moral Sentiments* and the *Wealth of Nations*, where the *Wealth* assumes an already socialized individual who encompasses the virtues—whether strong or weak—found in the *TMS*.

Nonetheless, the perpetuation of a "society of perfect liberty" is hardly sufficient to achieve a virtuous society, as unchecked moral decay would result in a citizen prone "to betake himself to drunkenness and riot."[3] Thus, we need education and individuals to emulate the truly virtuous individual from the *TMS* to prevent social and moral decay in *WN*. This is not the public that Smith came to see after writing the *Wealth*. It is in this changing view of society that Smith revisits the *TMS* with such vigorous emphasis on the moral sentiments that are necessary for a virtuous society. It is in his return to the *TMS* that Smith emphasizes "superior" to "inferior" prudence and "public spiritedness."

The invisible hand is, thus, predicated on socially minded individuals. If such values are removed from the system, it is not clear that the system functions for the benefit of society. Such a statement seems painfully obvious in the aftermath of the Great Recession. Memories, however, are particularly short when it comes to economics.

One could look at the bursting of the tech bubble in the late 1990s as the first in a continuous series of manias and crashes that have led us to the present precipice. As Papadimitriou details, when each bubble burst, money fled into new areas: tech money to commodities; commodities to consumer credit and real estate; real estate to bailouts; and now bailout to bailout? We have come full circle where nothing looks worth inflating. Even today, the major hope is that by keeping interest rates low, the economy will resume borrowing and revive the economy.

The regulatory response thus far has aimed at derivatives and preventing "bad" banks, all of this with the idea that no institution will be "too large to fail." Although not without merit, none of these responses addresses the issue of values in our society. Can we construct incentives for people to act "as if" they had values? Economists are surely working on models to test such a theory presently. Yet, this is the same short-termism that helped land us in our current debacle. The blind focus on GDP, the Dow, quarterly earnings, and the latest consumer confidence level pressures companies and individuals to skirt existing rules and lobbyists to erode such regulation in the name of efficiency in the market.

Our cyclical relationship to laissez-faire is ironic—demanding stronger regulation in the aftermath of periods characterized by relaxed rules. Moreover, this narrow focus diminishes the humanistic elements of the economy. New roadways and greater public transportation are worthy ends, but only in part because of what they add to the GDP. Equally important, albeit not in any economic model, are the gains such projects add to quality of life, reductions in stress, and potential greenhouse gases. This is a long way of saying that there are many aspects of the economy that we cannot easily model (or choose not to) but that still have far-reaching consequences for the agents in the market. The ubiquitous focus on bringing analysis down to the individual as the "agent" of analysis forgets that economics stems from *oikos*, the family. Keynes famously stated that "the biggest problem is not to let people accept new ideas, but to let them forget the old ones." We may be wise to remember what we have forgotten: that economics is *social* science.

To bring the discussion back to the beginning: We are living in an age of the "banality of finance," to paraphrase Arendt's most notable phrase. This is not to say that complex financial instruments and the financial industry itself are banal; rather, the *agents* of the system are largely thoughtless, pushing products that are not fully understood or with a blindness to the consequences of such actions. Whether the crisis took root on the back of greed and corruption or was simply the growing apathy and automation that accompanies prolonged periods of prosperity is a question I cannot answer. Hopefully, however, this volume offers the reader a range of lenses with which to view the issue. Whether we repeat or resolve these tendencies falls largely on individuals and their willingness to fight the currents of complacency that often grip society.

Notes

Introduction: The Burden of Our Times ✱ Roger Berkowitz

1. Charles R. Morris, *The Two Trillion Dollar Meltdown: Easy Money, High Rollers, and the Great Credit Crash* (New York: Public Affairs, 2009), 63.

2. George Soros, *The Crash of 2008 and What It Means: The New Paradigm for Financial Markets* (New York: Public Affairs, 2009), 84, 95.

3. See Bill Fleckenstein, "Why All Roads Lead to Inflation," *Contrarian Chronicles* (May 12, 2008). http://articles.moneycentral.msn.com/Investing/ContrarianChronicles/WhyAllRoadsLeadToInflation.aspx

4. John Stuart Mill, "Paper Currency and Commercial Distress," in *The Collected Works of John Stuart Mill*, vol. 4: *Essays on Economics and Society*, part 1, ed. John M. Robson (Toronto: University of Toronto Press, London: Routledge and Kegan Paul), 1967.

5. Joseph Schumpeter, *Can Capitalism Survive?* (New York: Harper Perennial Modern Classics, 2009).

6. Arthur F. Burns and Wesley C. Mitchell, *Measuring Business Cycles* (New York: National Bureau of Economic Research, 1946).

7. Hannah Arendt, *The Origins of Totalitarianism* (New York: Harvest Books, 1973), viii.

8. Hannah Arendt, *The Human Condition* (Chicago: University of Chicago Press, 1958).

9. Hannah Arendt, "The Crisis in Education," in *Between Past and Future* (New York: Penguin Books, 2006), 171.

10. Arendt, *Origins of Totalitarianism*, 125.

11. "The economy produces legitimacy for the state that is its guarantor. In other words, the economy creates public law, and this is an absolutely important phenomenon, which is not entirely unique in history to be sure, but is nonetheless a quite singular phenomenon in our times." Michel Foucault, *The Birth of Biopolitics: Lectures at the Collège de France, 1978–1979* (New York: Palgrave Macmillan, 2010), 84.

12. Max Weber, *The Protestant Ethic and the Spirit of Capitalism*, trans. Stephen Kahlberg (Chicago: Roxbury, 2001), 24.

Chapter 1: Can Arendt's Discussion of Imperialism Help Us Understand the Current Financial Crisis? ✱ Tracy B. Strong

1. All internal citations are to Hannah Arendt, *The Origins of Totalitarianism* (New York: Harvest Books, 1973).

2. Peter Mandelson, "Russia and the EU: Building Trust on a Shared Continent," *Information Daily*, June 23, 2008.

3. Hannah Arendt, *Men in Dark Times* (New York: Mariner, 1970), 87.

4. See Benjamin R. Barber, *Jihad or McWorld* (New York: Ballantine, 1996).

5. Jean-Luc Nancy, "La Comparution/Compearance," trans. Tracy Strong, *Political Theory* 20, no. 3 (1992): 392.

Chapter 2. "No Revolution Required" * Jerome Kohn

1. Hannah Arendt, *The Origins of Totalitarianism* (New York: Harvest Books, 1973).

2. That earmark can be concealed in the rhetoric of terrorism and nation-building but not erased. How blind must one be not to see the role played by the West's long and ongoing economic exploitation of the Middle East's oil, as well as (*sotto voce*) Afghanistan's opium poppy plantations, in the rise of Moslem "fanaticism"?

3. *The Origins of Totalitarianism* was published in 1951, exactly three hundred years after *Leviathan*. To avoid confusion, the gist of Arendt's discussion of Hobbes is not that he foresaw a totalitarian but an imperial form of government; it is she who discovers intimations of the former in the latter.

4. Hobbes's thought has been and continues to be diversely interpreted by and within philosophic, political, and historical fields of scholarship. Within that diversity, Arendt's primary focus on the future consequences of Hobbes's political analyses of new social phenomena in his day is unusual, if not unique.

5. The "liberty" of Leviathan's members is "to buy, and sell . . . to choose their own abode, their own diet, their own trade of life, and institute their children as they themselves think fit"—all good liberal values. Elsewhere Hobbes ridicules indeterminate freedom as the *feeling* of a spinning "wooden top" if it were unaware of being "lashed by the boys." Thomas Hobbes, *Leviathan* (Cambridge: Cambridge University Press, 1993).

6. Here Arendt refers to the *déclassés* of bourgeois society, who engaged in the "Great Game" of imperialist expansion with no moral scruples whatsoever, as forerunners of the mob that supported Hitler from the start.

7. Asked if she were a liberal or conservative, Arendt said she was accused of each by the other, adding "I don't think . . . real questions . . . get any kind of illumination from this sort of thing."

8. It is such borrowings and compromises between the private and public realms, and the consequent blurring of their boundaries, that constitute, for Arendt, the "social."

9. Gary Wills, "Entangled Giant," *New York Review of Books*, October 8, 2009, 4.

10. "The bourgeoisie . . . has accomplished wonders far surpassing Egyptian pyramids, Roman aqueducts, and Gothic cathedrals; it has conducted expeditions that put in the shade all former Exoduses of nations and crusades" (Karl Marx and Frederick Engels, *Manifesto of the Communist Party*.

11. Arendt's *Men in Dark Times* (New York: Mariner Books, 1968) is composed of the stories of men and women whose lives were sources of light in the darkest of times.

12. Charles Sanders Peirce, "The Doctrine of Chances," *Science Monthly* 12 (March 1878): 604.

13. It cannot be over emphasized that to Arendt the world is a human *artifice*, and sharply distinguished from the earth, humanity's *natural* home. The word "world" and its cognates "wordly" and "worldliness" refer always and only to the realm of human affairs, to what concerns the

citizens of a polity, and in the volatility of a technologically shrunken world, all humaniaty in common. If Hobbes was the first to understand politics as *"art,"* his notion of an "artificial man," an automaton with an "artificial *soul,"* has no place whatever in Arendt's human artifice.

14. Arendt herself finds something akin to it in the medieval thought of Duns Scotus, but there it has nothing to do with politics or the public realm. Aristotle admits the contingency of future events, but primarily as a logical and psychological obstacle to understanding them. Though not a *topos* in Oakeshott, contingency is implicit in his critique of "rationalism in politics."

15. From the beginning of her career as a political writer to its end, Arendt quotes the Roman poet Lucan: *Victrix causa deis placuit, sed victa Catoni* ("The victorious cause pleased the gods, but the defeated one pleases Cato"). Which is to say, as only a poet could say it, that action, even if its end is tragic, provides the primordial human experience of being free.

16. To speak of humans as a species instead of a *plurality* of unique beings would be misleading. It is rather as if the proverbial lion and lamb, representing two different and inimical species, lay down together in friendship; or better, as if animals representing many species clambered aboard Noah's ark, not two by two but one by one, not to survive God's flood but to subdue it. That two members of the same species are necessary for its propagation is, as far as humans are concerned, neither a political nor a public but a natural and private consideration. Needless

to say, *who* Socrates is and continues to be is not the result of his parents' sexual union.

Chapter 3. Judging the Financial Crisis * Antonia Grunenberg

1. "Notre héritage n'est précédé d'aucun testament" (see René Char, *Feuilles d'Hypnos* [Paris, 1946]).

2. Hannah Arendt, *The Origins of Totalitarianism* (New York: Harvest Books, 1973), 124. All further references to this title are given parenthetically in the text.

Chapter 7. Brazil as a Model? * Alexander R. Bazelow

1. See, for example, George Soros, *The Crisis of Global Capitalism: Open Society Endangered* (New York: Little Brown, 1998).

2. *The Everyman's Guide to the Financial Crisis* (Private Research report of "The Prism Group LLC," March, 2009), 5. All of the statistics pertaining to subprime mortgages, the composition of U.S. debt holdings, the collapse of Lehman Brothers, and the "profitability" or lack thereof of mortgage-backed securities can be found in these 177 densely packed and well-researched pages.

3. A version of this speech was given at the Rotonda Business Club, Cologne, Germany, November 30, 2009.

4. Data on U.S. consumption patterns, and in particular the distribution of wealth and debt, are summarized in an excellent article "The Consumer Isn't Overleveraged—The Middle Class Is," *Los Angeles Times*, August 14, 2009, which cites research from a private report by Bank of America-Merrill Lynch.

5. See Michael Lewis, "The Man Who Crashed the World," *Vanity Fair,*

August, 2009, and John Lanchester, "Bankocracy," *London Review of Books* 31, no. 21 (2009): 35–36, for profiles of Joseph Cassano of AIG and Richard Fuld, former CEO of Lehman Brothers. So secretive was Dick Fuld that it was not uncommon to find senior executives of the company who had never even met him.

6. The assertion that many of the mortgage-backed securities that blew up could never have been profitable once the full spectrum of risk is taken into account is demonstrated by Sanjeev Arora, Boaz Barak, Markus Brunnermeier, and Rong Ge, *Computational Complexity and Information Asymmetry in Financial Products*, Department of Computer Science and Department of Economics and Bendheim Center for Finance, Princeton University, October19, 2009.

7. Nassim N. Taleb, *Ten Principles for a Black Swan Robust World—Report on the Risks of Financial Modeling, VaR and the Economic Breakdown* (Private Report, "NYU-Polytechnic Institute, Principal Universa Investments L.P.," 2008), 8. Rule no. 2 reads: "No socialization of losses and privatization of gains. Whatever may need to be bailed out should be nationalized; whatever does not need a bail-out should be free, small and risk bearing. We have managed to combine the worst of capitalism and socialism. In France in the 1980s, the socialists took over the banks. In the U.S. in the 2000s, the banks took over the government. This is surreal."

8. Emmanuel Raufflet, "Creating the Context for Corporate Responsibility—The Experience of Instituto Ethos, Brazil," *Journal of Corporate Citizenship* 30 (Summer 2008): 95–106.

Chapter 8. Interview with Raymundo Magliano Filho *

Cláudia Perrone-Moisés

Alexander R. Bazelow supplied the questions. Ms. Jacqueline DeMelo provided the translation. Dr. Wolfgang Heuer, of the Free University of Berlin, was a most helpful facilitator. Their assistance is gratefully acknowledged.

1. SA Magliano Brokerage and Securities was one of the first companies to be listed on the Bovespa Stock Exchange.

Chapter 10. The Roots of the Crisis * Sanjay G. Reddy

1. Robert Shiller, *Macro Markets: Creating Institutions for Managing Society's Largest Risks* (Oxford: Oxford University Press, 2008).

2. See, e.g., Gillian Tett, *Fool's Gold: How Unrestrained Greed Corrupted a Dream, Shattered Global Markets and Unleashed a Catastrophe* (New York: Free Press, 2009).

3. It is appropriate here to recall the insistence of Hannah Arendt that the 'public' is not grounded merely in overlapping interests but rather in the recognition that we live together in the world, sharing it 'in common', and that it is from this recognition that our sense of public responsibility must stem. See, e.g., Kevin Quinn, "Markets, Politics and Freedom in the Work of Hannah Arendt," *Real-World Economics Review* 45 (March, 2008): 59–65.

Chapter 12. Managed Money, the "Great Recession," and Beyond *
Dimitri B. Papadimitriou

1. For a technical treatment see Wynne Godley, Dimitri B. Papadimitriou, and Gennaro Zezza, "Prospects for the United States and the World: A Crisis That Conventional Remedies Cannot Resolve," *Strategic Analysis*, Annandale-on-Hudson, New York: Levy Economics Institute of Bard College, December 2008; and Dimitri B. Papadimitriou, Greg Hannsgen, and Gennaro Zezza, "Sustaining Recovery: Medium-term Prospects and Policies for the U.S. Economy," *Strategic Analysis*, Annandale-on-Hudson, New York: Levy Economics Institute of Bard College, December 2009.

2. Axel Leijonhufvud, "Out of the Corridor: Keynes and the Crisis," *Cambridge Journal of Economics* 33, no. 4 (2009): 741–57.

3. Hyman Minsky, *Stabilizing an Unstable Economy* (New Haven, Conn.: Yale University Press, 1986), republished in *Hyman P. Minsky's Stabilizing an Unstable Economy*, ed. Dimitri B. Papadimitriou and L. Randall Wray (New York: McGraw-Hill, 2008), 328.

4. Hyman Minsky, "Uncertainty and the Institutional Structure of Capitalist Economies," *Working Paper* 155, Annandale-on-Hudson, New York: Levy Economics Institute of Bard College, 1996.

5. L. Randall Wray, "The Commodities Market Bubble," *Public Policy Brief* 96, Annandale-on-Hudson, New York: Levy Economics Institute of Bard College, 2008.

6. Hyman P. Minsky, "Securitization" (handout prepared for economics course 335A, Annandale-on-Hudson, New York: Bard College, Fall, 1987), published as *Policy Note* 2008/2, Levy Archives, Levy Economics Institute, June, 2008.

7. Minsky, *Stabilizing an Unstable Economy*.
For more on Minsky see also Hyman P. Minsky, *John Maynard Keynes* (New York: Columbia University Press, 1975), republished in *Hyman Minsky's John Maynard Keynes*, ed. Dimitri. B. Papadimitriou and L. Randall Wray (New York: McGraw-Hill, 2008); and Hyman P. Minsky, "Financial Instability and the Decline(?) of Banking," *Working Paper* 127, Annandale-on-Hudson, New York: Levy Economics Institute of Bard College, 1994.

8. David Greenlaw, Jan Hatzius, Anil K Kashyap, and Hyun Song Shin, "Leveraged Losses: Lessons from the Mortgage Meltdown" (paper presented at the U.S. Monetary Policy Forum Conference, February 29, 2008).

9. For a detailed discussion see Dimitri B. Papadimitriou and L. Randall Wray, "Time to Bail Out: Alternatives to the Bush-Paulson Plan," *Policy Note* 2008/6, Annandale-on-Hudson, New York: Levy Economics Institute of Bard College, 2008.

Chapter 13. Turning the Economy into a Casino * David B. Matias and Sophia V. Burress

1. Michael Hudson, "Saving, Asset-Price Inflation, and Debt-Induced Deflation," in *Money, Financial Instability and Stabilization Policy*, ed. L. Randall Wray and Matthew Forstater (Northampton: Edward Elgar, 2006), 104–24.

2. Mason Gaffney, *After the Crash: Designing A Depression-Free Economy*

(Chichester, West Sussex: John Wiley and Sons, 2009).

3. Adam Smith, *The Wealth of Nations*, ed. C. J. Bullock (New York: Barnes and Noble, 2004), 300. Originally published in 1776.

4. Hannah Arendt, *The Origins of Totalitarianism* (New York: Harcourt Brace Jovanovich, 1968), 145.

5. Ibid., 133.

Chapter 14. Capitalism: Neither Problem nor Solution—But Temporary Victim of the Financial Crisis * Liah Greenfeld

1. Max Weber, *The Protestant Ethic and the Spirit of Capitalism* (London: Unwin Hyman, 1930), 53.

2. Liah Greenfeld, *The Spirit of Capitalism: Nationalism and Economic Growth* (Cambridge, Mass.: Harvard University Press, 2001).

Chapter 15. Retrieving Chance: Neoliberalism, Finance Capitalism, and the Antinomies of Governmental Reason * Robyn Marasco

I am especially grateful to Justin Birru for several conversations about the financial crisis and recent developments in behavioral finance.

1. This is especially evident in the writings of Friedrich von Hayek, perhaps the most brilliant and far-reaching of neoliberalism's early crusaders. In *The Road to Serfdom*, Hayek posits that a competitive economy is to be preferred over a planned economy precisely insofar as human beings—and, especially, governments and bureaucratic agencies—*cannot* adequately model, predict, and plan for the future. A free market, for Hayek, is testimony to the *limits* of our predictive powers.

2. Kant also made reference to the black swan, but not in relation to questions of logic and falsification. In *The Metaphysics of Morals*, Kant describes moral friendship as a black swan in that "it is not just an ideal but . . . actually exists here and there in its perfection." Immanuel Kant, *The Metaphysics of Morals*, ed. Mary Gregor (Cambridge: Cambridge University Press, 1996), 217.

3. See Nassim Nicholas Taleb, *The Black Swan: The Impact of the Highly Improbable* (New York: Random House, 2007), and *Fooled by Randomness: The Hidden Role of Chance in Life and in the Markets* (New York: W. W. Norton, 2001).

4. Michel Foucault, *Security, Territory, and Population: Lectures at the Collège de France*, ed. Michel Senellart, trans. Graham Burchell (New York: Palgrave, 2007), 45.

5. See Wendy Brown, "Neoliberalism and the End of Liberal Democracy," *Theory & Event* 7, no. 1 (2003).

6. Martin Wolf, "The Challenge of Halting the Financial Doomsday Machine." *Financial Times,* April 20, 2010.

7. Karl Marx, *Capital*, vol. 3, ed. Friedrich Engels (1894), Institute of Marxism-Leninism, USSR (New York: International Publishers, 1959), 255.

8. Walter Benjamin, *The Arcades Project*, trans. Howard Eiland and Kevin McLaughlin (Cambridge: Harvard University Press, 1999), 513.

Chapter 18. Can There Be a People's Commons?: The Significance of Rosa Luxemburg's *Accumulation of Capital* * Drucilla Cornell

1. Hannah Arendt, *The Origins of Totalitarianism* (New York: Harvest Books, 1973), 148.

2. Rosa Luxemburg, quoted in Patrick Bond, "South African Sub-imperial Accumulation," in *The Accumulation of Capital in Southern Africa*, ed. Patrick Bond et al., (Berlin: Rosa Luxemburg Foundation, 1997), 91.

3. Ibid., 348.

4. Rosa Luxemburg, "Excerpts from *The Accumulation of Capital*," in *The Accumulation of Capital in South Africa*: *Rosa Luxemburg's Contemporary Relevance*, ed. Patrick Bond, Horman Chitonge, and Arndt Hopfmann (Berlin: Rosa Luxemburg Foundation; Durban: Centre for Civil Society, 2007), 11–12.

5. Ibid., 351. She continues: "Hence permanent occupation of the colonies by the military, native risings and punitive expeditions are the order of the day for any colonial regime. The method of violence, then, is the immediate consequence of the clash between capitalism and the organizations of a natural economy which could restrict accumulation."

6. S'Bu Zikode, "The Shackdwellers Movement of Durban," in *The Accumulation of Capital in South Africa*: *Rosa Luxemburg's Contemporary Relevance*, ed. Patrick Bond, Horman Chitonge, and Arndt Hopfmann (Berlin: Rosa Luxemburg Foundation; Durban: Centre for Civil Society, 2007), 165.

Chapter 19. An Economic Epilogue
* Taun N. Toay

1. Jerry Evensky, "The Evolution of Adam Smith's Views on Political Economy," *History of Political Economy* 21, no. 1 (1989).

2. Ibid.

3. Robert Heilbroner, "The Paradox of Progress: Decline and Decay in *The Wealth of Nations*," in *Essays on Adam Smith*, ed. A. S. Skinner and T. Wilson (Oxford: Clarendon Press, 1975).

Contributors

Raymond Baker Director, Global Financial Integrity Project

Alexander R. Bazelow Class of 1971, Bard College

Miguel de Beistegui Professor of Philosophy, Warwick University

Roger Berkowitz Associate Professor of Political Studies, Philosophy, and Human Rights, and Academic Director of the Hannah Arendt Center for Politics and Humanities, Bard College

Rebecca Berlow General Counsel, Sandelman Partners

Jack Blum Chairman, Tax Justice Network USA

Sophia V. Burress Vodia Capital, LLC, Concord, Mass

David Callahan Cofounder and Senior Fellow, Demos

Drucilla Cornell Professor of Political Science, Women's Studies, and Comparative Literature, Rutgers University

Olivia Custer Professor of Philosophy, Bard College

Liah Greenfeld University Professor and Professor of Political Science and Sociology, Boston University

Antonia Grunenberg Founder of the Hannah Arendt Center, University of Oldenburg

Zachary Karabel President, River Twice Research

Jerome Kohn Director, Hannah Arendt Center, New School for Social Research

Paul Levy Founder and Managing Director, JLL Partners

Hunter Lewis Cofounder, Cambridge Associates

Raymundo Magliano Filho Former President of Bolsa de Valores de São Paulo

Vincent Mai Chairman of AEA Investors, New York City

Robyn Marasco Assistant Professor of Political Science, Hunter College

David B. Matias Managing Principal, Vodia Capital, LLC, Concord, Massachusetts

Dimitri B. Papadimitriou President, Levy Economics Institute of Bard College

Cláudia Perrone-Moisés Associate Professor, Department of International and Comparative Law, University of São Paulo

Sanjay Reddy Associate Professor of Economics, New School for Social Research

Thomas Scanlon Attorney Adviser, U.S. Treasury Department

Tracy B. Strong Professor of Political Science, University of California, San Diego

Taun N. Toay Research Analyst, Levy Economics Institute of Bard College

Index